T0401172

Resisting Olympic evictions

Manchester University Press

Resisting Olympic evictions

Contesting space in Rio de Janeiro

Adam Talbot

MANCHESTER UNIVERSITY PRESS

Published by Manchester University Press
Oxford Road, Manchester, M13 9PL

www.manchesteruniversitypress.co.uk

British Library Cataloguing-in-Publication Data
A catalogue record for this book is available from the British Library

ISBN 978 1 5261 5629 7 hardback

First published 2024

Typeset by Newgen Publishing UK

Contents

List of figures		*page* vi
Acknowledgements		vii
Introduction		1
1	Contexts: Rio 2016, favela evictions and Vila Autódromo	18
2	The *Plano Popular da Vila Autódromo*: Sovereign power and rights	38
3	*Ocupa Vila Autódromo*: Space as resistance	60
4	*Espaço Ocupa*: Liminal placemaking in the protestival	81
5	RioOnWatch: Spreading place through the press	100
6	*Memória não se remove*: Heterotopia in the Museu das Remoções	121
Conclusion		140
References		155
Index		166

Figures

1.1 Map showing Barra da Tijuca in the city of Rio de Janeiro   *page* 22

1.2 Map showing the position of Vila Autódromo in Barra
da Tijuca   30

1.3 Rubble by the road in Vila Autódromo, November 2015   34

1.4 The rejuvenated children's play area, November 2015   35

1.5 Sketch map of Vila Autódromo   36

2.1 The *Planinho Popular*, February 2016   40

2.2 The 2016 version of the *Plano Popular da Vila Autódromo*   44

2.3 Graffiti details one of the favela's legal protections. March 2016   47

2.4 Mayor Eduardo Paes's initial plan for Vila Autódromo   57

3.1 A football game under way in Vila Autódromo. December 2015   62

3.2 *Espaço Ocupa* exhibit in the Museu das Remoções, May 2016   72

3.3 *Espaço Ocupa* during the Cultural Festival, November 2015   73

3.4 *Espaço Ocupa* without an event, March 2016   77

4.1 Graffiti on the back of the community church, April 2016   89

5.1 The new homes of Vila Autódromo, July 2016   101

6.1 The new sign at the entrance to Vila Autódromo, July 2018   133

6.2 Remains of homes from Vila Autódromo on display in the
Museu Histórico Nacional   137

Acknowledgements

This book marks the culmination of a decade-long research project and as such there are a great many people who have helped along the way. First and foremost, I want to thank all those activists in Rio who welcomed me into their lives and helped me, particularly Penha, Luiz, and all their fellow residents of Vila Autódromo, who tolerated an awkward gringo asking questions with endless warmth and good humour. The team at Catalytic Communities, especially Theresa and Cerianne, were an invaluable source of understanding about Rio and its favela communities, but also provided a community away from home. Other activists, from the Comitê Popular and other groups, were also friendly and considerate, welcoming me into their world and enduring questions that must have seemed strange to them at times.

Numerous researchers have guided this book to fruition along the way. Thomas F. Carter, Mark Doidge and Kepa Artaraz at the University of Brighton gave invaluable support in the initial research period, helping me to guide and focus the research. Fernando Marinho Mezzadri at the Federal University of Paraná supported me in a similar way in Brazil, as well as aiding with a research visa for Brazil. Matt Graham was an invaluable mentor in developing the detailed proposal for this book. Others have provided helpful comments and feedback that have refined the ideas discussed here, including Jules Boykoff, Marie-Bénédicte Dembour, Aidan McGarry, John Horne, David McGillivray and Bryan Clift. Tony Blackshaw, Donna Woodhouse, Jim Cherrington and Jon Dean all played a part in equipping me with the skills and sensibility needed to conduct this research. Support to undertake fieldwork in 2018 came from the Carnegie Trust for the Universities of Scotland, with the support of Scott Hardie at Abertay University enabling me to spend a summer away from my day job. Finally, none of this could have been achieved without the good humour and support of colleagues who worked with me along the way, including Rachel Handforth, Claudia Dolezal, Maria Gebbels, Jenni Holland, Rhiannon Lord, Chloe MacLean,

Tom Bason and countless others, who provided camaraderie even when academic life became overwhelming.

Tom Dark helped me overcome doubts about whether writing a book was the right approach for me and had the patience to explain the process to me in detail, bringing me into Manchester University Press. Laura Swift and Shannon Kneiss have guided me in the production process, providing invaluable guidance on things I know very little about. In particular, their unfailing good humour as I repeatedly asked for just one more month to finish things was deeply appreciated. Thanks must also go to the anonymous reviewers who have commented on this book, whose insightful and generous engagement with the work not only gave me practical steps to clarify key points, but also reinvigorated me to pursue this project. I would also like to thank Tanis Eve at Newgen Publishing for invaluable support with the production process and Sophie Richmond for her thorough proofreading which caught many (if not all) of my mistakes.

Last but not at all least, Débora Picorelli Zukeran, who I met while conducting fieldwork for this book and married a few months before its completion, has been a source of constant support and love. From helping me feel comfortable in her city, introducing me to her family and network of friends, to putting up with countless questions checking my translations, she has been a source of both inspiration and practical support. Above all, her unwavering belief in me pushed me through the moments when I felt unable to complete this book.

Introduction

Rio de Janeiro, International Women's Day, 2016

I woke up early, at around 6 a.m., as my phone buzzed on the nightstand. Groggily, I reached over and peered at the blue screen, seeing a message in the WhatsApp group for supporters of Vila Autódromo, a favela community threatened with evictions.[1] The message, from one of the few remaining residents, explained that shock troops – the municipal police who protect the people carrying out demolitions – were invading Vila Autódromo and asked for supporters to come to the community; these have become fairly regular occurrences in the last few weeks. I sent the message on to some of my international friends though Facebook, speculating about what could be happening. Simultaneously, I got up and started to dress, ready to head out to the community if necessary, when a message came through from another resident in the WhatsApp group: 'THEY'RE GOING TO DESTROY MY HOUSE'.[2] Fully awake only a few minutes after the first message, I raced out of my flat close to Downtown to find a taxi driver who was prepared to drive the long distance from the city centre to Vila Autódromo. The journey to the favela, located next to the building site for the main Olympic Park, had become familiar over the past six months as I followed the resistance to evictions in the community that this book documents.

During the long drive to Rio's West Zone, I chatted on WhatsApp to some of my international friends. We were all working with the favela advocacy non-governmental organisation (NGO) Catalytic Communities on a project called RioOnWatch, which sought to promote the voices of favela residents during Rio's Olympic preparations. We arranged how to

---

1 Throughout this book, I use the terms 'favela' and 'community' interchangeably. This reflects residents' use of both terms ('favela' and 'comunidade') to refer to Vila Autódromo. As such, this does not reflect a theorising of community, which is beyond the scope of this study.

2 All translations are mine, except where otherwise noted.

act to achieve this aim and support residents once we arrived, dividing up duties of live-tweeting, taking down quotes and notes to write up later, and filming and photographing events to pass on to international media. In the WhatsApp group for supporters of the community lifts were arranged to reach the community and traffic updates sent frantically, advising others that it was better to take the more direct route along the coast than the highway north then west.

When we arrived at Vila Autódromo, the community was abuzz with activity, but not in the positive, hopeful ways it had been when activists had been drawn there for the launch of an alternative plan for development the previous weekend, as discussed in chapter 2. This was a more menacing atmosphere; the buzz a panicked frenzy, not the collective effervescence from the coming together of like-minded people. I made my way along the dusty road towards Penha and Luiz's home, slated for demolition that day. The couple, particularly Maria da Penha, had been prominent in the movement to resist eviction that had been running for several years, and Penha was seen as an unofficial spokeswoman of the community by many. A few days earlier, when the injunction preventing the demolition of her home was finally dismissed by the courts, along with around thirty other activists I had helped the family move their belongings out of their large, airy home, some going into the community church and the rest to a nearby community for safekeeping. The road into the community followed a metal fence which cordoned off the Olympic construction site next door. Until around a month before, a concrete wall had served this purpose, built decades ago around the racetrack that once stood adjacent to the community. In recent weeks, the wall had been demolished and the corrugated metal fence had steadily encroached into the community, claiming more land for the construction works. The fence itself was plastered with graffiti denouncing the government's actions, claiming that 'When the Olympics arrive, justice gets dirty' and calling for 'Rio without evictions'.

As I walked into the community, passing the rubble of the Residents' Association, which had been demolished the previous week, I saw dust rising from Penha and Luiz's house – the demolition already under way. According to the regulations on demolitions, water should be sprayed on the building to reduce dust clouds, but this was often ignored, despite residents' protestations (Comitê Popular 2015). I made my way to the house, where a small crowd had congregated with a police cordon keeping them away from the demolition. Dozens of Guarda Municipal (City Hall's security service), in their beige uniforms, surrounded the building, ensuring nobody could get near. Luiz hugged his daughter before she started shouting her indignation at the demolition of the home she grew up in, screaming 'WE DEMAND OUR RIGHTS!' and leading the small crowd of some twenty activists in a chant of '*URBANIZA JÁ, A VILA VAI FICAR!*'[3] The demolition was paused as I arrived: one of the activists who had got there before me explained that they were waiting for an engineer to arrive to ensure that damage to neighbouring homes would be avoided and to disconnect the electricity from the now semi-demolished house. During the pause in proceedings, I had chance to talk to Melissa, a RioOnWatch volunteer, who had been live-tweeting the demolition for the site. We both started to well up and shared an embrace to comfort each other. Luiz looked on forlornly, not speaking, his face a picture of stoicism as the building where he had married his wife and lived for over twenty years was torn down. Penha, usually front and centre of community protests against evictions, was nowhere to be seen.

As the morning wore on, journalists arrived to cover the demolition and a professional film crew came to record the scene. As we watched, the house itself seemed to be putting up a fight. The set of concrete steps which led up to the first floor was strong, taking several strikes from the backhoe before it was dislodged. The demolition was taking significantly longer than others I'd witnessed in the past few months. Those gathered to watch occasionally called out their condemnation, as well as asking 'Where is Globo?', referring to Brazil's largest news network, widely seen to be ignoring the community's plight. When the house was finally reduced to rubble and the Guarda Municipal had made their way out of the community, Luiz spoke to some of the press as a bulldozer tidied up the pile of debris behind him. While Penha was still nowhere to be seen, supporters of the community were now present in force, many of whom I recognised from the past few months of resisting evictions. The tense atmosphere had relaxed somewhat with the departure of the Guarda Municipal, as activists consoled each other and began to carry the family's last remaining possessions, which had been moved into the dusty road before the demolition started, to the community church some 200 metres away, across the rubble of homes that had been destroyed over the last two years of evictions.

Suddenly, the guards were back. The atmosphere was panicked. Shouts and cries came from the edge of the community. The Guarda Municipal had suddenly stormed into the community and surrounded another resident's house. Fear abounded as residents, activists and journalists scrambled for information. Was this house protected by law? Could it be demolished legally? Some activists ran to the house to try to form a protective circle, but the Guarda Municipal got there first. A small cadre of activists and

---

3 '*Urbaniza já, a Vila vai ficar*' (Upgrades now, the Vila will stay) was a common refrain of activists, sometimes also shortened to '*Urbaniza já*'. Translating literally, *urbaniza* means 'urbanisation', but 'upgrades' better captures the meaning: asking for development of infrastructure in and around the favela.

residents made it inside their cordon, some filming on smartphones as others tried to negotiate. Amanda, a resident prominent in the resistance movement who had made it inside the cordon was shouting: 'You can't demolish this house.' Luiz tried to push through the police cordon and was pushed back with a riot shield. Tensions were high and the situation threatened to descend into violence. However, Luiz and the activists nearby showed restraint, shouting their anger in place of resorting to physical violence, and the Guarda Municipal in question chose to remain in line instead of taking further action.

Moments later, the owner of the house and a lawyer arrived and, after a short conversation with the Guarda Municipal leaders, the guards walked off as one, to the sound of thunderous applause from the assembled crowd of residents and activists. It was over as suddenly as it had begun. Amanda addressed the clutch of journalists, explaining that the guards were trying to move the fence which demarcated the Olympic Park construction site so as to isolate the house inside the site and away from the community, a tactic they had used previously to break community ties, facilitating further demolitions. Finally, Penha appeared, walking towards us from the direction of the church with a warm smile on her face, as so often. Standing little more than 5 feet tall and with a wiry frame, the near ever-present smile on her rugged face exuded warmth. She shared a hug and some quiet words with her family. A journalist took a photo of their brief conversation and she hugged him as well. Cheerfully, she took her position in front of the rubble of her home and orchestrated the cameras and journalists so she could speak with the debris behind her.

'Today', she explained, 'is International Women's Day. My name is Maria da Penha, I have a church,[4] I have a law,[5] I just don't have the right to housing. Today I am being totally disappropriated from my home – I was taken out, I didn't receive anything, I don't have anything. I am here only with my face, my courage and my bones, to continue fighting for my housing in my community.' In her short speech, she explained that the courts had decided to build a road where her home was, and 'unfortunately our justice system is like this ... this is how things work in this country. For mega-events, they take your house and you're in the street.... Now the fight is for me to stay in the community.' She explained that she would stay with her family in the community church, and challenged Mayor Eduardo Paes to keep to his promise that 'those who want to stay can stay'. Reaffirming her desire to continue fighting, she asserted: 'I am firm and strong, they can demolish

---

4 A reference to the Igreja de Nossa Senhora da Penha in Rio's North Zone.
5 A reference to Lei Maria da Penha, a domestic violence law named after a survivor and activist of the same name.

my house but they can't destroy me.' A smattering of applause from both journalists and activists greeted the end of her speech.

After speaking to journalists, Penha headed back towards the church to coordinate the activists who were moving her possessions into the building. With time to stop and think, I felt the hot sun beating down on my neck as midday approached. Along with Melissa, I headed into another resident's house, gratefully accepting the offer of water and the chance to charge our phones. Penha had been due to speak on a panel downtown in the afternoon, part of a series of events marking International Women's Day, before being awarded a prize to celebrate the contribution of women citizens in the State legislature at an event organised by the State Commission for the Defence of Women's Rights. Her attendance at the first event had already been called off, but she was still intending to receive her prize in the assembly that evening. After an hour or so recuperating from the events of the morning, word rippled around the community that the Mayor had called a press conference in the afternoon at his official residence in Botafogo, in Rio's South Zone. Hopeful whispers wondered whether he would be announcing the implementation of the *Plano Popular* (Popular Plan),[6] the community's proposal for coexistence with the Olympic Park, or some other plan for the remaining thirty or so families to stay in their homes. The press conference would be at 5 p.m. and residents set about planning their own press event outside the Mayor's residence at 4 p.m., intending to attend the Mayor's event afterwards, to learn what would happen to them and their homes.

Once we had made our way back into the city and called up more RioOnWatch volunteers, we arrived at the small event outside the gates of the Mayor's residence to find a swarm of TV cameras around Penha and some twenty activists waving banners and placards at the passing traffic. A small group further down the road, at a set of traffic lights, stood in the road displaying placards when the lights were on red. The microphones thrust in front of Penha and other residents bore the logos of all the major Brazilian TV networks, including Globo, the dominant network, which is often accused of biased reporting, particularly against favela residents (Rosas-Moreno and Straubhaar 2015). I could not recall ever seeing a Globo journalist at a Vila Autódromo event previously. As a group, we set about filming, taking photographs and tweeting about the demonstration. Penha was asked about the award that she would receive that evening for being a strong woman citizen. She explained that 'the medal that I will receive tonight will serve to strengthen me in the struggle'. After the interviews, journalists

---

6 While the literal translation of the Portuguese word '*popular*' gives the same word in English, the Portuguese term is used in this sense to clearly mean 'of the people', so much so that RioOnWatch chose to translate the term as the 'People's Plan'.

filmed residents holding their banners and placards as supporters chanted their refrain of '*Urbaniza já! A Vila vai ficar!*' The hastily assembled placards held by the small band of supporters had a clear gendered theme to them, from 'The women of Vila Autódromo teach us how to fight' to 'Today City Hall presents its policy for women: VIOLENCE'. A member of the Comitê Popular da Copa e Olimpíadas (Popular Committee for the World Cup and Olympics, generally referred to as the Comitê Popular), held up a printout of the *Plano Popular* calling out to Eduardo Paes: 'Mayor, if you are going to upgrade the community, here's the plan.' Another member of the Comitê Popular passed out factsheets explaining the plan for journalists: both of these activists are urban planners who worked on developing the plan.

After residents had spoken to the press, word went around that the Mayor had moved his press conference: it would instead be held at the City Hall in Cidade Nova at 4:30. Cidade Nova is on the other side of Rio's downtown business district – getting there in the half hour before it started would be impossible. I later learned that a couple of RioOnWatch volunteers had made it to the event, but were barred from entry as their names were not on the approved press list. All hope of a positive development in this favela's story ebbed away with the realisation that the Mayor didn't want the residents there when he announced what would happen to them. Indeed, *Folha de São Paulo* later reported that the change was made as a direct result of residents organising their own event outside the municipal government's planned press conference (Vettorazzo 2016). After a hasty discussion, we all made our way towards the State assembly for the prize-giving event that evening, some taking cars, but many walking as a group to the Metro station to make our way to Praça XV, where a feminist demonstration was under way prior to the event inside the legislature.

As we approached the building, we saw a crowd of several hundred people, mostly but not exclusively young women, gathered in front of the grandiose Palácio Tiradentes, where the State legislative chamber is located. A large purple banner on the steps leading up to the building called for the legalisation of abortion. A group of drummers led the crowd in feminist chants between speeches from various women's rights activists on a microphone set up for the event. Towards the end of the demonstration, as darkness fell, Penha addressed the crowd. She told the assembled feminist activists that, 'Today, more than ever, those of us who have gathered together in this square can see a better tomorrow.' The tone of this speech was typical of Penha, somehow able to strike a positive, hopeful and inspiring tone even on this day, the day she later called the worst day of the entire process. After she spoke, the crowd were led in a chant of 'We are all Maria da Penha, we are all comrades, we are all Vila Autódromo.' Penha then made her way into the colonial palace for the awards ceremony. We followed, although many fellow supporters of Vila Autódromo, who hadn't had a chance to change into long trousers and who were carrying placards and banners, were stopped by security. Some seemed to have made it in though, as had lawyers from the State of Rio de Janeiro's Public Defender's Office, which exists to provide legal support to those who are unable to pay for it, and who have long supported the community's struggle for permanence. We found seats in the chamber and watched the room fill up. Clearly, the activists who had been stopped by security outside had found their way in eventually, as half the room seemed to be there for Penha, overflowing into viewing galleries at the sides of the chamber.

The event opened with a short speech from the chair of the assembly, which is on a raised platform at the front of the chamber, by Enfermeira Rejane, State Deputy for the Communist Party of Brazil (PCdoB), who had organised the event and spoke even as the room continued to fill with activists, some of whom were hanging Vila Autódromo banners around the chamber. As she mentioned Penha for the first time, the crowd erupted into a standing ovation, which brought a lump to my throat and a tear to the eye of some around me. Rejane went on to chastise the authorities, explaining that, 'It's not just about a house, it's a lack of dialogue', typified by residents' exclusion from the municipal government's press conference earlier in the day. There were several awards to be given, all to strong women citizens, who came up to receive their award and a bunch of flowers, and each made a short speech. For all of them there was polite attention and applause, but it seemed clear that most people were there for Penha, who received her award towards the end of the ceremony.

When she was announced the crowd erupted again, chanting their familiar refrain of '*Urbaniza já*', demanding upgrading and permanence for the community. Standing on the platform, Penha seemed even smaller than usual as she looked out at the chanting crowd. Across from me I spotted her husband Luiz, a picture of pride as his wife was presented with her award. She gave a short speech that seemed almost timid by her standards, thanking her family and her supporters, dedicating the award to them and vowing to continue fighting. Applause rang through the chamber, followed by more chanting. I began to well up and many of my RioOnWatch colleagues were in tears too, as the sheer scale and range of emotions throughout the day finally surfaced. We filed out after the ceremony and news started to spread from the Mayor's press conference: there would be upgrading, but very different from that envisaged by the *Plano Popular* developed with residents' input. I caught up with one of the urban planners who been involved in creating the *Plano Popular* on the way out. He dismissed the Mayor's plan as 'ridiculous', as it had much smaller homes and lacked any communal space, saying it had been designed simply to give the appearance of a community.

Space, power and resistance at Rio 2016

This book is a story of resistance to evictions like the one detailed in the previous section. It is a story of one community which, supported by others, stood up to a globetrotting, destructive behemoth. As such, it is a story about power, about who decides what and who urban space is for. These events, captured during fieldwork in the lead-up to the Olympic Games, provide a snapshot of the dynamics of state violence and resistance I studied: contested legal rights, different notions of what the space represents, the use of social media and smartphones, and the importance of speaking to journalists. These residents, in collaboration with supporters in organisations across the city, used innovative strategies to stand up against eviction, drawing on new technologies as well as the supercharged international attention focused on the Olympic Games to force their issue into public consciousness. Where the Olympic Games has historically driven forced evictions and gentrifications in host cities (Centre on Housing Rights and Evictions 2007; Boykoff 2014a) from Seoul and Beijing to Vancouver and London, these activists were able to affect outcomes in ways others have not.

Rio's (in)famous favelas – informal, self-built communities which emerged due to an unmet need for housing and are generally treated with a combination of neglect and outright violence by the state – were always going to be threatened by mega-events in the city (a more detailed discussion of the emergence of favelas and their position in the city is included in the following chapter). Vila Autódromo was not the only favela in Rio faced with evictions during the pre-Olympic period – far from it: 22,059 households were evicted in at least thirty favelas according to data compiled by the Comitê Popular (2015) – but Vila Autódromo came to be seen as an emblematic case for a number of reasons. First, it was the only favela where the local government admitted evictions were caused by mega-events; its location adjacent to the Olympic Park construction site making this impossible to deny. Other favelas across the city suffered evictions either directly, from legacy projects like the Bus Rapid Transit system, or indirectly, from the climate of real estate speculation encouraged by mega-events, muddying the waters for journalists seeking to report on Olympic preparations. Second, residents of Vila Autódromo had clear legal rights and a well-organised Residents' Association, which had fought off eviction attempts in the past, particularly in the 1990s. These rulings made this particular case an important precedent: 'If they can remove Vila Autódromo, they can remove anywhere', as one activist put it. Third, and relatedly, those seeking to remove Vila Autódromo represented a cornucopia of powerful interests in Brazil, including the construction sector, their political allies, and the International

Olympic Committee. This created an opportunity to set a similarly power-ful precedent: that even the interests of these groups could not quash the rights of *favelados*, as favela residents are known. For these reasons, Vila Autódromo was able to garner support from groups across the city, as well as nationally and internationally in their fight against eviction.

In 2018, having returned to Rio for a second period of fieldwork, I asked Luiz what he thought the legacy of the Olympic Games was. Luiz responded that it was 'a joke', and he outlined what he thought the legacy could have been:

> Vila Autódromo is a peaceful and orderly community, a community that is never in the headlines as an aggressive community, bringing danger to society. It's a community without militia, without traffickers, a community where you don't see shootouts, rape, you don't see assault, you don't see people killing each other, as you see in so many other communities. It was a perfect commu-nity to be embraced by the municipal government and to have infrastructure development as a real social legacy.

Luiz wanted to see the political and financial capital unlocked by the Olympic Games used to show how favelas could be integrated with the city, based on residents' priorities and needs. This approach to urban upgrading in place of slum clearance chimes with contemporary best-practice approaches in urban planning, which emphasise participatory planning and legal rights as reflected in the United Nations' New Urban Agenda. Although Luiz's wish for government support for this vision did not come to pass, residents and their supporters sought to demonstrate a different conceptualisation of their informal community, based on its safety and homeliness: in essence, a good place to live.

This sits in direct contrast to what Janice Perlman (1976) described as the myth of marginality nearly fifty years ago, the (misplaced) idea of favelas as marginal, disease- and crime-ridden havens of poverty, which serves to justify blanket evictions and slum clearance. As Perlman (1976: 195) notes 'favela eradication expresses basic and sometimes calculated misunderstandings of the favelados, and is best understood as a specific instance of upper-sector policy carried out at the expense of lower sectors using the ideology of the myths of marginality'. Despite fits of progress in the intervening decades, these myths still perpetuate poor policy making, with Perlman (2010: 149) noting recently that 'the concept of marginality with its multiple and shift-ing connotations provides a window into the thinking of the general public and some policy-makers, inflamed by the near hysteria in the mass media'. The rehabilitation of removals as a legitimate policy of government in the pre-Olympic period is similarly based on a 'metaphor of abandonment', in the terms of anthropologist Alexandre Magalhães (2013: 104–105).[7] The popular conception of favelas as marginal, as blights on the city, creates an imperative for removal, particularly in the context of sporting mega-events, when the city will be on show to the world. For Magalhães (2019), 'the repertoire of removal' developed in the early 21st century, discussed in more detail in the following chapter, clearly plays on these myths of marginality.

Residents of Vila Autódromo and their supporters showed a version of their community that defies the myth of marginality and sought to promote this alternative perspective, with a view to countering not only their own eviction, but favela removals more broadly. This book outlines how they constructed a different vision through the urban space of the community and the social relations that took place within it. In doing so, I argue, they created a sense of the place that transcended the physical space of the community, spreading across geographical scales through social and traditional media. This sense of place is bound up with a radical transformation of housing politics and serves a heterotopian role of presenting a localisable utopian reality, reinforcing the feasibility of this approach. A range of innovative strategies, from urban planning to museology, were used to make this a concrete and clear alternative, and promote a different, more integrated relationship between the formal and informal parts of the city. This book describes the process of creating, reinforcing and spreading this different conception of the favela as a tool of resistance to eviction.

Being there, doing ethnography

This book is based on 14 months of ethnographic fieldwork in Brazil, conducted initially between September 2015 and September 2016, followed by a second period of fieldwork in July and August 2018. This involved a range of specific data-gathering methods but was principally based on participant observation, complemented by interviews, document analysis and archival research at the National History Museum in Rio de Janeiro. Following the advice of Emerson et al. (2011), I recorded this data in a notepad at the time, noting key words and phrases from what people told me alongside my own observations, and writing these up later in the day when I had returned home, fleshing out the keywords while the events were still fresh in my mind. This formed a corpus of over five hundred pages of typed field notes on which this book is primarily based.

---

7 The Portuguese word *remoção* literally translates as 'removal', but is also used to mean 'eviction'. Both translations are used in this book based on context, with removal generally used to signify a broader policy of favela clearance.

The first period of fieldwork was punctuated by time away from Rio de Janeiro at the Federal University of Paraná in the southern city of Curitiba, which was an opportunity to take stock of the field notes I had gathered and refocus. This allowed me to take a very broad scope on entering the field of researching activism related to the impacts of the Olympic Games, and progressively narrow the scope of the research to the specific issue of evictions in Vila Autódromo, based on events in the field. On arrival in Rio de Janeiro, I was only peripherally aware of Vila Autódromo's case, but through the first few months it became clear that this was one of the major ongoing contestations in the city. I had attempted to make contact with a range of groups before my arrival in Rio through email and was invited to the weekly meetings of favela advocacy NGO Catalytic Communities. Through contacts made at these meetings, I also began attending weekly meetings of the Comitê Popular, an umbrella group for anti-Olympic movements. In both these forums, the issue of evictions in Vila Autódromo was among the most frequently discussed topics. Importantly, even in late 2015, the struggle over Vila Autódromo was widely recognised as being symbolic of struggles of other favelas against arbitrary eviction, for the reasons outlined above.

Ethnography, it is important to note, is a methodological approach to research and to writing. It does not prescribe particular data-gathering methods such as observations and interviews but is rather characterised by an approach to research and the way researchers should interact with the people they study. Ethnographers, in some sense, live the social reality we seek to study with our 'participants': we share in their victories and commiserate in their defeats. We walk alongside them as they engage in their day-to-day lives and we become part of their lives as they become part of ours. Of course, this is not to say we experience the rhythm of life in the same way: my status as a white, Western man means my own interactions often differed dramatically from those of many of the people I worked with, not least my interactions with the authorities. But embedding ourselves in the social worlds of others allows us to become better acquainted with the 'texture of other life', as Borneman and Hammoudi (2009: 14) put it. Ethnography, then, is an 'immersion in others' worlds in order to grasp what they experience as meaningful and important' (Emerson et al. 2011: 3). Being there, to borrow Geertz's (1988) phrase, allows us to gain rich insights into the way that social world functions, giving a far deeper, more detailed and nuanced experience than a detached observer would enjoy.

Does this compromise our objectivity, our distance, and ultimately the quality of our analyses? Maybe, but this must be balanced with a closer reading of social life. I cannot dispassionately analyse whether evictions in Vila Autódromo were justified while having watched tears roll silently down

Luiz's face when his home was being demolished. Luiz was my friend, he welcomed me into his life, inviting me to play on his football team in tournaments, showing me his photos of wildlife in the community, sharing jokes and conviviality at a range of events. To take a step back from all that is to lose the great value of ethnography: its insight into everyday interactions and relations and the meaning attached to them. This, in turn, influences the way ethnographers write. I want these people to leap out from the page – for you, the reader, to get to know them in the way I have and to understand their joys and despairs, their hopes and fears. Above all, I hope to convey a sense of what the fight against eviction felt like, not just the academic details, but the emotions and rhythm of how this affected people on a day-to-day basis.

For this reason, I eschew many of the terms used by researchers for the people they work with: participants, respondents, interlocutors, informants. They are all unsatisfactory in that they define these people by their relationship with me, the researcher. Instead, I refer to them as residents or, when speaking about the broader group of people who supported the fight against eviction, as activists. This, I hope, allows them to come to life more freely in these pages, albeit still filtered through my own experiences and relationships. I also, in some cases, use their real names. Many of these people are public figures, and so being able to connect their public utterances in journalistic reporting with more private discussions that I bore witness to and participated in reveals some of the tactical framing they are engaging in, among other things. Similarly, the well-reported nature of their views limits the likelihood of harm from my using their names, but I have nevertheless taken care to ensure any potentially harmful disclosures are protected by anonymity, usually by avoiding naming any specific person (either real name or pseudonym) as the source for information. I only use real names where I have explicit permission to do so. At the end of formal interviews, I asked all interviewees whether they wanted me to use their real name, with separate questions about quoting from the interview and describing my observations. All those who were asked replied in the affirmative in both cases, often after a brief discussion of what the consequences might be. As I will explain shortly, I did not interview everyone I observed, and therefore I did not have a chance to discuss using real names with all the people who are discussed in this book. Where this is the case, these people's identities have been concealed through the use of pseudonyms, and where their public utterances are quoted, care has been taken not to connect these to the individual's pseudonym in any way.

For a number of reasons, I did not conduct formal interviews with activists in the lead-up to the Olympic Games, preferring instead to rely on questions asked in naturalistic contexts than sitting down with a dictaphone.

Primarily, this was because these activists were incredibly busy during this period, particularly residents, many of whom continued to work and support their families while fighting for their homes. One of the main constraints on their time was journalists' interviews – I was concerned that if I conducted interviews before building rapport I would get the same answers as journalists. Over time, I came to sit in on some of their interviews with journalists and other visitors, in some cases helping out by translating into English. Given that I was seeking to pull back the curtain on what lay beyond beyond the public face, I found it more fruitful to drop my questions into everyday situations, in the hope of gleaning less polished responses (see Walford 2007). However, this inevitably meant that answers were not recorded as accurately, with my notes often containing just a few key words of quotation, and the rest of the picture built up through paraphrasing. As a result, while I have endeavoured to place prominence on activists', and particularly residents' voices where possible, a higher proportion of my own voice appears than I would necessarily like.

In 2018, two years after conducting the bulk of the fieldwork upon which this book is based, I conducted semi-structured interviews with leading activists as part of my follow-up fieldwork, to allow space for those involved to explain the issues in more detail. While those I sought to speak to were less busy than in 2016, they were not all easily accessible: some had moved to other cities, others I found it difficult to arrange interviews with due my limited time during this period. These interviews, conducted after a large part of the analysis for this book had been conducted, allowed me to clarify important details while recording lengthier explanations of events in activists' own words. In total, ten semi-structured interviews were conducted, ranging from 30 minutes to 75 minutes. While some questions were asked to all, such as what the legacy of the Olympics was in their view (see Talbot 2021), many questions were tailored to the individual's experiences, seeking to understand their role in the story this book tells. It is important to note that this book is an ethnography of the resistance movement, not an attempt to understand everyday life in the community. While residents are, of course, a fundamental part of the movement, it also includes other groups who broadly termed themselves as supporters (*apoiadores*) of the community. In particular, Catalytic Communities and the Comitê Popular played key roles in the events presented and analysed in this book, alongside residents.

This research is explicitly and unapologetically partisan. This has important implications for the nature of knowledge produced and the scientific endeavour. These implications, however, are not to be shied away from, but to be embraced. As Becker (1967: 239) puts it, 'the question is not whether we will take sides, since we inevitably will, but rather whose side are we on?' Becker's (1967) ensuing call for an underdog sociology is too simplistic, however, as who deserves the underdog label in any given scenario is in itself a value judgement. Following McDonald (2002) and Gouldner (1968, 1973), I argue that this taking of sides must be underpinned by a set of explicit values, allowing the reader to understand why the sides have been chosen. Broadly speaking, this research has been grounded in principles of social justice and democracy: the ideas that we should all be treated with a certain fairness and should have a significant voice in changes that affect our lives. It is through this lens and set of values that I find myself on the side of residents of Vila Autódromo and their allies in fighting against evictions. Echoing Magalhães (2019: 10), 'those who follow situations like these and don't feel them have lost their humanity'.

As is the case with any ethnography, and arguably any research whatsoever, my own subjectivities have filtered through the observations and analyses. While engaging in reflexive practices, such as taking time away from the field to refine the scope of the research, this remains a study based on my experiences. As such, it is important to clarify some of the fundamental principles with which I approached this research, so that you, the reader, can understand my position and how this may have had a bearing on the research itself (Dean 2017). At times, it is clear that the data gathered has been influenced by my own position in the field and these instances are clearly highlighted, with explanations of why this was the case and its implications. It is certainly the case that my focus on Vila Autódromo was driven by a number of factors, including the ease with which I was able to gain access (see chapter 3). The focus on international media perspectives was guided by my work with Catalytic Communities, with whom I felt very much at home as a *gringo*, as Westerners are known in Rio (see chapter 5).

I learned Brazilian Portuguese for this research. Often, the trials and tribulations of language learning and its processes are left out from ethnographic accounts, to the detriment of the reader's understanding (Gibb and Danero Iglesias 2017). The reasons for this are understandable: to admit that at some points in our fieldwork we didn't understand the very words people were saying to us makes us vulnerable to well-worn critiques of ethnography as unrepresentative. However, to ignore these elements of research practice does a disservice to readers, researchers and the researched. Indeed, issues with fluency explain why I was more comfortable and therefore better embedded with the English speakers at Catalytic Communities than the Portuguese-speaking Comitê Popular. My fluency in Portuguese developed over time. On arriving in Brazil, I struggled to keep up with conversations, often sitting quietly listening to others talk as I was unable to simultaneously understand the speech of others and organise my own thoughts into coherent words at the pace of conversation. During this initial period of fieldwork, I would often reflect that I seemed to be missing key information due to a lack of fluency, frequently scribbling profanities in the margins of my notebooks as an expression of my frustration. This informed the particular style of ethnographic data collection, often jotting notes in my books in the background, not fully participating. This is also part of the reason I elected not to undertake formal interviews in the opening months of the research. After a month or so of struggling along and taking more Portuguese classes, my fluency improved: I stopped missing information and was able to participate more and more in conversations, and to ask questions and gain clarifications on my observations, as described above. I stopped taking classes somewhat accidentally: during an exceptionally busy period in February and March I had no time to attend classes, but during this period I realised I was no longer struggling in the same way. While I continue to find working in Portuguese difficult and at times draining, for the vast majority of the fieldwork I did not find myself missing information as a result of conducting the research in a second language.

Throughout fieldwork, I took on a range of roles, being simultaneously an ethnographer, activist, journalist and fixer. Without exception, I was always an ethnographer first and fulfilled the other roles only when they were useful and appropriate for furthering the ethnography, either through gathering data or negotiating access. Participating in activism not only helped me to understand what it is to be an anti-Olympic activist, but also served to reinforce whose side I was on, building trust between myself and other activists. Similarly, performing the role of a journalist, writing about the favela for RioOnWatch and other outlets, allowed me to contribute to the movement in an appropriate and useful way, fulfilling what Gillan and Pickerill (2012) call the ethic of immediate reciprocity: immediately reciprocating activists for time lost to my research with the benefits of publicity. In this, I was also a witness to events, with the presence of a *gringo* with a camera-phone in the favela increasing the likelihood of bad press for the municipal government. Residents perceived (rightly or wrongly) that this affected the calculus about the level of violence that could be tolerated by the state, particularly during the process of evictions such as the one detailed at the opening of this introduction: would the Guarda Municipal have refrained from escalating the situation with Luiz had there not been cameras around? Acting as a translator and fixer for journalists visiting the favela allowed me to gain crucial access to the process of research as performed by journalists, observing first-hand the way they shape their reports through engagement with the favela. By taking on this range of roles throughout the ethnography, I gained a more holistic picture of the various groups and individuals involved in resisting evictions in Vila Autódromo.

How the story unfolds

In the following chapter, I provide a more detailed context for the research by delving into the history of Brazil and Rio de Janeiro, pulling out important elements of this history which help explain the position of favelas in Brazilian cities and the way housing rights have developed in the Brazilian context. This is followed by a detailed history and description of Vila Autódromo, the community whose struggle against eviction is explored in later chapters. The chapter also includes a brief literature review, situating this research in the context of existing knowledge about mega-events like the Olympic Games and social movements, particularly in the Brazilian context.

Chapter 2 provides an overview of the way the episode of contention unfolded, exploring the broader ideas about favelas that frame these events, one based on the myth of marginality (Perlman 1976) and another on an idea of favelas as safe, homely, legitimate communities. This chapter explores the long-contested relationship of Brazilian citizens to the state, examining the way a discourse of rights permeated the struggle against evictions. In doing so, this chapter elucidates the role of sovereign power in the context of evictions and violations of human rights in the lead-up to the Olympic Games, critiquing the overused notion of a state of exception and demarcating its proper application to this context. This is achieved through an examination of the *Plano Popular da Vila Autódromo*, a blueprint for urban upgrading developed through a collaborative process with urban planners from Rio's universities, which presents a clear alternative conception of favelas.

Chapter 3 starts to explore the way this alternative conception of favelas was constructed by describing a football tournament held in Vila Autódromo in December 2015, one of many social events held under the banner of *Ocupa Vila Autódromo* (Occupy Vila Autódromo). I argue that these events played an important role not only in bringing people to the community and demonstrating support to residents, helping them to continue fighting for their rights, but also by constructing the space of the favela in a particular way. Through a range of techniques, from physically inscribed messages in graffiti and posts about events on social media, to the ways in which residents greeted and made themselves available to foreign visitors, these events served to construct the space of Vila Autódromo as a welcoming, safe and homely community. This requires some critical unpacking of Henri Lefebvre's well-known triad of perceived, conceived and lived space to deconstruct the biases of Lefebvre's work and the challenge of applying these ideas to informal communities.

Chapter 4 details the ways in which this transitory and ephemeral construction of space was transformed in a more permanent sense of place, an idea of what the community represented, while conceptually staking out the distinctions between space and place. I argue that the liminal nature of the *Ocupa Vila Autódromo* events played a crucial role in this process of placemaking. Such liminality brings with it the possibility, or at least the potentiality of a radical transformation, based on Victor Turner's notion of anti-structure, wherein existing social structures can be either reaffirmed or transformed through liminal events. Importantly, the sense of place forged through these liminal events is not limited to those who have experienced the events first hand, and can be spread across geographical scales through social media, as I outline through the example of live-tweeting.

Chapter 5 continues this focus on spreading the sense of place, bound up with its radical political connotations, across geographical scales, exploring the role of journalistic reporting on events. Based on experience of supporting journalists to report on Vila Autódromo, the chapter examines the particular role Catalytic Communities carved out for itself as a translator of not just language, but culture and politics. This involves an examination of the everyday practices of negotiation over the portrayal of favelas in the traditional media and the symbolic struggle this represents. More broadly, the chapter examines the challenges posed by existing preconceptions in the process of dispelling the myth of marginality through spreading this sense of place.

The last of the substantive analysis chapters, chapter 6 considers the Museu das Remoções (Evictions Museum) set up by residents in the heat of their resistance and continued after their specific housing conflict seemed to be resolved. This museum was set up to 'participate in the struggle against evictions, preserving the symbolic connection, emotional memory and social practices of evicted communities' (Museu das Remoções 2017). In particular, this chapter focuses on the role of this sense of place in the museum, and the ways in which residents continue to seek to mobilise this notion of what their community is for political purposes. In particular, the chapter considers the role the museum plays as a totem of a different kind of favela, as an actually localisable utopia, or heterotopia.

The Conclusion then summarises Vila Autódromo's resistance to eviction in relation to the myth of marginality. It considers the implications of this resistance in Rio, considering some of the developments in the city since the events described in this book, notably the dehumanising discourses promoted by now former President Jair Bolsonaro and Eduardo Paes's return as mayor in 2020. It also considers the relevance of Vila Autódromo's struggle, and the wider movement against Rio 2016, with regard to the Olympic Games, exploring some of the ways the event has attempted to reduce the likelihood of similar cases in future host cities. Finally, it concludes with a discussion on whether Vila Autódromo's case should be seen as a success despite the fact that 97 per cent of the community was evicted.

1

Contexts: Rio 2016, favela evictions and Vila Autódromo

The greatest show on earth?

The Rio 2016 Olympic Games are the backdrop to the story outlined in this book. Closely following on from the 2014 FIFA World Cup, the final of which was hosted in Rio's Maracanã stadium, the Games were the culmination of a decade of hosting mega-events in the city, stretching back to the 2007 Pan-American Games and including the World Military Games in 2011 and World Youth Day in 2013. In the early 21st century, hosting of these mega-events spread beyond traditional hosts in the global North to include cities and countries in the global South, notably including the Beijing 2008 Olympics and the South Africa 2010 FIFA World Cup, alongside the events in Brazil. While the hosting arrangements were seen as a risk by event owners like the International Olympic Committee, and Rio was required to successfully host the 2007 Pan-American Games to demonstrate its capability to host the Olympic Games, holding the Games there was seen as an opportunity to use the biggest events in global sport to support sustainable development around the world.

Mega-events, defined as events which have dramatic character, mass popular appeal and international significance (Roche 2000), have long been purported to bring benefits to host locations, from enhancing local tourism to new sporting and transport infrastructures, despite relatively limited evidence. In Rio's case, as with other hosts in the global South, there were also attempts to use these events for geo-political purposes, with Brazil using its hosting of events as part of a broader campaign to take up a permanent seat on the UN Security Council (Resende 2010). However, in the early part of the 21st century, events like the Olympic Games massively expanded in scale. As the price tag for the event has ballooned, the notion of leaving a legacy of sustainable development has emerged as an attempt to justify the levels of public expenditure. Evidence from the early adopters of a legacy framework suggests that this is largely ineffective in creating a sustainable event (Müller et al. 2021). More practically, the discourse of legacy tends to elide the deleterious impacts of mega-events on host cities and is used to persuade host populations of the benefits of hosting (Talbot 2021).

Jules Boykoff (2014a) theorised the approach to hosting mega-events like the Olympic Games as Celebration Capitalism, with six specific elements. First, he argues the Games create a state of exception in host cities by introducing a deadline, thereby enabling governments to ride roughshod over certain laws, particularly environmental regulations (this is discussed in greater detail in chapter 2). In this state of exception, the Games are delivered through a series of lopsided public–private partnerships, where the state commits to underwrite any overspend while private corporations are able to gain sizeable profits. A festive commercialism accompanies the event, using spectacular imagery and corporate sponsorship to transform urban space into 'idealised visions and Disneyland geographies' (Giulianotti and Brownell 2012: 203). Given the scale of the event and in response to the threat of terrorism since 9/11, the Olympic Games enables local security forces to secure the best training and equipment – the tooling up of the police being an important legacy objective (Boyle and Haggerty 2009), frequently threatening rights of political activists. All this is wrapped up in a language of sustainability, both environmental and social, that is divorced from reality given the record of evictions (Centre on Housing Rights and Evictions 2007), repression of marginalised groups (Kennelly and Watt 2011) and greenwashing (Boykoff and Mascarenhas 2016). The process is cheered on by a broadly uncritical mass media which provides little space for critique, although mega-events held in the global South seem to attract more criticism, with the hosts as object of critique, not the flawed model of event hosting (Manzenreiter 2010).

By the time Rio was preparing to host the Olympic Games, these critiques were well established in academic literature, and were bleeding into public discourses about the Games, building on growing contention around the hosting of mega-events over the previous decades (Lenskyj 2000, 2008; Boykoff 2014b). Brazil's strong culture of social movement organising since re-democratisation in the 1980s (see Gohn 2009) surely suggested there would be activism surrounding the event well before the mass protests of 2013 during the Confederations Cup, a test event for the World Cup, followed by smaller protests the following year during the FIFA World Cup. While the 2013 protests were surely not focused on sport mega-events, but were more amorphous and anarchic, there was a current of critique that followed through to the World Cup in 2014, particularly focused on corruption in FIFA (Omena 2015).

We know then, as academics, that the Olympic Games have severely deleterious impacts of host cities. The starting point for this research, unlike previous studies of the Games, was to consider how the local population responds to this juggernaut. How are the impacts of the event contested, challenged and resisted by local populations? To what extent are these multi-faceted impacts linked together, and how are alliances created among oppositional movements? Mega-events like the Olympic Games present local activists with a global platform on which to air their grievances, an unenviable political opportunity, to use the language of political scientist Sidney Tarrow (1996). Thirty thousand journalists, three times the number of athletes, descended on Rio de Janeiro for the Games, a significant chunk of whom sought to tell the story of the city and its people. This presented a unique opportunity to introduce a global audience to Brazil and Rio de Janeiro – how would Brazil's famously strong social movements use this opportunity?

Brazil, Rio, favelas

Brazil, as composer Tom Jobim famously claimed, is not for beginners. A former colony of the Portuguese empire, with an economy highly dependent on the transatlantic slave trade, it was the last major country to abolish slavery in 1889 and legacies of colonialism and slavery remain firmly entrenched, despite the popular myth of racial democracy – the flawed idea that miscegenation means anyone can be Brazilian, which ultimately serves to obfuscate racial discrimination. Brazil's political landscape has long been dominated by clientelism and a relative disregard for the poor and marginalised (Fischer 2008). This is epitomised by the common phrase 'for the English to see', used to dismiss projects targeted at foreign investors and tourists, which dates back to the lack of enforcement of the abolition of slavery, enacted under pressure from the British government. In the years following the abolition of slavery, what we now call favelas began to appear in Brazil's cities, particularly the capital, Rio de Janeiro. A commonly told story of how Rio's first favela, Morro da Providência, came into being stems from this period, which Valladares (2019) calls the myth of Canudos, having become a socially constructed origin story for the favela. An uprising in the Canudos region of Bahia state threatened the new republic, so the government told local peasants that if they fought for the government and quelled the uprising they would be given land in Rio de Janeiro. Persuaded, the local population defeated the insurgents and made their way to Rio and the Ministry of War to take up their new homes. On arrival however, they were told there was no land available and were directed to camp on a nearby hill until something could be done. Nothing was done, and their descendants still live on the hill, having built more permanent homes and infrastructure over the past century. While this folk history may well be riddled with exaggerations, half-truths and misremembered details, it serves to help understand what favelas are: self-built communities resulting from an unmet need for housing, often occupying leftover spaces within cities. Indeed, for Valladares (2019), the story of Morro da Providência served to define favelas more broadly for Brazilian society and elites.

In the early 20th century, under the mayoralty of engineer Francisco Pereira Passos, Rio de Janeiro went through a major redevelopment process, inspired by Haussmann's redevelopment of Paris, widening boulevards and creating grand buildings befitting a capital city, gaining the nickname *Cidade Maravilhosa* (Wonderful City) as a result (Benchimol 1992). The period gained the nickname *Bota Abaixo* (knock-it-down) as a result of the large-scale evictions and demolitions of *cortiços*, the high-density tenement housing occupied by working-class Brazilians in the 19th century, which were in some ways precursors to favelas (Valladares 2019). The demolition of *cortiços*, motivated in part by the poor hygiene and spread of disease in these buildings, was not accompanied by any provision of alternative housing, leading to the proliferation of favela communities (Chalhoub 1993). As Carvalho (2013) notes, these reforms were partially driven based on concerns related to Brazil's image abroad, seeking to make the national capital a more attractive urban landscape. In many ways, this period helped to create the dynamics of the city we still see today.

Rio de Janeiro is commonly split into four zones: Downtown and West, North and South zones, as shown in Figure 1.1. Broadly speaking, the Downtown area is the commercial centre of the city, with economic activity also spreading into the middle-class, touristic South Zone, which is home to the world-famous beaches of Copacabana and Ipanema. The North Zone is densely populated with mostly working-class Brazilians, as is the Baixada Fluminense, as the suburban region to the north of the city limits is known. The West Zone is also home to mostly working-class Brazilians, but is more sparsely populated, in part due to the significant distance to the economic centre of the city. The exception to this is Barra da Tijuca, technically part of the West Zone but similar to the South Zone in demographics, where, since the 1970s, gated condominiums have sprung up to dominate the landscape. Vila Autódromo lies across the Jacarepaguá lagoon from Barra, with the growth of this neighbourhood providing a key pressure for removal.

The oligarchical first republic survived until the 1930s, when Getúlio Vargas took control in a military coup. His 'New State' was based on economic nationalism and despite his fervent anti-communism, Vargas gave some rights to workers as he sought to industrialise the country (Fischer 2008; Holston 2008). Favelas had long been seen as havens of criminality and uncleanliness, going back to the original myth of Canudos (Valladares 2019) and were now made illegal by decree, resulting in the forced eviction

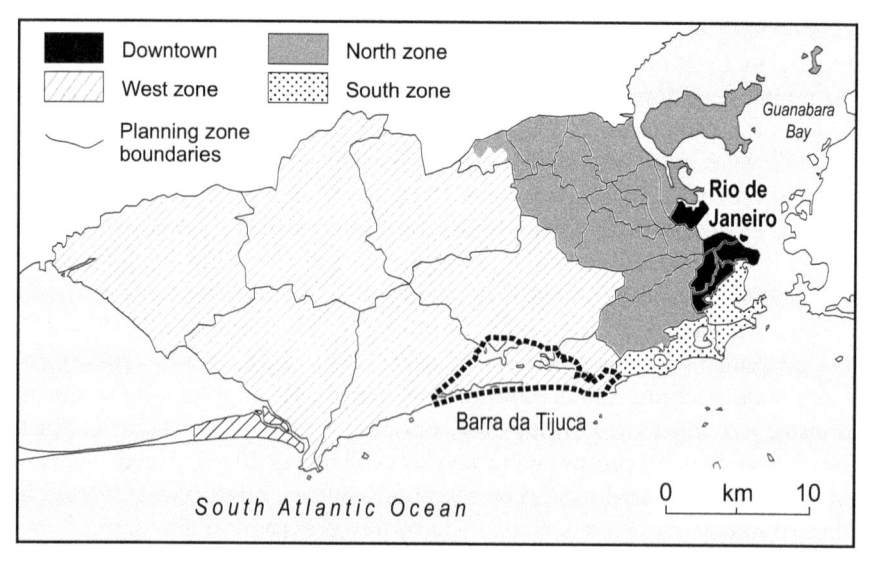

Figure 1.1 Map showing Barra da Tijuca in the city of Rio de Janeiro.
(Map created using data from OpenStreetMap.)

of numerous favelas (Rial y Costas 2011). Democracy returned after the Second World War, following a bloodless coup, and successive governments pursued development plans, including moving the federal capital to a new, purpose-built capital: Brasília. Vargas's policies of economic nationalism and industrialisation were, broadly speaking, continued, as was the steady eviction of favelas across Rio, until a US-backed coup deposed the elected president and installed a military junta in 1964.

The military dictatorship continued the emphasis on industrialisation, but now without Vargas's emphasis on workers' rights. The early years of the military government saw rapid development, known as the Brazilian economic 'miracle'. But while the middle class reaped the benefits of authoritarian rule, disappearances, torture and paramilitary death squads became a fact of life for the Brazilian poor (Scheper-Hughes 1992). Opposition to the government was met with brutal force, with kidnappings and torture common for political activists, including future President Dilma Rousseff. The government invested heavily in expanding telecommunications networks, with the largest television network, Globo, broadcasting pro-dictatorship messages across the country in return. This period was marked by the callous brutality of the state towards the poor, particularly from the military police, with scant regard for human rights (Scheper-Hughes 1992). Rights were reserved for the wealthy elite (Fischer 2008; Holston 2008). In Rio, principally under Mayor Carlos Lacerda, the military regime proceeded with a 'policy of massive eradication of the *favelados* from their existing dwellings and their removal to "embryo-houses" and apartments in the periphery of the city' (Portes 1979: 5).[1] Essentially, the government sought to destroy favelas in Downtown and the South Zone while moving residents to government-built housing on cheaper, sparsely populated land to the west of the economic centre of the city.

A gradual process of re-democratisation began in the 1980s, known as the *abertura*, or opening. A new constitution was written from scratch, with heavy involvement of social movements. Approved in 1988, the new constitution provided an egalitarian framework for the new republic, as well as enshrining constitutional protections against the possibility of a military coup. In particular, the new constitution included provisions guaranteeing the right to housing. Article 6 of the constitution, following a constitutional amendment in 2000, guarantees the right to housing as a social right (Constituição Federal 1988), meaning the state has an obligation to ensure citizens have access to housing. Prior to the constitutional amendment in 2000, the right to housing was included in Article 7 of the constitution indirectly, listed as part of the rights of urban and rural workers (Constituição Federal 1988).

As a result, favela removals dropped sharply following the return of democracy, partly due to the sheer size of favela residents as a voting bloc (Perlman 2010) and partly due to the egalitarian laws of the 1988 constitution (Earle 2012). While evictions still happened, their frequency was vastly reduced, as successive local governments pursued policies seeking to integrate favelas with the formal city, with varying degrees of success. The development of the City Statute, an internationally lauded federal law that seeks to prioritise the social function of urban space, and the addition of a constitutional right to housing, both supported by social movements, added further barriers to evictions. In line with these changes at federal level, Rio's *Prefeitura* (City Hall) passed a law allowing the designation of Areas of Special Social Interest (AEIS – *Area Especial de Interesse Social*), which obliged the authorities to support service provision and integration with the formal city.

As the new democracy flourished, particularly under the presidency of former union leader Luiz Inácio Lula da Silva, known as Lula, the country took a larger role on the global stage, aiming to secure a permanent seat on the UN Security Council – leading to successful bids for the 2014 FIFA World Cup and 2016 Olympic Games (Resende 2010). In 2013, during

1 The Portuguese word *remoção* literally translates as removal, but is also used to mean eviction. Both translations are used in this book based on context, with removal generally used to signify a broader policy of favela clearance.

the Confederations Cup, Brazil (then under the leadership of Lula's protégé Dilma Rousseff) erupted into protest. Initially sparked by transport fare increases in São Paulo, the protests rapidly became much more amorphous and anarchic, particularly as a consequence of heavy-handed policing. As Gutterres (2014: 904, emphasis added) notes 'police acted in accordance with their military training, *a form of action rarely seen by those living outside of the favelas*', revealing the brutality of the military police to society at large. This mobilisation, for which the World Cup test event served as an important catalyst (Carvalho 2016) morphed into a movement against corruption concurrent with Operation *Lava Jato*, a federal police investigation initially centred on contracts awarded by the state oil company, Petrobras, but which became much broader. This investigation ultimately led to Rousseff's removal from office during the Paralympic Games and ensnared many of those involved with organising Rio 2016: then-Governor Sérgio Cabral Filho (2007–2014) and his replacement Luiz Fernando Pezão (2014–2019) were both found guilty of crimes including corruption and money laundering related to mega-event construction contracts. Carlos Arthur Nuzman, head of the organising committee for the 2016 Games, was also found guilty on similar charges. Rio's Olympic Mayor, Eduardo Paes (2008–2016 and 2020–), has so far avoided prison despite numerous allegations and investigations.

Evictions

As discussed, the first favelas developed in the late 19th century, largely built by migrants from rural Brazil to make up for the lack of housing. This self-built nature is the fundamental quality of a favela; that it is built by those who live there through a process known as *autoconstrução*, or self-construction (see Holston 1991). Favelas are therefore developed without the power of the state. As Maricato (1982) notes, this form of building often takes place through a communal process known as *mutirão*, a form of construction based on mutual cooperation in direct contradiction to capitalist forms of production based on extracting profit, translated by Earle (2012: 107) as 'mutual self-help building'. Favelas continued to form throughout the 20th century as rural Brazilians migrated to the cities in search of work, occupying unused land in the urban periphery when housing was unavailable, often due to high costs (Perlman 2010). Given their informal and unplanned development, favelas can be very different from each other. In the built-up areas of Rio, such as Downtown and the South Zone, this led to the traditional stereotype of favelas climbing up the steep hills in the city, as this was the only available space. In the North and West Zones, however, which were less densely populated, favelas sprawled across unoccupied marshes and lowlands and, particularly in the West Zone region of Barra da Tijuca, the formal city later developed around these favela communities.

Over twenty thousand families were evicted from favelas in the run-up to the Olympic Games (Comitê Popular 2015: 36). Mega-events brought a new wave of favela removals, unlike anything seen since re-democratisation (Magalhães 2019). The municipal government argued that the six hundred or so families evicted from Vila Autódromo were the only *favelados* evicted due to mega-events. Statistics compiled by the Comitê Popular (2015) dispute this, suggesting the figure increases to over four thousand families in over thirty favelas if evictions to clear land for legacy projects are included. While additional evictions during the lead-up to the Olympic Games and 2014 FIFA World Cup cannot be directly linked to mega-events, activists argued that many can be blamed on the climate of real estate speculation these events engendered. Seen through the lens of real estate speculation, the clearance of favelas throughout the city not only creates space for new development, but increases the value of existing properties close by, as proximity to favelas acts as a drag on land values due to associations with criminality and poverty. Faulhaber and Azevedo (2015) note that more favela residents were evicted during Eduardo Paes's first two terms as mayor than any other mayor in Rio's history, including the infamous periods of favela removal under Pereira Passos and Lacerda. The geography of these evictions follows a clear pattern of removing favelas particularly in the Downtown and South Zones while moving residents to government-built housing on cheaper, sparsely populated land in the far West Zone. This is eerily reminiscent of the approach taken to favelas under military rule in the 1960s and 1970s. The formal city had spread westwards in the latter part of the 20th century and these Olympic evictions served to remove favelas like Vila Autódromo from the newly developed parts of the city.

While the favela removal policies pursued in the run-up to the Olympic Games physically removed residents to publicly built housing complexes, this was simply one side of a policy to incorporate favelas into the formal city and, by extension, the market. Favelas were also incorporated into the formal city through the controversial pacification programme, whereby specialist military police units occupied favelas. As Boykoff (2016: 225–226) points out, this policy was instituted to attract the Olympic Games to Rio, giving the appearance of safety and security to a notoriously violent city. While noble in its aims of removing trafficking gangs from favelas and creating safer communities, pacification ultimately continued the 'same old variety of oppressive state action in the favela' (Robb Larkins 2015: 139), providing little security for residents. The police have been heavily criticised by human rights groups, blamed for over 2,500 people having been killed by police annually in the years leading up to the Olympic Games. Where the programme was successful in pushing out trafficking gangs, especially in South Zone favelas such as Santa Marta and Vidigal, the subsequent increase in rents led to gentrification, pushing traditional residents out and further contributing to the spatial segregation of the city (Ost and Fleury 2013).

The Brazilian anthropologist Alexandre Almeida de Magalhães (2019) explored this new wave of favela evictions in the city, based on ethnographic work with public defenders and residents' groups. He argues that the discursive groundwork for this wave of evictions was laid previously through discourses in media outlets such as Globo, as commentators and politicians sought to, quoting an interview given by Eduardo Paes in his first year as mayor, 'break the taboo of evictions' (Magalhães 2019: 21). The argument in favour of wholesale favela removal as policy – the city's development plan aimed to reduce the area occupied by favelas by up to 3.5 per cent – was based on favelas being part of a broader problem of urban disorder, as well as environmental justifications for preserving natural landscapes (Mendes 2016a). Such a justification bears similarity to the largely discredited 'broken windows' theory, which argues that removing visible signs of disorder has the effect of reducing crime. This link between favelas and urban disorder has been well established in political discourse in Rio de Janeiro for decades, particularly since the rise of drug trafficking gangs in the 1980s (Cocco 2016). My own experience of favelas in the field is similar to Perlman's (1976: 136): that these communities are 'internally safe and relatively free from crime and interpersonal violence', although this is likely heavily influenced by my own whiteness. Violence is a part of everyday life for many favela residents, a result of the dehumanising discourses surrounding poor, black Brazilians (Costa Vargas 2006) coupled with unequal distribution of rights in Brazil (Fischer 2008; Holston 2008).

Shortly after Rio de Janeiro won the right to host the Olympic Games in 2009 and the municipal government announced its intention to remove certain favelas, the region suffered heavy rains in April 2010, which led to multiple landslides across the city, killing numerous favela residents and leaving many more homeless. These events served to reinforce the discursive work of breaking the taboo against evictions, consolidating what Magalhães (2019: 93) calls a 'repertoire of removal'. According to Brazilian law, favela evictions should only be used as a last resort and only where there is risk to life that cannot be addressed through development. The narratives promulgated by politicians and mass media implicitly positions *favelados* as incapable of understanding the danger they are in, privileging elite conceptualisations of levels of risk. In this sense, Magalhães' (2019) notion of the repertoire of removal clearly draws on the myth of marginality described by Perlman (1976, 2010), positioning favelas as marginal to justify their removal. The rains and resulting landslides therefore provided the state with a powerful argument for engaging in widespread favela removal, while mega-events provided a clear deadline by which to do so. Interestingly though, when evictions were occurring for mega-event led development projects, the term eviction (*remoção*) returned to being taboo (Magalhães 2019). As I will argue in chapter 5, this is likely due to the heightened international interest in these particular cases of eviction.

These evictions had severe impacts on those affected. Residents often complained of the dehumanising treatment, not only regarding the fact of eviction itself but also the lack of information and the process by which municipal government officials pressured them to leave. Magalhães (2019) calls this a moral disqualification, a treatment of people as less than human, which has deleterious effects on their human dignity. Former residents also complained of the health impacts of the trauma they went through at the hands of the municipal government. In one extreme case, detailed by Faulhaber and Azevedo (2015: 95), an elderly resident of Vila Autódromo, who had lived there for thirty-four years, died just one week after being evicted from his home.

In response to the renewed repertoire of removals at the beginning of Paes' first term as mayor, a network of groups came together to form a web of resistance (Magalhães 2019). This was formed principally around the Catholic Church's favela outreach group, the Pastoral de Favelas, a network of residents' associations known as the Conselho Popular (Popular Council), and the State of Rio de Janeiro public defenders' Nucleo de Terras e Habitação (NUTH: Nucleus of Land and Housing). These groups had begun to act together to provide support for favela residents threatened with eviction, with NUTH developing a broader, more participatory approach to working alongside residents (Mendes and Cocco 2016). The collaboration between these groups ensured a wide outreach, as well as significant resources, most notably legal support, but also technical support to produce reports that contested the municipal government's designation of favelas as at risk. Vila Autódromo played a key role in the constituting of this network, largely due to its well-organised Residents' Association and legal status, the result of previous struggles (which will be discussed in more depth shortly). The community was also identified at this early stage as having symbolic importance in the struggle against evictions: at a meeting to plan a protest, the president of the Residents' Association stated that 'if Vila Autódromo falls, all the others will fall', and a city councillor argued that 'if Vila Autódromo doesn't build this movement, all [the other favelas] will be "devastated" as there will be a "domino effect"'' (Magalhães 2019: 238–239).

Once the state has determined an eviction will occur because the land is needed for public use, it becomes very difficult for residents to legally contest the eviction, although they can contest the amount of compensation received (Faulhaber and Azevedo 2015). For this reason, public defenders had to be creative in their legal challenges, avoiding asking courts to rule on the outright legality of evictions and aiming to halt or disrupt the process through other means. For example, in the Estradinha favela, public defenders sued the government for leaving the rubble of former homes on the grounds that it was damaging the health of residents who remained, winning an injunction that effectively halted demolitions until the rubble had been cleared (Magalhães 2019). In other cases, the Pastoral de Favelas and Conselho Popular organised 'counter-reports' to challenge the municipal government's determination that homes were at risk (Mendes 2016b). While this web of actors had numerous early successes in the struggle against evictions, it was eventually disrupted by the state: Rio's State Governor appointed a new head of the Public Defender's Office in 2011, who significantly reduced NUTH's personnel and resources, limiting the ability of the organisation to support communities.

Resistance

This is the combustible mix of circumstances that faced Rio's favelas before the Games. Massive infrastructure spending intending to reshape the city in a short period of time, coupled with a municipal policy of removing favelas despite long-term protections. This book explores the case of Vila Autódromo, a community which resisted eviction despite the odds stacked against them. This serves not only to illustrate what became the emblematic case of Olympic evictions in Rio de Janeiro, but also provides insights into the ways in which communities on the receiving end of what David Harvey (2004) would call accumulation by dispossession can effectively resist. Drawing on a number of creative resistance strategies, this book explores the way Vila Autódromo's residents and their supporters in social movements mobilised the space of the favela to resist eviction.

Residents of Vila Autódromo found themselves in a unique situation. While many favelas have previously faced and continue to face threats of eviction, the community of Vila Autódromo did so in an exceptional context because of their physical proximity to the impending mega-event. What Sidney Tarrow (1996) calls the political opportunity structure was fundamentally altered by the Games. While scholars have frequently explored how the political opportunity structure is transformed in the years leading up to mega-events from the perspective of the state, creating a state of exception, analysis of the effects of this on civil society more broadly have been under-explored.

The literature on anti-Olympic resistance offers some instructive lessons. From Lenskyj's (2000) groundbreaking work on anti-Olympic bid campaigns, a lesson that has become clearer in recent years as the International Olympic Committee (IOC) struggle to find willing hosts (Boykoff 2016; Lauermann 2019) is that the bidding phase of events is a key period for influencing changes, as plans remain in flux and effective opposition can shut down bids. Once the bid is accepted though, resistance becomes more challenging. As Boykoff (2014b) illustrates in the context of Vancouver 2010 and London 2012, grassroots resistance to the Olympic Games is an often marginalised and ignored position, despite global media attention, with activists relying on humour and other creative forms of resistance to make their case in the face of hegemonic power.

Events like the Olympic Games are often presented as a steamroller that destroys everything in its path for the sake of showing the best face of the host city. When activists have attempted to work with the Games to ameliorate local impacts, attempting to redirect the vast resources from the event towards their own priorities, evidence from numerous cases shows they tend not to be successful. However, Vila Autódromo's partial success shows that resistance can be effective: residents and activists were, albeit in a limited way, able to influence outcomes through their actions. This provides an illustrative case study of the way a relatively small community was able to contend with a multi-billion dollar global juggernaut. While this case is obviously about the Olympic Games, the lessons from this struggle are broader. They enable us to rethink the neoliberal capitalist system and understand how the seemingly powerless can effectively resist accumulation by dispossession.

Vila Autódromo

Given our focus on the Vila Autódromo community, it is worth tracing the history of this favela closely. This selective history is drawn from a synthesis of stories told by residents and activists and my own experiences, as well as published sources, including media and activist sources. Vila Autódromo was initially settled as a fishing community on the banks of Jacarepaguá lagoon in the 1960s, squeezed between the lagoon and the Nelson Piquet International Racetrack, from which the favela takes its name. The sign at the entrance to Vila Autódromo claimed that it had been 'a peaceful and orderly community since 1967'. Then a sparsely populated area due to its distance from the economic hub of the city, residents moved there for the safety and the space. As Barra da Tijuca, the middle-class neighbourhood of gated communities and condominiums across the lagoon, expanded in the 1970s and 1980s, construction workers

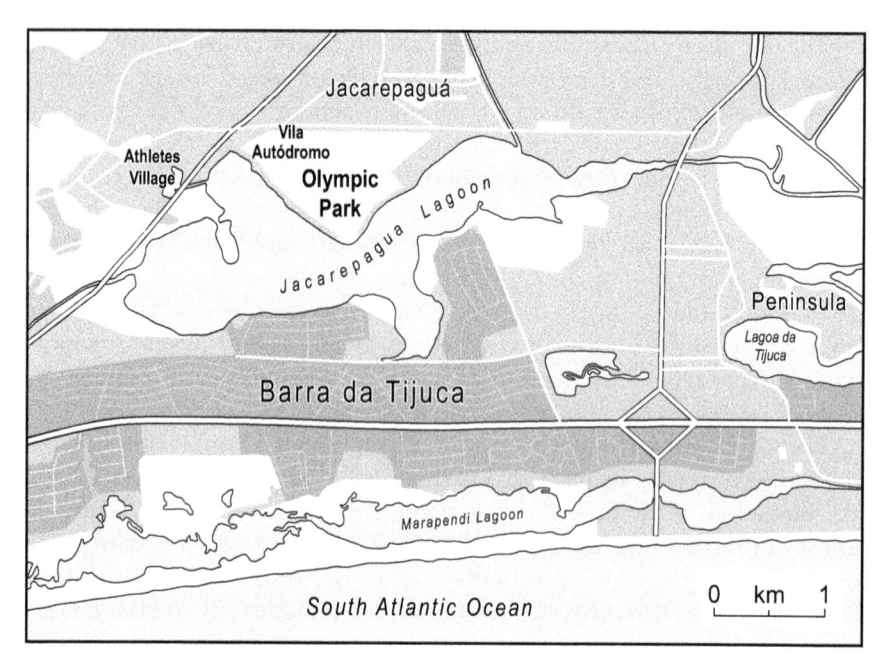

Figure 1.2 Map showing the position of Vila Autódromo in Barra da Tijuca.
(Map created using data from OpenStreetMap.)

settled in Vila Autódromo, enlarging the community to some 600 families
(Cavalcanti et al. 2016) (Figure 1.2).

The expansion of Barra (as the neighbourhood is commonly known) in
this period and beyond is, fundamentally, what threatened residents of Vila
Autódromo. Although technically part of the West Zone, Barra is seen by
many of its residents as an extension of the middle-class, touristic South
Zone of the city. As the value of land around Vila Autódromo increased,
threats of eviction began. The favela not only took up space on valuable
land but also acted as a drag on the value of nearby land and buildings.
In 1993, Mayor César Maia evicted several favelas in the area, arguing
they caused environmental damage, despite the fact that the lagoon was
being heavily polluted by ongoing construction works. Maia attempted to
remove Vila Autódromo, but was stopped when the Governor of the State
of Rio de Janeiro, which owned the land on which the community had
been built, granted residents a 99-year lease to the land (NEPLAC/ETTERN
2016). Maia's eviction attempt had been overseen by an ambitious young
politician who had recently been appointed Deputy Mayor for the region, a
young, clean-cut white man from Rio's South Zone by the name of Eduardo
Paes. He went on to serve as Mayor of Rio de Janeiro from 2009 to 2016,
overseeing Rio's transformation into the Olympic city and the eviction of

hundreds of families from Vila Autódromo, as well as tens of thousands more across the city. He was re-elected as mayor in 2020, after having been term-limited from running for a consecutive third term in 2016, when his preferred candidate and former chief of staff, Pedro Paulo, finished third, and was eliminated in the first round of voting.

In the years that followed this first eviction attempt, life was by no means secure for Vila Autódromo's residents. The Residents' Association, formed in 1986 to promote community interests, continued to fight for greater legal protections for residents. As a result of the struggles for permanence, as well as the government resettling families from other favelas in Vila Autódromo, the community was designated an Area of Special Social Interest in 2004 (Associação de Moradores e Pescadores da Vila Autódromo 2016).[2] This obliged the municipal government to provide services such as refuse collection and mail delivery, as well as a plan for improving the community. This, along with the 99-year lease to the land, made Vila Autódromo one of the most strongly protected favelas in Rio, with significant legal rights alongside a well-organised Residents' Association with experience of fighting eviction. As Luiz explained, when he had initially moved to Vila Autódromo in the 1980s he and Penha weren't used to this, 'but we got used to the idea of resistance, of fighting for territory, for home, for housing, for the right to the city'. When Rio hosted the 2007 Pan-American Games, seen as a test of Rio's ability to host sport mega-events, Vila Autódromo successfully resisted eviction attempts with the support of activists across the city (Gaffney 2016).

In 2009, a decision made thousands of miles away changed the course of the favela's future. In Copenhagen, the IOC awarded Rio de Janeiro the right to host the 2016 Olympic Games, with the main Olympic Park to be built in Barra da Tijuca, on the site of the Nelson Piquet racetrack. At the very least, part of Vila Autódromo would be removed, if not the entire community. An access road into the Olympic Park would cut through the favela and the homes on the banks of the lagoon would be removed for environmental remediation. Others would be removed for the widening of roads and the construction of a new Bus Rapid Transit (BRT) line. The vast and ever-changing number of reasons given for removal created challenges for residents who never knew what the specific reason for their removal was, one of a number of tactics documented by RioOnWatch editor-in-chief Theresa Williamson (2016a) in the years preceding the Olympic Games. While the finalised design for the Olympic Park maintained much of the community, the private consortium that would actually build the park and gain the land afterwards required removal to make the endeavour profitable

2 Sometimes also referred to as a Zone of Special Social Interest.

(Rolnik 2015; Medeiros 2019). As one resident, Amanda, described it to a group of visitors from Amnesty International: 'with the Olympics, the government started to remove Vila Autódromo'.

Over the following years, the municipal government identified those residents who wanted to leave, those who could be persuaded to leave, and those who had no interest in leaving in an attempt to divide and conquer, another tactic identified by Williamson (2016a). This was undertaken through a painstaking campaign of knocking on residents' doors and pressuring them to sign up for housing in the nearby Parque Carioca public housing complex. In the background of the offer of alternative housing was the implicit and (usually) unspoken threat that the entire community would be removed and residents would be left with nothing. In response, residents collaborated with urban planners at the Federal University of Rio de Janeiro and the Federal Fluminense University to create the *Plano Popular da Vila Autódromo* (Associação de Moradores e Pescadores da Vila Autódromo 2012). This plan 'affirms the right and the possibility of permanence for the community in the current area and rejects the involuntary removal of any resident' (Associação de Moradores e Pescadores da Vila Autódromo 2012: 11).

During this time, Vila Autódromo residents were also linking up with other favelas across the city threatened with eviction, as well as the Comitê Popular, an umbrella group bringing together different groups protesting about mega-events in the city. This led to several protests against evictions of Vila Autódromo and other favelas, as well as documentation of human rights abuses in the Comitê Popular's dossiers on the subject (see Comitê Popular 2015). In August 2013, Mayor Paes announced a change of course, committing to fair compensation and promising that those who wished to stay could stay (RioOnWatch 2013). Throughout these protests against eviction, Rio's public defenders had been working with the community to defend their legal rights to the land and numerous residents had accepted offers of compensation or alternative housing and left the community. By mid-2014, many residents were in negotiations with the municipal government, but nearly 200 families remained steadfast in their desire to remain in the community (Comitê Popular 2014).

In March 2015, the municipal government announced eminent domain orders marking fifty-eight families for eviction – essentially forcing evictions through the courts (Parkin 2015). Demolitions became a regular occurrence in the favela, sometimes with little warning for the inhabitants of the homes. While the official reasons for these evictions constantly shifted, the commonly held belief among residents and activists was that the removals were occurring to clear the apparent eyesore of the favela from the margins of the Olympic Park and thereby increase the value of the ongoing real estate development in the area. In June 2015, an attempted demolition led to an altercation with police, leaving several residents injured and attracting global media attention (Watts 2015a). Key figures, including Residents' Association president Augusto and long-time activist Yasmin, were evicted in the months that followed. With evictions proceeding despite the legal efforts of public defenders, residents and activists developed new strategies of resistance through attracting press attention and holding a campaign of social events in the favela, starting in August, in response to the violence in June.

These social events and the broader social movement organising around the community form the central elements of the analysis presented in this book. Having arrived in Brazil in September 2015, I visited the community for the first time in early November, when many demolitions had already taken place. I went with a RioOnWatch volunteer, Steve, to report on a *mutirão* that had been organised to renovate the children's play area, a week after the community's table tennis table had been destroyed. We travelled via metro to Del Castilho in the North Zone to pick up a bus that took us to Vila Autódromo in the West Zone. As we left the air-conditioned metro we were hit by sweltering heat, forecast to reach over 35° Celsius that day. The bus was full, with limited air conditioning despite the overwhelming heat. Looking out of the window as we headed along the Linha Amarela highway, the houses were small and dirty, many entirely hidden behind high walls, a mass of low-rise housing: the largely working-class North Zone neighbourhoods. We drove through a tunnel, under the Tijuca Forest and, as we emerged, the view changed from run-down hovels to run-down condominiums. After we passed Cidade de Deus, the housing complex-turned-favela made famous by the eponymous film, the condominiums became steadily nicer until we reached Barra, when all of a sudden we were surrounded by glass buildings that looked like they were built yesterday: shopping malls and gated communities. The dusty areas to the side of the road were replaced with palm trees and manicured gardens that were oddly devoid of life.

We missed the stop and had a short walk back to Vila Autódromo. There were no pavements for us to walk on. We had to cross the busy Avenida Salvador Allende, where construction work was ongoing. We spotted the favela on the right ahead of us, behind a thicket, as we walked along the edge of the busy highway. On first appearance, it seemed like a motley collection of buildings scattered across a fairly small area, perched in front of the looming Olympic construction site. We were currently separated from it by a canal of black sludge, its putrid stench rising in our nostrils. A rusty footbridge crossed the canal from the highway into the dusty ground of the favela. Above this bridge is a sign with an aerial photograph of the favela before demolitions began with the word 'Welcome' in Portuguese, English and Spanish. Below, again in three languages, it asserts that this is 'a peaceful

Figure 1.3 Rubble by the road in Vila Autódromo, November 2015.
(Image: author's own.)

and orderly community since 1967'. The rusty bridge moved as we stepped onto it; Steve and I shared an anxious look. The surface of the bridge was sheet metal and through holes eaten away by rust, we could see the canal below, a black mire slowing leaching into the lagoon. Surveying the community ahead of us, there were a few houses and some clearly defined roads, while some parts were covered in rubble left from previous demolitions, interspersed with trees and other vegetation (Figure 1.3).[3] The dirt roads were uneven, with large puddles formed from recent rainfall.

After a minute or so of walking, we came to a clearing that had not always been a clearing. The rubble on the ground around us indicated that this used to be a built-up area. A burnt-out backhoe and a rusty shipping container stood nearby. Steve commented that it looked like a warzone and I can't think of a better way to describe it. Houses were dotted around the community seemingly at random, with rubble-filled gaps where homes had previously stood. About half of the eighty or so buildings seemed uninhabited: chunks had been knocked out of the walls to ensure people couldn't move back in. Graffiti covered the walls and fences as far as we could see – not artistic ones, but political slogans. Steve summarised for me as I struggled to translate all the words, saying that all of it basically said 'fuck the government'. To our left, we spotted the *mutirão*, under some trees close to a concrete wall that marked the edge of the community. As we approached, nobody looked up from what they were doing. The play area was colourful and full of people, mostly women in their early twenties, most of them

3 All photos are by the author.

Figure 1.4 The rejuvenated children's play area, November 2015.
(Image: author's own.)

white. As Steve started chatting to them, I spotted an activist I'd met at a Comitê Popular meeting and headed over to catch up. He told me that he'd been there since 9 a.m., along with some twenty-five others. 'All the vibrant colour was added today', he explained, as he rolled light green paint onto the concrete wall separating the favela from the Olympic construction site next door. 'Most of the people here are university students', he said, 'brought here to do this as part of a project for an urban studies class.' 'There are more researchers here than residents left', he lamented, jokingly suggesting we could organise a football match for the two sides.

Steve interviewed a Black woman who appeared to be organising things, asking pre-planned questions he'd drawn from RioOnWatch's extensive contributors' guidelines, before taking her photo with some of the flowers that had been planted in the background. As we continued chatting to people, a young woman came and asked if we'd like food. We followed the woman, whose name was Ana, into the Residents' Association building across the road from the play area where we were served a lunch of chicken and rice, along with a can of coke, for 10 reals (about US$2.50).[4] We grabbed our drinks from an old fridge in the corner and sat at a long table in the centre of the room to eat, Steve chatting to some of the students. Various certificates and old photos of the favela adorned the walls, along with a well-stocked bookcase, and papers were strewn across other tables: this was clearly an important hub of community life. After lunch, Steve interviewed Rosa, the lecturer who had brought the students, before we left. On our way out,

4 All currency conversions are based on 2016 exchange rates unless stated otherwise.

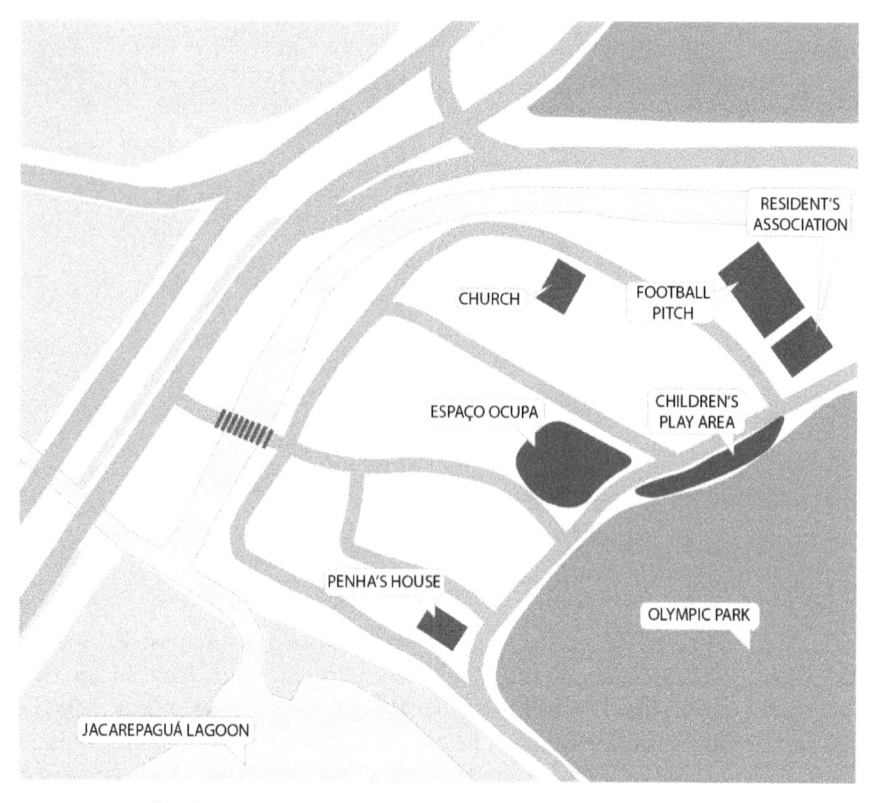

Figure 1.5 Sketch map of Vila Autódromo. Given that demolitions were constant throughout fieldwork, it is impossible to provide a map showing all buildings; instead, this map shows important buildings that will be discussed throughout the book. (Map by Débora Picorelli Zukeran, using data from OpenStreetMap and author sketches.)

we explored the small favela a little more, taking the photos we had been hesitant to take when we arrived. While at times the devastation was jaw-dropping, making it hard to understand why people continued to live here, we both agreed that the favela seemed like quite a friendly place. Some of the houses, even with the devastation surrounding them, looked like good places to live: colourful, spacious and surrounded by nature. It must have been a really nice place before the Olympics came along, we agreed as we left.

By this point, demolitions had already gutted the community, leaving some fifty buildings scattered across the favela. The constantly shifting nature of the favela makes it impossible to capture this on a map, but these buildings were scattered around the community, with roughly 10–15 per cent of the white space in Figure 1.5 occupied by buildings. The buildings were more dense in the central part of the community, around the *Espaço Ocupa* (see chapter 3), and particularly sparse along the shore, with just a couple of homes overlooking the lagoon. The renovation of the park was part of a series of events known as *Ocupa Vila Autódromo* that continued to unfold until the Olympic Games a year later, as residents fought to remain in their homes, displaying a resolute determination that the community would remain. The following chapters discuss several events from this series, as well as other meetings and actions related to the community. Ultimately, this series of events is the key focus of the analysis of this book, which argues that they served to effectively mobilise the space of the favela in the campaign against eviction.

Conclusions

This chapter has provided important background for understanding the unique context in which the story of Vila Autódromo's resistance to evictions took place. Understanding how the Olympic Games are hosted through a collaboration of local elites and global corporations, with very little democratic control, enables us to recognise the challenge that residents and their supporters faced. Awareness of how the normal standards of what can be done by states change in the lead-up to these mega-events is crucial to understanding the resurgence of evictions as a public policy. The long history of Brazil and the historical emergence of favelas also brings important insights regarding how legal routes to resist evictions were utilised by the community, but also the broader history of political contention over the space occupied by favelas in the city. In particular, understanding how these evictions sit in a broader policy framework designed to reduce the number of favelas in the city, stimulated by real estate speculation, helps us understand how these developments intersect with favelas. This raises the question of how resistance can be successful in the face of such overwhelming odds, which is explored in the remainder of the book.

The next chapter explores the *Plano Popular da Vila Autódromo* and its role in disrupting the myth of marginality, presenting Vila Autódromo not as a haven of criminality and poverty but as a legitimate community with an exciting future. In doing so, the chapter explores the complex relationship working-class Brazilian citizens have with the state and the way a language of rights was used to contest evictions. This leads us to an understanding of the sovereign power shaping events in the community, enabling us to see the outcome of this struggle as a de facto recognition by the Brazilian state of a communal right to city, albeit in a limited form. The book then goes on to explore the way residents and their supporters constructed an alternative image of the community through their actions and sought to spread that image across geographical scales in the run-up to the Olympic Games and beyond.

2

The *Plano Popular da Vila Autódromo*: Sovereign power and rights

As the Olympic Games began, twenty families from Vila Autódromo were settling into their new homes in the community.[1] This conclusion to the struggle was by no means certain and at times seemed unthinkable. At the end of February 2016, the contest over evictions in Vila Autódromo's resistance had reached its zenith. After a court had judged that the Residents' Association building could be destroyed, activists had flocked to the community to support residents. Over the following week, many activists slept in the favela to be ready for demolitions, which usually happened early in the morning. The Residents' Association was demolished on Wednesday, as was Carol's home along with her Candomblé spiritual centre. On Saturday, residents hosted an *Ocupa Vila Autódromo* event. The event had been planned for months, but happened to coincide with what was, in hindsight, one of the busiest weeks of the entire campaign of resistance. A video had been produced and shared on social media with various residents inviting people to the event, and invitations had been sent to Mayor Eduardo Paes, State Governor Luiz Fernando Pezão and Brazil's President Dilma Rousseff. There were two events scheduled: in the morning lots would be marked out for new buildings and a clown troupe would provide entertainment followed by a launch event for the updated version of the *Plano Popular* in the afternoon.

The plan was a clear contrast to the notion of favelas based in the myth of marginality (see Perlman 1976). It showed how the favela was not a drug-addled slum, but a self-made community. In this, the *Plano Popular* served as a manifesto for this understanding of favelas as places of sanctuary and security. This chapter examines how the understanding of favelas as safe,

---

1 While this is how residents explain the resolution of their struggle and I follow them in doing so throughout this book, it elides some complexity. Twenty government-built homes were given to residents, although some families who had previously lived in one (usually larger) home were split across multiple homes, meaning, in a sense, that fewer than twenty families remained after the agreement. In addition to this, one resident refused to accept the rehousing agreement and his home, which did not stand in the area the City Hall required for Olympic infrastructure, was never demolished.

communal spaces clashed with municipal government policies derived from myths of marginality, exploring how power shaped the outcome of this episode of contention. I examine the nature of rights in Brazil using Holston's (2008) concept of insurgent citizenship to frame the way rights are understood and applied in the Brazilian case. This examination of Brazilian rights necessarily draws in the question of sovereignty, of who has the right to decide. In this case, it is the sovereign who has the right to decide on which understanding of favelas shapes the future of Vila Autódromo. While examining the nuances of the agreement by which twenty families stayed in the community reveals implicit acceptance that residents should have a voice in shaping their community, the agreement itself is a clear repudiation of residents' right to define their own space and place. The favela is no more (in a material sense at least): the space has been transformed into a condominium, removing the so-called impurities of the favela and driving up land values.

Presenting a plan for the future

It was a baking hot day, the temperature close to 50° Celsius. I headed out to Vila Autódromo for the morning session on my own, spending around an hour on a crowded bus without air conditioning. The place was already busy when I arrived, a hive of activity. There were around a hundred people spread across what remained of the favela in small groups. I headed over to the church, where I could see a small group marking out lots supervised by Augusto. A leader by virtue of his experience of evictions, he came to Vila Autódromo after being evicted from Cidade de Deus in the 1990s, where he had lived after being evicted from his home at the edge of the Rodrigo de Freitas lagoon in the South Zone when he was a child in the 1970s. Those evictions ignited his political awareness and he was instrumental in securing several legal protections for the favela in earlier struggles. He appeared a little rough around the edges, with short greying hair atop his roughly shaven face. With light brown skin, he stood around 6 foot tall, with a small pot belly, and he commanded the respect of residents and activists alike.

A builder by trade, he was giving instructions to the group of youths around him. They appeared to be students and were working from A3 printouts of the plan for the community. A clown troupe moved around the favela, entertaining the students and generating a friendly, relaxed atmosphere. I could recognise about half of the people here, excluding the clowns. I chatted briefly with a few people I knew before heading towards Penha's house, the de facto hub of the community since the demolition of the Residents' Association earlier in the week. Children were gathered outside the building, a group of them being supervised by a couple of adults. They were creating a '*Planinho Popular*' (little popular plan), including things they wanted to have in Vila Autódromo (Figure 2.1). Repeated numerous times was the

Figure 2.1 The *Planinho Popular*, February 2016.
(Image: author's own.)

common mantra '*A Vila vai ficar*' (the *Vila* will stay), while drawings of trees and the lagoon drew attention to the value placed on nature.

After a little while, people stopped marking out the lots to have lunch as home-cooked food for the massed crowd seemed to appear out of nowhere. Some sheets had been rigged up to provide some respite from the unrelenting sun, with a few tables set up underneath them. People spilt out from the tables onto the ground, sprawled around the limited shade in the *Espaço Ocupa*, an open space in the centre of the community (see chapter 3). A steady trickle of visitors continued to flow into the favela and join the growing crowd. People were chatting in small groups, catching up on what had happened in the community during the week. A few of RioOnWatch's team arrived as lunch wrapped up. We caught up briefly as the lunch break ended and everyone made their way towards Penha's house. We met Penha in the courtyard and I asked where they would do the launch. 'Here!', she replied, a beaming smile across her face, gesturing around the shaded courtyard in front of her three-storey home, as if the answer was obvious.

Surely no more than 5 foot tall and 50 kilos in weight, Maria de Penha (commonly known as just Penha) is living proof that people are far more than just their bodies: she had become an almost inspirational figure among activists. This seemed to be due to a combination of her steadfast determination to remain in her home, her erudite way of speaking publicly about the evictions process and her seemingly endless optimism and joy, which clearly originated from her strong Catholic faith. Originally from the northeast of Brazil, she moved to Rio as a young girl, living in Rocinha (Brazil's largest favela, located in the South Zone of the city) before moving to Vila Autódromo with her husband Luiz. Her small, wiry frame, her short, curly black hair and the wrinkles of her light brown skin displayed a frailty of body which belied her fortitude. In an interview conducted in 2018, she explained how she became a leader of the community through her determination to remain as other leaders were evicted:

> I became a leader somewhat by accident, it wasn't my idea, it came naturally, because when the evictions started, in 2013, when Eduardo Paes started talking about this, I hadn't been involved, I never participated in the Residents' Association, me and my husband, we helped out, but it was different, through the church and he as a teacher had social projects in the community.... When I started to understand my right, that I have the right to remain on this land, I started to say that I will not leave and I really didn't want to leave because I understood that I had the right to this land and if I had the right why would I have to leave.... Then, with the trajectory of everything that went on for two and a half years, nearly three years of eviction, I started to become a bit of a leader because I would say that I don't want to leave and I stayed firm in saying that I would not go, with my family's support, and so we together, were able to stay on this land.

Photos of the plan adorned the walls of the courtyard, as well as photos from the events in June the year before, when there had been a violent altercation with the Guarda Municipal. More people had arrived, meaning there must have been close to two hundred people in the community: I'd never seen that many people there. We found a space on the roof of Penha's garage and from our vantage point, up high, it quickly became clear that not everyone would fit in the courtyard: it was already full and there was still a significant throng of people outside.

A decision was taken quickly by some of the residents and soon after the assembled crowd started to leave the courtyard. The launch event was being moved to the children's play area: the only unoccupied public space left in the community with enough shade to shelter the crowd from the baking sun. Speakers were set up in front of the slide and the crowd gathered, with cameras filming at the front. Augusto stood in front of the crowd, next to the brightly painted slide. Holding a microphone, he called out for Penha, but she was nowhere to be seen. Luiz walked around filming on a digital camera, describing what was happening as a voiceover to his video, so he could post it on the community Facebook page later. All of a sudden, applause started from the back of the crowd, slowly rippling forward until Penha emerged at the front, wearing a neat checked shirt and denim shorts, ready to address the mass of people.

She started by proclaiming that over the past week 'the association fell, but we didn't', to a huge cheer. She spoke about how they would continue to resist eviction, even saying at one point 'Long live the Olympics', affirming her desire to coexist with the Games. Amanda took the microphone next, attacking Eduardo Paes; 'he promises that whoever wants to stay can stay, but that's not how the municipal government acts on the ground'. Amanda, along with Penha, is one of the most frequently interviewed residents of the favela. A mother to four children, hers was one of the few remaining homes where children lived – many others had chosen to leave to secure safety for their children. She appeared to be in her early forties, her light brown skin showing the beginnings of wrinkles on her face. She was particularly well-connected with social movements and the Comitê Popular, and when she spoke about the evictions she often tied the problem to larger political issues of real estate speculation and capitalist exploitation, as she did on this occasion. As she spoke, however, the crowd chanted '*A Vila vai ficar*': the chant was started by Penha, a mischievous grin on her face as the chanting interrupted Amanda.

After a couple more speakers, including a representative of the Public Defender's Office who pledged their continued support, Carlos Vainer, professor of urban planning at UFRJ (Federal University of Rio de Janeiro) and co-coordinator of the *Plano Popular*, took the microphone. He declared that the plan rejected removals and that adequate housing is not merely a house but integration with the city. He went on to attack the hotel, gesturing to the Olympic construction rising behind him, which, he argued, doesn't want the view of Vila Autódromo, hence the community was being removed. He explained that Vila Autódromo's resistance was an example not just to others in Brazil but across the world, thanking the residents for 'the class they are giving' in resistance. He offered an anecdote to elucidate how global the story had become, saying he had been to a conference in India where people there fighting eviction had gained strength from Vila Autódromo. He argued that 'the *Plano Popular* is part of the struggle' for all these communities, saying 'this fight isn't over'. He concluded by adapting a popular phrase among the residents, saying 'Vila Autódromo exists *because* it resists' (normally this is 'Vila Autódromo exists and resists').

Next the co-coordinator from UFF (Federal Fluminense University), Regina Bienenstein, spoke about some of the details of the plan. Like Vainer, she asserted that the point of the plan was to show that 'it is possible for Vila Autódromo to stay', and that staying in the community was 'the dream of the residents'. The crowd chanted again after she had finished, indicative of the febrile atmosphere. Ana made her way up to the front to speak next, seemingly nervous, and Penha went to stand by her. Ana was similarly short and lean, with light brown skin, long curly black hair and square glasses. She didn't usually speak to crowds at events, instead preferring to help coordinate things behind the scenes. In this eventful week, however, she had begun to assert herself more than she had previously. She started by saying it was hard to follow everyone, as they had spoken so well. She thanked the people who had come on this day and throughout the week for their support through the human rights violations that had happened here. She declared that, without this outpouring of support, it would have been very difficult to continue the struggle. Each of her statements was punctuated by applause from the rapt crowd. Penha spoke again after her, thanking others who couldn't be here for their support, gesturing to the banners hung around, showing support from various organisations and nearby favelas.

Yasmin spoke next about the violence of her own eviction and the toll it took on her health. Approaching her sixties, her short black hair was beginning to grey, but even after eviction had a detrimental impact on her health, she continued to be a regular presence in the favela, fighting for her former neighbours' rights. The sadness in her eyes, shining out from her brown face as she addressed the crowd, tell their own story of what this community means to her. Prior to eviction, she had represented the favela across the city, linking with social movements to build support for the favela. She broke into tears as she spoke, at which point Penha went to stand with her, comforting her with a warm embrace. Children played on the slide behind Yasmin as she spoke, apparently oblivious to the event that was going on around them. The microphone was then offered to anyone else who wished to speak. The crowd had started to thin; the event was coming to an end. A few more people spoke, including Federal Deputy Chico Alencar, who spoke of his support for the community, accusing city councillors of being in the pockets of developers. After the speeches ended, Amanda thanked the crowd of around two hundred and fifty people for coming, while I made my way with the crowd to the exit from the park, where copies of the updated *Plano Popular* were available in exchange for a donation to support events.

As I will argue throughout this book, the removal process and the resistance to evictions in Vila Autódromo is part of a larger contest over what favelas are – an emblematic case that sits in the context of a wider wave of removals. In this, the contestation over evictions is a contest over place, over how the place of the favela is defined and how these places are incorporated into the city. The visibility brought by the Olympic Games gave increased importance to Vila Autódromo's case, expanding the available avenues for mobilisation and contention. This is not to say it made resistance either harder or easier, as similarly strengthened opportunities and incentives applied to the municipal government's case for eviction. Rather, the global spotlight served to increase the stakes in the contest, with this case likely to set precedent for future struggles over favelas as a key moment in defining what favelas are. In this chapter, I explore how this contest is played out in the wider context of rights in Brazil. In essence, this chapter explores who has the power to decide which conceptualisation of favelas becomes dominant.

The right to the favela?

The *Plano Popular* was formed by residents with the support of students and academics at two of Rio's Federal universities (UFRJ and UFF). The plan, developed over numerous meetings between residents and planners, included a particularly fierce insistence on public space. This, along with the strong emphasis on participation, was a key reason the plan won the Deutsche Bank Urban Age award, a US$80,000 prize awarded by the London School of Economics. The plan itself was constantly updated to reflect the changes in the community, with the plan shown in Figure 2.2 being the iteration presented in February 2016, with space for fifty homes.

Reading the plan, it is clear from the first page of the introduction that this is a demand for the right to the city. Highlighted in a box on the first page (Associação de Moradores e Pescadores da Vila Autódromo 2016: 9) is the statement: 'The Plan for Vila Autódromo is a *Plano Popular*. It is the community that decides and establishes the priorities!' along with the assertion that 'we, residents of Vila Autódromo, took on the challenge of creating a plan where we show the city that we want, to which we have the right, and how to build it'. This desire to shape their own space can also be seen in the way residents protested when the Residents' Association building was

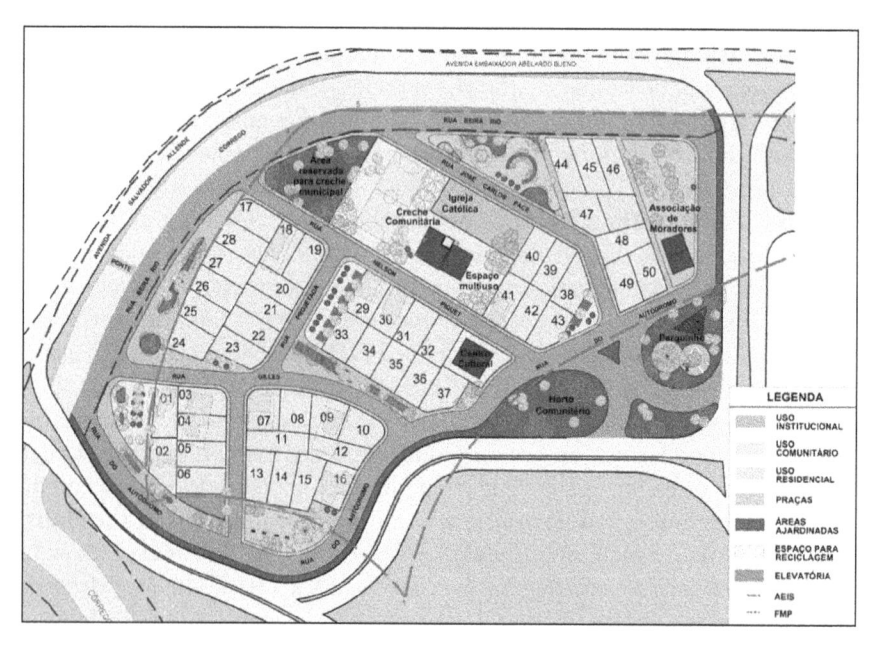

Figure 2.2 The 2016 version of the *Plano Popular da Vila Autódromo*. (*Source:* NEPLAC/ETTERN/IPPUR/UFRJ and Associação de Moradores da Vila Autódromo.)

destroyed, earlier that week. As Guarda Municipal swarmed around the building, fencing it off for demolition, they stood outside silently with their mouths gagged, symbolising the lack of voice they feel they have in shaping the future of Vila Autódromo.

The right to the city is a concept first introduced by Henri Lefebvre (1996 [1968]) in his book of the same name. Lefebvre himself was rather vague on what the right to the city entails, only that it is focused on 'all those who *inhabit*' (1996 [1968]: 158, emphasis in original). He bemoans the 'Olympians of the new bourgeois aristocracy' (1996 [1968]: 159) who no longer inhabit cities, but move from place to place, hotel to hotel, yacht to yacht. David Harvey, himself heavily influenced by Lefebvre's work, provides much needed clarity to the concept. Harvey (2008) grounds the right to the city in the observation that cities are shaped by people but also shape behaviour; as such, 'in making the city man [sic] has remade himself' (Park 1967: 3). Building on this, Harvey (2008: 23) offers the following definition of the right to the city:

> The right to the city is far more than the individual liberty to access urban resources: it is a right to change ourselves by changing the city. It is, moreover, a common rather than an individual right since this transformation inevitably depends upon the exercise of a collective power to reshape the processes of urbanisation.

The marking of lots before the launch of the *Plano Popular* can be described as a *mutirão*. The demarcation of lots that morning was by no means the only example of *mutirão* in Vila Autódromo, the renovation of the children's play area discussed in the previous chapter and the beginnings of building a community crèche were both processes of *mutirão*. *Mutirão* is a clear expression of the right to the city. It involves transforming the city to suit the needs of those involved, usually *favelados*. It is, in its purest sense, 'the exercise of a collective power' (Harvey 2008: 23), but this power is not directed, as Harvey suggests, at reshaping the processes of urbanisation, but at reshaping the city directly. This perhaps reflects Harvey's Western experience, whereby transforming the city is possible only through modification of the laws and structures which guide urban policy. In favelas, however, urban policy is decided upon by residents, sometimes haphazardly, and evolves according to need. Taking the two specific *mutirão* events in late 2016, we can see that residents of Vila Autódromo considered the welfare of their children important and in need of development; hence the renovation of the play area and the beginning of work on a community crèche. Collectively transforming the built environment transforms the conditions of their own existence: in this way, residents are exercising their right to the city.

The right to the city was an idea that was strongly supported among those who were critical of Rio's mega-events. It was a guiding theme of the

Comitê Popular's criticism of the Olympics, that the event was not held for the benefit of those who inhabited the city, a theme expressed in the commonly posed rhetorical question 'Olympics for whom?' Several academic members of the Comitê co-authored a book chapter examining the impact of sporting mega-events from the perspective of the right to the city, concluding that 'there have been profound and on-going transformations to the urban dynamics of Rio de Janeiro … characterised by the subordination of public power to agents of the market' (Castro et al. 2015: 434).

The right to the city is a concern for Brazilian political parties too. As Caldeira and Holston (2015) note, in recent years, Brazilian laws and institutions have developed in ways that lend themselves to popular participation in urban planning, particularly under Presidents Lula and Rousseff of the PT (Worker's Party). Chico Alencar, the federal deputy who spoke at the launch of the *Plano Popular*, is a member of the Freedom and Socialism Party (PSOL),[2] a party formed following a split in the ruling PT government, broadly speaking to the left of the PT. PSOL, in the months leading up to the municipal elections which followed the Olympic Games in October 2016, initiated a programme called 'If the city were ours', which held public meetings throughout the city to generate discussion about the changes residents would like to see. In essence, this programme was intended to generate urban policy as a manifestation of the right to the city. PSOL, a relatively small party, had their best electoral showing ever in Rio's October 2016 elections, becoming the second largest party in the council while their candidate for mayor, Marcelo Freixo, made it through to the second round. Freixo regularly spoke in support of Vila Autódromo and his election materials included photographs with residents of the favela.

Residents' claims of rights were a common feature of the graffiti dotted around the favela. These ranged from generic claims that they had 'the right' to stay, to more specific claims based on legal protections afforded to the community, such as those expressed in Figure 2.3. The *Plano Popular* (Associação de Moradores e Pescadores da Vila Autódromo 2016) also emphatically claims the right to housing for the community. A history of the community is included, including a section titled 'The conquest of the right to housing', detailing previous struggles against eviction and the specific legal protections won through these struggles. Affirming this right to housing is one of the key objectives listed in the plan, including a detailed list of the various legal elements to right to housing:

THE RIGHT TO HOUSING

- The Federal Constitution of 1988 **establishes housing as a fundamental social right**, in Article 6.

2 PSOL is pronounced '*pessoal*', the Portuguese word for 'people'.

Figure 2.3 Graffiti details one of the favela's legal protections: 'Complementary Law 74, Area of Special Social Interest. We have the right to live here, all that remains is to see if there is still any morality in the justice system or if the corruption starts there. Not everyone has a price.' March 2016.
(Image: author's own.)

- A United Nations General Assembly Resolution from 1966, subscribed to by Brazil in 1992, defends the right of all to adequate housing, characterised by accessible cost, by availability of services and infrastructure, accessibility, location, and cultural adequacy of housing. Included in this concept is **legal security of tenure and protection to the citizen from threats and forced evictions.**
- Federal Laws 11,124/2005, 11,481/2007 and 11,977/2009, as well as the State Constitution and Organic Municipal Law, determine the **priority use of lands owned by Public Power for housing as a social interest.**
- The residents of Vila Autódromo have titles from a **concession of the real right of use,** an instrument of urban policy used in land regularisation processes, that gives the right to use of public lands for popular housing. Legal provisions are in Decree-Law no. 271/1967, Art. 183 of the 1988 Constitution, Art. Of the City Statute and Art. 7 of Law 11,481/2007.
- Vila Autódromo was declared a **Zone of Special Social Interest (ZEIS)** for popular housing through Complementary Law No. 74/2005 of the Municipality of Rio de Janeiro. The ZEISs have legal provision in Art. 182 of the 1988 Constitution, Art. 4, item V, paragraph f of the City Statute (Law 10,257/2001) and Art. 47, item V of Law 11,977/2009. (Associação de Moradores e Pescadores da Vila Autódromo 2016: 26, emphasis in original)

I will return to some of the specific legal protections shortly, but before going any further, we must first consider the nature of rights. Academic research, Dembour (2010) explains, has traditionally approached human rights from four distinct schools of thought: as a natural element of the human condition, as political values adopted by societies, as claims made on behalf of the poor, and as an imperialist imposition. Rights are often asserted to be inalienable protections afforded to particular aspects of human life, apparently applicable to all humanity. This understanding of rights, for Dembour (2010: 2–3), is 'the most common and well-known definition of human rights' and has 'traditionally represented the heart of the human rights orthodoxy'. Such protections are considered to be the duty of the nation-state, and as such the conferring of rights is the responsibility of the state. As Hannah Arendt (1958 [1951]: 299) observes 'not only did the loss of national rights in all instances entail the loss of human rights; the restoration of human rights ... has been achieved so far only through the restoration or establishment of national rights'. As such, human rights are indelibly tied to the nation-state, conferred by sovereign power, not by some transcendental, natural source. International agreements and bodies such as the United Nations, with its Universal Declaration of Human Rights, or the Inter-American Court of Human Rights, are significant only because national governments choose to subscribe to them. They do not establish rights above national governments.

Claims of rights made by social movements, then, are necessarily claims on governments to provide or enforce protections for their citizens. As David Harvey (2013) notes, rights are generally conceptualised as individualistic and property-based, sustaining a neoliberal capitalist order grounded in private ownership. As a result, urban land conflicts tend to be seen through the lens of private property, which leads to compensation for evictions not including the land value, and negotiations being conducted individually instead of collectively (Müller 2016). As such, rights are contested, with social movements seeking to utilise the radical potential of rights to empower the powerless, while powerful interests seek to use rights to preserve existing unequal power structures (Tagliarina 2015). Stammers (2009) refers to this difficulty as the paradox of institutionalisation, whereby, once codified in law, rights stand in an ambiguous relation to power: 'while they can still be used to challenge power, their origins and meanings as "struggle concepts" can get lost or be switched in ways that result in human rights becoming a tool of power, not a challenge to it' (Stammers 2009: 3).

The right to housing is a good example of this paradox. Used by social movements, including Vila Autódromo residents and the Comitê Popular, it represents good quality housing for all with access to the city and amenities including education and health as well as protection from eviction, as described in the second bullet point from the list of housing rights. For many nation-states, however, housing is provided by the private sector, with profound implications for housing rights (Rolnik 2013). This individualises the problem of housing, suggesting that the lack of adequate housing is a matter of individuals' own failure, ignoring the exclusionary politics of exploitative capitalism (Hoover 2015).

Throughout their resistance, residents of Vila Autódromo complained that the judicial system was not fulfilling its role in supporting the favela. Holston (2008) points out that Brazilian law has long been used by elites to preserve inequalities, particularly through land ownership laws, through a system of differentiated citizenship, whereby universal citizenship also serves to exclude certain parts of the population from rights. As Earle (2012: 99) summarises, 'people were not discriminated against as non-citizens, but because they were particular kinds of citizens'. Through various legal and political strategies, land ownership laws are used to maintain the privileged economic position of Brazilian elites, an example of rights being used to maintain the status quo. As Holston (2008: 19) observes, 'this use of law not only sabotaged universal application but also estranged most Brazilians from the institution of law'. The allegations of judicial corruption regularly made by residents of Vila Autódromo appear to confirm this estrangement.

As I have argued elsewhere (Talbot and Carter 2018), the demand for the recognition of and respect for the right to housing was an implicit element of the resistance to evictions in Vila Autódromo. At times, this became explicit, such as in Carlos Vainer's speech, which situated the resistance in the global context of housing struggles. However, established human rights NGOs such as Amnesty International and Human Rights Watch focused their attention on police violence in the lead-up to the Olympic Games, with limited discussion of housing rights. The critique of market-based housing provision inherent within the right to housing as it was understood by residents was deemed unacceptable in pre-Olympic Rio (Talbot and Carter 2018).

The claims to rights made throughout the *Plano Popular* draw on Holston's (2008) notion of insurgent citizenship, claimed by the poor through meeting traditional markers of citizenship such as home ownership, taxation and consumption. Beyond the reference to specific laws in pamphlets, graffiti and speeches, the action of hoisting the Brazilian flag over the remaining houses in January 2016 made explicit the claim to citizenship and its associated rights. Holston (2008) proposed three core elements of urban citizenship which exist simultaneously: citizenship earned through autoconstruction, the differentiated nature of rights, and text-based rights in new legal frameworks. Earle (2012) cogently argues that Holston focuses on the first two, underplaying the importance of text-based rights. As can be seen in examples cited previously, such as the list of rights quoted from the *Plano Popular* and the graffiti scrawled across the walls of Vila Autódromo (see Figure 2.3), residents placed significant importance on text-based rights as a crucial tool in their resistance to eviction. As Penha explained in an interview in 2018, knowledge and understanding of rights was crucial to sustained resistance:

> I think that the difference [between Vila Autódromo and other communities that were evicted] was about knowing what you want. I think that the people, especially workers, poor people, they don't have awareness of their right and what it needs … to have rights be respected, you have to fight until the end, you cannot give way.

Luiz, also speaking in 2018, explained the work that public defenders had engaged in to ensure that residents were aware of their rights: 'The public defenders, in meetings, would always make it very clear that we have a right, that while we would suffer a lot of pressure, that if we resisted we would stay because we had the document that gave us rights.' However, as historian Brodwyn Fischer (2008: 5) notes, legal inequality in Brazil occurs due to a misfit between Brazilian law and the communities it is applied to, meaning that 'legal inequality thus has to be sought not in the letter on Brazil's laws but instead in the assumptions that underlay them, and in the processes that enforced them'. Further, as Alves (2018) effectively argues in relation to police violence in São Paulo, while rights have been extended on paper, the racial politics of Brazil inscribes *favelados* and their communities as inherently violent, rendering the exercise of violent state power acceptable.

While Holston (2008) rightly emphasises the potential of the constitution of 1988, he provides limited examples of the usefulness of text-based rights. Drawing on the analyses of Brazilian jurists (in Ferreira and Fernandes 2000) and the list of rights outlined in the *Plano Popular* (Associação de Moradores e Pescadores da Vila Autódromo 2016: 26), it is clear that the constitution grew in importance for social movements as laws were passed to support the right to housing. The concept of social rights as a guide for government policy appears to have resulted in the passage of laws providing stronger protections for the right to housing. Following Earle (2012), we can conclude that while contradictions still exist, laws supporting constitutional rights such as the right to housing have strengthened insurgent forms of citizenship, giving new rights and influence to marginalised populations and social movements. However, the wave of evictions in Rio in the build-up to the Olympic Games demonstrates that such text-based rights are not a panacea; Fischer's (2008) historical observation that the law as written differs from the law in practice still holds true, at least to some extent.

Sovereignty and rights

Despite the advances that have been made in guaranteeing the right to housing, outlined in the previous chapter, almost all the homes in Vila Autódromo were demolished, with new homes built by the municipal government for just twenty families. We can see here a discrepancy, between the right to housing as conceptualised by residents, including security against arbitrary eviction, and the right to housing as applied in law. Brazil, like most modern states, reserves the right to remove people from their homes for public works through eminent domain orders. Many of the homes in Vila Autódromo were removed through such orders. Others were removed through a process of negotiation, whereby residents agreed to leave in exchange for an agreed level of compensation, in this case either money or alternative housing, or both. These negotiations were conducted with the implicit and, at times, explicit threat that refusing to negotiate would mean being left with nothing. I want to focus on one particular case which didn't fit either of these descriptions, as an example of the state of exception.

The state of exception is a well-used concept in relation to the Olympic Games. It refers to the temporary suspension of legal order enabling the extra-legal denial of rights (Agamben 2005). Boykoff (2014a) suggests that the Olympics induce a state of exception in host cities, allowing for the passage of laws which would not otherwise be palatable due to the impending mega-event. There appears to be significant consensus around this analysis of the effect of mega-events on host cities (Vainer 2011; Coaffee 2015; Gray and Porter 2015; Rolnik 2015; La Barre 2016). While there are clearly examples where mega-events engender a state of exception, the concept has been applied broadly and its theoretical utility has been somewhat lost. While these scholars have surely hit upon a genuine phenomenon, an exceptional condition in which cities find themselves when hosting sport mega-events, this is not a state of exception per se. The state of exception is specific concept, referring to a moment in which the rights of citizens are denied by the sovereign with impunity.

Some of the examples given as evidence of a state of exception, such as the passage of legislation altering construction requirements and limiting civil liberties (Boykoff 2014a), or the use of compulsory purchase orders (Gray and Porter 2015), do not constitute a denial of rights through the state of exception. Indeed, as Vainer (2011: 10, emphasis added) explains, in his elaboration of the city of exception, '*Notwithstanding the (formal) functioning of the typical mechanisms and institutions* of the representative democratic republic, the formal institutional apparatuses progressively abdicate portions of their responsibilities and powers.' While the governance processes of pre-Olympic Rio de Janeiro may have enabled a denial of rights, this occurred through the normal process of governance: there is nothing *legally* exceptional about it. While Agamben (2005) does trace the normalisation of states of exception as a form of contemporary governance, with particular focus on Guantanamo Bay, the use of the state of exception to analyse political and governance changes that sit within an existing legal framework is flawed. The exception is an extra-legal concept, in that it occurs outside the normal rules of jurisprudence (Schmitt 1985 [1922]). The examples above may be states of political exception, but not legal exception – and would therefore be better theorised as an alteration to the political opportunity structure, a change in what is politically possible. Legal protections are twisted and bent beyond their original purpose in the abnormal political context of hosting mega-events, but these are not cases of the state breaking laws with impunity.

This distinction matters due to the wider connotations of the state of exception. The exception reveals sovereignty – only the sovereign can define the exception (Schmitt 1985 [1922]). For this reason, the state of exception is important in our present discussion of rights. Where the state of exception occurs, sovereign power is at play, shaping events. Agamben (1998) explains the relationship between sovereignty and rights through *homo sacer*, the person who can be killed with impunity. In essence, *homo sacer* represents a person with no rights, the polar opposite of the sovereign. By virtue of national citizenship, the sovereign confers rights upon *homo sacer*, creating citizens. In the context of favelas, the insurgent citizenship won through autoconstruction generates a recognition of the rights of *favelados* which previously did not exist. As Holston (2008) acknowledges, this is a conflicted and contested recognition. Indeed, as Alves (2018: 8) argues, contrary to gaining rights, 'the racial alterity of the favelados … renders them, in the gaze of the state, as ungovernable subjects and thus subjected to the decisive power of state terror'.

In the case of Vila Autódromo, however, I argue that sovereign power is at play in the reshaping of the community. While the majority of the demolitions occurred within established (albeit contested) legal norms of practice, I will focus here on one exceptional case. Through seeing this eviction as occurring in a state of exception, we see the influence of sovereign power on the outcome of the community's struggle. As such, we are able to analyse the agreement made between the municipal government and residents to build new homes as an agreement between the sovereign and citizens, conferring rights on residents.

First, in order to establish that a state of exception existed, I must first expound the details of the norm of demolitions. Those who negotiated with the municipal government were given the chance to leave in their own time, before workers demolished their homes or, where demolition was unfeasible, homes were made uninhabitable by knocking chunks out of the walls with sledgehammers. Negotiations were conducted privately with individual families, meaning different families with similar houses received different compensation packages, a sore point with many former residents. In particular, residents and activists condemned what they called a campaign of psychological terrorism to create inhospitable conditions for those living in the favela and force them to negotiate with the city. Those whose homes were demolished under eminent domain provisions faced a different process, with demolitions conducted with little warning, these being among the most controversial evictions in the favela. The example I provide here is of the Residents' Association building, as that is the only demolition during which I was present throughout. From my partial attendances at other demolitions, as well as descriptions from residents and other observers, the demolition of the Residents' Association followed the usual process for such demolitions, albeit with a heightened sense of importance given the symbolism associated with the building.

I had stayed in Vila Autódromo for the two nights before the demolition, since an injunction preventing the demolition of the building had been struck down. When I first arrived, an activist had explained the situation, saying that the building could be demolished legally, but still complained about immoral laws and the corrupt judiciary. I woke early and made my way over to the Residents' Association building, where other supporters of the community were gathering. The Guarda Municipal arrived in force at 7 a.m. sharp, at least a hundred of them literally bussed into the community. They set about cordoning off the building, easily moving residents and activists who were shouting their protests against the demolition, encountering little physical resistance. Someone, I think an official from the municipal government, handed demolition papers to Augusto, President of the Residents' Association. He stood in a corner checking the legal documents thoroughly, occasionally joined by residents. Having read through the documents, he had no complaints, implying the papers were all in order. The residents had heard from the public defenders a few days before that there was nothing more they could legally do to halt this demolition. The Guarda Municipal brought in a backhoe to do the actual work of demolishing the building. A few activists half-heartedly attempted to block it, joining hands to form a barricade across the road. The backhoe simply drove around them. Watching this, part of me wondered why residents and activists didn't do more to try to stop the demolition, but there was nothing they could do – as it was perfectly legal.

This account of demolition in Vila Autódromo, expounded in more detail in chapter 3, represents the norm. Aspects of this process were decried by activists as violations of the right to housing (Comitê Popular 2015: 38–39).

Specifically, Raquel Rolnik (2015: 364), former UN Special Rapporteur for the right to adequate housing, lists the following violations that occurred in pre-Olympic Rio:

> lack of information about the projects, lack of definition of routes [of public transit], implementation of works without any public debate or possibility to present alternatives, individualised procedures and 'case-by-case' negotiations, diverse forms of pressure and threats, failure to remove the rubble of demolished homes, insufficient compensation for families to gain alternative housing.

While these are serious violations that caused significant hardship and pain for residents, the omission from this list of evictions per se indicates that at least some evictions were conducted legally, through established processes.[3] As such, they do not constitute a legal state of exception and would be more accurately described as occurring in a unique political context. While they are often challenged through the justice system, these challenges are not always successful (see Mendes and Cocco 2016). Indeed, since favelas first sprang up in Rio at the end of the 19th century, they have faced threats of violent evictions. By taking a historical view, it becomes clear that the removal of favelas does not constitute a state of exception – even if it may not have been legal, favela removal is an established norm (Perlman 2010), based on the disparity between the law as written and law as practised described by Fischer (2008). However, after the end of military rule in the 1980s, favela evictions were dramatically curbed, by all accounts (see Perlman 2010; Faulhaber and Azevedo 2015). A combination of new rights contained in the 1988 constitution and the political difficulty of abusing a significant section of the electorate created a degree of stability and reduced the threat of eviction.

Nevertheless, mega-events brought the reality of evictions back to Brazil's favelas (Magalhães 2019). Rio was clearly more affected by this trend than any other city due to the comparatively high proportion of residents living in favelas and, in particular, the greater scale of concentrated urban development required to host the Olympic Games compared to the World Cup, which saw smaller-scale increases in favela evictions in host cities across the country (see Santos Junior et al. 2015). This, however, is not a state of exception, as scholars such as Boykoff (2014a) argue, due to the legality of these removals. The hosting of the Olympic Games created a political climate in which these evictions could be conducted. This is distinct from the state of exception, however, evidenced by legal due process throughout the lengthy legal battle over evictions in Vila Autódromo and other favelas

---

3 It is important to note, however, that the violations listed by Rolnik (2015) could have served to mask illegal demolitions – by not providing information or public debate, for example, the true reasons behind the eviction, which may not have been legal, remained obscured.

(see Mendes and Cocco 2016). This unique political context is fundamentally different to the legal concept of the state of exception.

Despite the laws passed by the federal government, there remains little protection for residents whose homes sit on land designated for public use. As is common around the world, the Brazilian government reserves the right to claim land for public works, which in this case includes the construction of stadia for mega-events. Of course, there is a legitimate question of whether building a stadium should be classified as a public good, but that is not at stake here. The important point is that whether removals were completed through eminent domain provisions or through negotiations and compensation, these processes abided by Brazilian law. While activists claimed such processes were immoral, or that the law was unjust, or that the judiciary was corrupt, they did not claim that these removals were illegal. As such, these evictions did not occur in a state of exception.

However, focusing on one particular demolition in February 2016, I argue that sovereign power was exercised in Vila Autódromo. The home of Augusto, President of the Residents' Association, was demolished illegally. I should make it clear here that I am not a lawyer; I rely on what residents told me and my knowledge of the usual eviction process in determining the legality of this act. This allows me to determine that this was an exceptional event. I was not there for the demolition itself – myself and a couple of other volunteers from RioOnWatch responded to a call for coverage from the residents that morning but it took around an hour to get there because of the distance. When we arrived, the demolition had been completed, the dust was settling on the rubble behind the football pitch, close to the entrance to the favela. However, Augusto was nowhere to be seen, instead Penha was standing near the rubble answering questions from a journalist. Listening in, we heard that Augusto had been away, staying with family – our first clue that this was not a normal demolition. When we asked why the residents who were there didn't try to stop the demolition, she responded with a simple question: 'What could we do against armed troops?'

Aware that we had not had breakfast, Penha offered us some food and we followed her to the church, where she explained what had happened in more detail. As we walked, a new minibus full of Guarda Municipal arrived: a changing of the guard it seemed, as nobody panicked. Penha explained that Guarda Municipal were now a constant presence in the community, even overnight, camping in their minibus close to the playground. She suspected that they had noticed Augusto was not there and seized the opportunity to demolish his home. Augusto's home was in a strange situation, Penha explained, as she filled plastic bottles from a water dispenser on the wall at the back of the church. He had previously been evicted and his old home demolished but, unwilling to leave the community, he had built a new home on a small patch of land behind the Residents' Association. It was this home, along with another, unoccupied home, that had been demolished that day. This land was part of the Residents' Association and therefore covered by an injunction preventing demolition of that building, Penha explained. Another RioOnWatch volunteer had heard a different story from Amanda, however; she apparently said that there was a garden that had been used by residents which was not covered by the injunction. Someone had begun to build a home there and had then accepted an offer of compensation from the government, which provided the pretext for the demolition of all the homes.

Penha explained that while 'we [residents] will never give up' resistance, it was much harder to stop a demolition when it is not your home, as you don't know all the details, evidenced by the differing accounts from different residents. The situation is even worse when there are lots of what she called 'shock troops' (Guarda Municipal in heavy body armour) surrounding you. Augusto was on his way back to the favela and Penha talked more broadly about the process while we waited, explaining that she didn't really know why they were being evicted, but her sense was that they wanted to clear 'these shacks from the ground' and remove the 'ugly association', chiming with what others had said about these evictions being a beautification project. After a short while, Augusto arrived back in Vila Autódromo. Clearly hurt by this demolition, he stood in front of the rubble that used to be his home and spoke to us and a few other journalists who had made the trip here, with the demolition papers in his hands. These papers, Augusto pointed out, had someone else's name on them as the owner of the home: someone he had never even heard of, despite his role as President of the Resident's Association. He affirmed clearly that the municipal government had no legal right to demolish his home. With emotion straining his gruff voice, he complained that 'justice doesn't exist for the poor', criticising Brazil's reputation: 'People think that Brazil is wonderful, but for whom? Not for the poor.'

We can see clear contrasts between the account of this demolition and others. In other cases, residents didn't resist because the demolition was legal, in this case it was due to fear of violence. In normal demolitions, the demolition papers were checked by the resident before the demolition was started – which was not the case for this one as Augusto was not there. Instead of waiting for him to return, the demolition proceeded without his permission. Had he been there to check the papers, he would have spotted an irregularity, with another person's name listed as the owner. As President of the Residents' Association, Augusto could reasonably be expected to recognise the names of residents, past and present, yet he did not recognise the name on the papers authorising the demolition of his home.

As such, what we see in the case of Augusto's eviction was an abnormal, illegal denial of rights by the municipal government – a state of exception. Having identified this as a state of exception, we can therefore see, from the example of Augusto's eviction, that sovereign power was reshaping Vila Autódromo, transforming it from a 'peaceful and orderly community' into an area primed for real estate development. While in most cases evictions did not occur in a state of exception, that some do ultimately reveals who has the right to define the territory that is Vila Autódromo. From this, we can also examine the agreement reached between residents and the municipal government as an exercise in sovereign power.

On 8 March 2016, in the events described in the introduction to this book, Mayor Eduardo Paes announced that twenty families would be able to remain in Vila Autódromo and that the government would build new homes for these residents, based on the plan presented in Figure 2.4. After this was announced, there was a period of around a month of negotiation, when residents pushed for changes to the plan before accepting it. Several modifications were made to the plan as a result and, while the agreed plan still differs dramatically from the *Plano Popular* (see Figure 2.2), meaningful modifications were made. The homes were enlarged from 46 to 56 square metres, as well as each home being on a single lot, not connected. More public space, a key feature of the *Plano Popular*, was added, including a new Residents' Association building as well as space for commercial use. Initially, the residents were required to leave while construction took

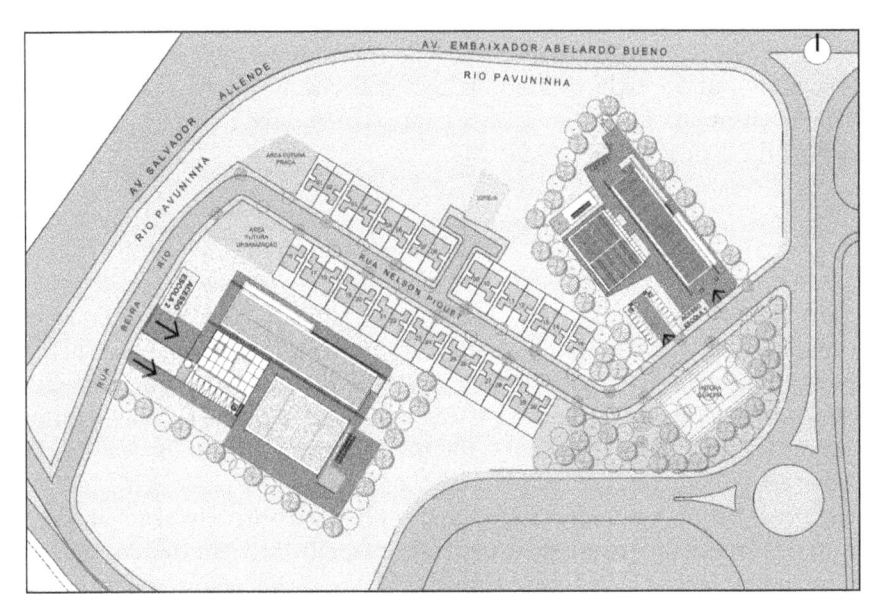

Figure 2.4 Mayor Eduardo Paes's initial plan for Vila Autódromo. The large buildings nearby are schools, which the community insisted they didn't want or need.
(*Source:* Photo from Prefeitura do Rio de Janeiro, 2016.)

place, whereas it was agreed that only those houses that were in the way of the new construction would be demolished, and temporary housing would be provided within the community. While I was not present at the meeting between residents and the municipal government, the relative dearth of major changes in the plan is indicative of the power exerted by the authorities to keep the more radical ideas contained within the *Plano Popular* off the table.

Importantly, however, the plan was agreed between the city and community, not between the city and individuals. As Penha proudly explained to me in May 2016, as she showed some visiting researchers around the community, this was the first time a favela housing agreement had been reached collectively. Theresa, founder of Catalytic Communities, a favela advocacy NGO that had worked in the city for over two decades, confirmed this was the case. Even with these successes the agreement had its critics, including myself at the time, arguing that the municipal government was seeking to erase the favela from the territory by constructing new whitewashed homes, motivated by increasing the value of nearby land (see Talbot 2016). As such, the plan to change the community was communally agreed with the intention of changing the character of the area. As we have seen from the demolition of Augusto's home, the process of evictions in Vila Autódromo was enforced through the exercise of sovereign power. From this we can conclude that this plan represents the sovereign ceding the right to remain living on the land to the residents of Vila Autódromo. This was not only a recognition of the right to housing, as a collectively agreed plan including significant emphasis on public space, it also represented a sovereign recognition of the collective right to the city.

Conclusions

The *Plano Popular da Vila Autódromo* showed that an alternative urban policy was compatible with the Olympic Park, even that such a policy was attractive, with lower costs than the municipal government's policy of evictions. Developed by leading urban planners following principles of participatory planning, the plan placed strong emphasis on the value of public space. This plan was a key prong of residents' fight to remain in their community. Through this plan and other elements of activism, residents emphasised their rights, principally the right to housing and the right to the city. The right to housing holds some basis in Brazilian law, but is nebulous and difficult to enforce, and is considered more as a guideline for public policy rather than a firm guarantee for citizens. Through examining the laws residents claim were violated, we can see the paradox of institutionalisation (Stammers 2009), as the meaning of the right to housing shifts from protection against eviction to protection of real estate values.

Against a historical context where traditionally rights have not been respected, favela residents claim their rights and citizenship through insurgent forms of citizenship (Holston 2008). By constructing their own neighbourhood in Rio's periphery, residents of Vila Autódromo claimed their citizenship by conforming to traditional standards of citizenship, including home ownership and taxation. Through resisting eviction attempts in the past, specific legal rights were gained, including a 99-year lease to the land and its designation as an Area of Special Social Interest. As such, Vila Autódromo residents had protections conferred upon them through sovereign power. While the majority of evictions did not explicitly contradict these protections, there were some examples where evictions occurred in a state of exception, revealing the work of sovereign power. Importantly, these exceptions were limited and temporary, not a lengthy state of exception as some contend the Olympics engender. Given that sovereign power was reshaping Vila Autódromo, the agreement that twenty families could remain in the community can be seen as a significant victory for activists, as an implicit recognition of the legitimacy of the right to the city. As Orlando, a member of the Comitê Popular put it, Vila Autódromo's struggle against evictions 'was able at least to alter the correlation of forces of the public authorities'. In subsequent chapters, we explore how the ideas about the community contained in this plan were inscribed on the space of the favela and ultimately spread around the world in order to pressure City Hall into these concessions.

3

Ocupa Vila Autódromo:
Space as resistance

Vila Autódromo hosted the *Taça Libertadores* (Liberators Cup) football tournament on 26 December 2015 and I made the two-hour journey to the community with the intention of writing a report for RioOnWatch, along with another volunteer. We struggled slightly getting to Vila Autódromo, going a different route to the one I'd taken before. We first went to the Alvorada bus terminal in Barra da Tijuca, planning to catch a bus the short distance to the favela from there. At the terminal we discovered that there were no direct buses to Vila Autódromo: when we asked an attendant for help in getting there his response was simply 'fuck man, that's hard'. Unable to find a bus to this apparently remote location, we took a taxi for the last section of the journey. As we arrived at the community, I was surprised by how much things had changed since I was last there only a few weeks ago. A permanent barricade blocked the vehicle entrance, stopping works trucks from using the roads in the community, erected in protest at the heavy traffic flowing through the community a few weeks ago. There were gaps where there had previously been buildings. The space of Vila Autódromo was constantly changing in this way throughout fieldwork, with new demolitions a regular occurrence.

In this chapter, I explore how residents actively shaped the space of the favela, promoting spatial meanings associated with homeliness, community and friendliness. In doing so, residents were engaged in a discursive contest over the nature of favelas, challenging the conceptualisation of favelas as dangerous, poverty-stricken slums which underpins the policy of eviction. Through events organised as part of a campaign known as *Ocupa Vila Autódromo* (Occupy Vila Autódromo), residents carved out moments in which they could articulate their community largely on their own terms, challenging the logic behind the municipal government's policy of displacement. During these events, the community was vibrant and alive, in stark contrast to the 'sense of abandonment' that was evident otherwise. Residents were not the only actors producing space in Vila Autódromo, as the municipal government sought to exert its influence to shape the favela (or perhaps more accurately, to remove it). This chapter examines these contested constructions of space in Vila Autódromo. The following section describes a football tournament organised as part of the *Ocupa Vila Autódromo* campaign, before I discuss Lefebvre's conceptualisation of space in relation to favelas. I then move on to discuss how the movement produced space as part of their contestation of evictions and the role of *Ocupa Vila Autódromo* in resisting evictions.

Taça Libertadores da Vila Autódromo

A few people were standing around chatting in front of the Residents' Association when we arrived, so we went over to introduce ourselves. A guy in his late forties, sporting a purple baseball cap, seemed to be in charge; he introduced himself as Luiz Claudio Silva, Penha's husband. The baseball cap covered trimmed black hair and he was well built, clearly an impressive athlete in his youth. His face was unusually expressive; his smile would warm the heart while his frowns would break it. His dark brown skin was unmarked, with wrinkles only just beginning to show on his hands. Players arrived in dribs and drabs, heading to the small football pitch, boxed in by crumbling walls and fencing behind the Residents' Association, to warm up. The vast majority of the visiting players were white, while the Vila Autódromo residents' team was largely made up of black players.[1] All the players were men, although a few women had also come to enjoy the football and support their friends and partners.

We headed around to the pitch, following Luiz. As he pumped up a ball, I mentioned that we were from RioOnWatch and that we planned to write a report about the tournament. He became visibly more comfortable, speaking very highly of other members of RioOnWatch who had come there. He explained that he was happy to talk to us because we were helping their struggle. He told us a little about himself, including that he had lived in the community for twenty-three years. I asked him what the event was for and he explained that 'the idea forms part of a wider strategy', aiming to emphasise that 'Vila Autódromo lives, exists, and resists'. In essence, this event was about 'giving visibility' to the vibrant community within this space, welcoming visitors to the favela to show that it wasn't 'abandoned'.

Luiz headed off to organise drinks for everyone and we chatted to a guy from one of the teams. His team was called *Peladas da Esquerda*, or 'players of the left', and was formed to play for fun as a political statement, hence

---

1 Following Perry (2013) I use the term 'black' to refer to racialised minorities, instead of using Brazil's complex multiracial self-classification system. As she notes, Brazilian institutions, including the police and justice system, have no difficulty determining who is black when physically and symbolically attacking them.

Figure 3.1 A football game under way in Vila Autódromo. The graffiti reads 'Carlos Carvalho [local real estate developer], we are not poor, you are poor.' December 2015.
(Image: author's own.)

'of the left'.[2] A couple of other teams had arrived too: *Radical Contra* was a group who, like the *Peladas da Esquerda*, played informal football across the State of Rio de Janeiro with political motives, and *Remo(vidas)* was a group of students who came to play football and support the community.[3] When everyone was ready, the four teams (including the Vila Autódromo residents team) gathered in front of the Residents' Association to agree the rules for the tournament, with some debate about the length of games due to the strong heat. *Peladas da Esquerda* (white with green and red highlights) and *Radical Contra* (black with thin white stripes) both had their own kits, while the Vila Autódromo team used light blue Fluminense vests and *Remo(vidas)* played topless.

Luiz pointed out where the toilets were and showed everyone a cool-box full of ice, beer and Coca-Cola to which everyone was welcome, having contributed R$10 (around US$2.50) each. He explained that there would be a *churrasco* (barbecue) after the football, also paid for by this small fee. During the games, a player from one of the other teams officiated, although the referee is fairly redundant as fouls tend to be admitted to, even without appeal from the other players. The atmosphere was convivial, with the

2 *Pelada* is a slang term, usually meaning a football game: specifically a non-competitive, recreational game with loose informal rules. In this case, the term is used to refer to footballers who play this form of the game.
3 *Removida* means removed or evicted, while *vida* means life: these brackets formed a deliberate pun emphasising the impact of evictions on lives.

humdrum sound of construction work in the Olympic Park next door frequently drowned out by the shouts of players and laughter among the small crowd of spectators. Breaks between games often lasted longer than the 15-minute games themselves, with players (and spectators) fetching drinks and using a water hose to cool off in the shade of the trees, taking a brief respite from the scorching summer sun. The tournament here couldn't stand in starker contrast to the Olympics which took place a few hundred metres away, eight months later.

I was offered the chance to play on the *Peladas da Esquerda* team, but I declined, saying it was far too hot. It was around 35° in the shade, but, to be honest, I was more worried about embarrassing myself given the quality of these teams, particularly the *Peladas da Esquerda* and *Radical Contra*. Shortly afterwards, Luiz again asked if I wanted to play. I tried to wriggle my way out of it, but eventually he persuaded me, handing me one of the vests the Vila Autódromo team were using. As we headed over to the pitch, Tobias asked whether I played back or front: I chose back in an attempt to reduce the amount of running I would need to do in the heat. We huddled up with the rest of the Vila Autódromo team and Luiz gave a short team talk, explaining that we play with two at the front and two at the back, and stressing the importance of keeping them under pressure all over the pitch. Luiz's insistence on including me in the games was characteristic of the atmosphere of *Ocupa Vila Autódromo* events.

Even though the event was advertised on Facebook as a five-a-side tournament, *Radical Contra* seemed to have ten or eleven players present, with those who weren't playing sitting and chatting with others who'd come to watch and enjoy the day. After recovering from the game, I took some food and joined in the conversation with some of the players. As we talked, I asked the players why they had come today. One of the *Remo(vidas)* players explained that this wasn't his first time here: 'I, at least, already came to other events. I have followed the resistance of Vila Autódromo and, hey, to play football, to celebrate this year of resistance, of struggle, to end the year well, with a light mood, as I've seen very heavy things here …'. To the same question, a *Radical Contra* player explained that 'the team was created with the intention to be on the political left. Because, in truth, in these places, we are very well received, normally.' These teams had made the long journey to Vila Autódromo that day for two main reasons, encapsulated by these quotes. First, they came to support the resistance movement in the favela, broadly agreeing that the eviction of residents was wrong. Second, though, they came for enjoyment; to enjoy the day playing football, drinking beer and eating *churrasco* in a friendly, welcoming atmosphere. It is difficult to separate these two motivations for making the trip to the favela, they remain entangled and to some extent they are connected by the emphasis on comradely participation in place of oppositional competition.

Once the games had finished, with *Peladas da Esquerda* beating *Radical Contra* in the final, the *churrasco* got under way, with food passed around as the players and residents drank beer and socialised. Luiz then stood up to present the trophy and give a short speech. Many more residents had arrived by now, to enjoy the food at the end of the day. Luiz held a cheap plastic trophy, which had been decorated with one of Vila Autódromo's stickers, cut down to fit nicely on the small trophy. Before presenting the trophy to the winning team, Luiz gave a short speech to the assembled crowd of some forty people, detailing the community's struggle and speaking about the importance of *Ocupa Vila Autódromo* events:

> This campaign lifts our spirits, because we feel that we are not here alone and we are not abandoned.[4] Because when people come here to our community, it has a sense of abandonment, it has a sense of a community that already surrendered, but this is not true. Our struggle is a struggle for justice, and we hope for a time when justice will wake up and do its part. We are an established community, we have tenure, we have the Supplementary Law 74, which gives us full right this place here, which is an area of interest for social order and housing. So we are not invaders, as the mainstream media sometimes describes us, O Globo in particular has already said this several times. We are a community of around fifty years, so it's very clear that the invaders are those who are arriving now.

Luiz was making the point that most days, when there are no events in the favela, it appears abandoned, as if the community has surrendered, but that during these events the community appears vibrant and alive. By organising the space of Vila Autódromo as a vibrant, friendly community for these events, residents and visitors were challenging the everyday 'sense of abandonment' Luiz spoke of. He went on, to explain the legal issues and protections the community had, and the way these had been ignored, in great detail. During his speech, Penha heckled him, telling him to stop going on so people could eat and drink, a wide smile beaming across her face. Once the trophy was awarded, residents took photos to post on the community Facebook page before everyone returned to the *churrasco* and beers. Chatting to Luiz afterwards, he was keen to organise another football tournament in future, saying 'It's a good event, people enjoy the game, the food, the drinks and the socialising', placing particular emphasis on the social aspects of the event.

This football tournament was part of a series of events held in Vila Autódromo, a campaign known as *Ocupa Vila Autódromo*. Other events included book launches, musical performances, documentary screenings, and Catholic masses. Held in the favela, these events served to highlight the continued existence of the community while also strengthening the community's ties with their supporters. As detailed in the *Plano Popular* (Associação de

---

4 I have translated the Portuguese word *ânimo* here and in other quotes as 'lifting spirits', but its meaning is broader, referring to good mood and courage.

Moradores e Pescadores da Vila Autódromo 2016: 49), 'the presentation of bands, film projection, theatre, exhibitions, graffiti, etc. provided new ways to reaffirm the [community] life built over the years and its right to remain'. As an activist from the Comitê Popular told TV news network Record News at one event, 'one of the tactics which City Hall seeks to use is to create an extremely hostile environment that obliges residents to accept compensation and leave' (Rocha 2015). The *Ocupa Vila Autódromo* events, characterised by festive celebrations of the community, served as an antidote to this tactic: as Luiz said, it lifted residents' spirits, enabling them to continue resisting.

In this chapter, I will argue that the political significance of these events was derived not only from the events themselves, but from the space in which they occurred. This space was constructed as a welcoming, friendly space, challenging the logic of removals based on the myths of marginality. This was contested by the actions of the state, which sought to make the favela an inhospitable environment through a combination of demolitions and psychological pressure. By holding events in the favela, residents drew attention to their struggle on their own terms, as opposed to the attention gained when the municipal government demolished homes. To think through how the space of the community played this role I first explore the work of Henri Lefebvre, to draw out how his theorising on space applies to informal communities such as Vila Autódromo.

Lefebvre in the favela

'Space', Henri Lefebvre (2009 [1979]: 186) plainly asserts, 'is social'; that is, space is 'a product of interrelations ... that is always under construction' (Massey 2005: 9). It is imbued with social meaning through the practice of individuals and groups within space and their construction (both physical and social) of space. Lefebvre (1991) developed an analytical triad of conceived, perceived, and lived space to understand how meaning is socially created and ascribed to space. Perceived space refers to the way societies attach meaning to spaces through everyday social life and is bound up with the complex power relations which exist in modern societies (Martin and Miller 2003). Meaning is generated through social interaction in and with spaces, imbuing them with meaning(s). In essence, space is socially constructed, with all the complex relationships between structural constraints and social agency that characterise social constructions. Conceived space refers to the 'official' meanings ascribed to spaces. For Lefebvre, these meanings are imbued through both the physical production of built space and dominant power relations which privilege certain understandings of space (Soja 1996: 60–70). Perceived and conceived space illustrate the potential for a single space to hold conflicting meanings and it is in lived space that these conflicting meanings are contested.

Lived space then, is 'seen by Lefebvre both as distinct from the other two spaces and as encompassing them' (Soja 1996: 67). This chapter, in Lefebvre's (1991) terms, examines the lived space of Vila Autódromo by examining the contest between perceived and conceived space in the favela.

Yet before we turn to the case of Vila Autódromo, we must further interrogate these theoretical tools. This triumvirate holds particular complexities for conceptualising the urban landscape of Rio de Janeiro, specifically favelas. Lefebvre's analysis is primarily based upon European cities, particularly Paris. This is problematic when applying his theoretical ideas to cities across the global South, where informal communities are far more common. In particular, Lefebvre presupposes an 'official' understanding of space, a pre-planned meaning intended for urban space. This is set against understandings of space which are clandestine, contesting the 'official' meaning of space. As Merrifield (1993: 525, emphasis in original) summarises, for Lefebvre 'space is always set to a particular *conceived* representation because it is the dominant conception', that is, the conception of the state. In essence, Lefebvre assumes a conflict between what we might call popular meanings and 'official' meanings attached to material urban space, and sets the 'official' meanings in clear dominance. This is based on the architectural design of built space conforming to 'official' desires: the state can physically design spaces to engender particular meanings. While contestation of these meanings is possible based on social action and small, temporary changes to material space such as street art, 'official' meanings are, quite literally, set in stone.

As such, Lefebvre's analytical tools cannot be applied easily to favelas where the physical space is designed and built organically from below. However, that residents build their own communities does not automatically give dominance to their preferred conception of space. As Penglase (2014: 69) observes, 'Lefebvre tends to see built spaces as reinforcing the dominance of structures of oppression [whereas in favelas] understandings of the neighbourhood were tools used for a variety of purposes, some reinforcing domination and others seeking to find spaces of autonomy and creativity.' As such, considering informal communities using Lefebvre's triad reveals a deeper level of analysis which too often goes ignored; that is, by whom are spaces perceived and conceived. Lefebvre takes it as given that the state conceives space while the masses perceive space: the reality is far more complex and multi-faceted and requires detailed examination of the production of the space of the favela.

This privileging of 'official' meanings is not limited to Lefebvrian thinking, but runs through many conceptualisations of space. Brazilian geographer Milton Santos (2006 [1996]), for example, theorises space along the twin axes of verticality and horizontality, where verticality refers to conceptualisations of space imposed from the top down, while horizontality refers to bottom-up meanings attached to space. However, Santos's (2006 [1996]) focus on the *técnicas* that produce spaces calls on us to be attentive to the multiple processes by which space is constructed, and the interplay of power and time within this. For Santos (2006 [1996]: 29) '*técnicas* are a set of instrumental and social means by which an individual makes their life, produces, and at the same time, creates space'. As Davies (2019: 589) points out, translating the Portuguese term *técnicas* as used by Santos is highly complex, as 'it goes beyond technology and technique into a way of understanding historical conjunctures and the production of space'. As such, while Santos's theorisation of space, itself heavily influenced by Lefebvre, remains problematic for thinking about the space of the favela, retaining a presumed dominance of 'official' spatial meanings, his insistence on paying close attention to the *técnicas* by which space is produced provides an instructive approach for disentangling the contested spatial understandings of Vila Autódromo.

Applying this analysis of the *técnicas* that produce space to the Vila Autódromo favela, then, clarifies the differing conceptions and perceptions of space, revealing a conflict inherent in favelas across Rio, Brazil, and in informal communities more generally. Through *técnicas*, living in and adapting the space, residents made Vila Autódromo their home, and a space of safety and security. The sign at the entrance to the community embodies these understandings of space, declaring that it has been 'a peaceful and orderly community since 1967'. Built through autoconstruction and *mutirão*, both examples of Santos's (2006 [1996]) *técnicas*, the physical form of the favela reflects this understanding of the space as a friendly and welcoming community. This can be seen in the lack of walls and fences compared to the formal city of Rio, and particularly of the immediate surroundings of the middle-class Barra da Tijuca, where gated communities are the norm.

Conversely, 'official' narratives about favelas emphasise danger, poverty and criminality. This chimes with what Magalhães (2019) calls 'the repertoire of removal', the narrative built up over time to justify evictions. In this narrative, favelas represent dirt, impinging on the purity of the city, to use Mary Douglas's (1966) terms. The formal city, planned and controlled by trained professionals, represents purity, with the messiness of the informal city posing a danger to this purity. The narrative about favelas put forward by activists and residents turns this on its head, with corruption in government and the judiciary posing a danger to the purity of communal life in favelas. In the official perspective, favelas are pollution, desecrating the *Cidade Maravilhosa* with peril and destitution, in direct conflict with the image of the safe, modern, global city the municipal government wished to promote in the Olympic spotlight. As such, it follows, these impurities must be removed.

This narrative of favelas as dirt to be removed has been built up over many years. In the cultural arena, favelas have been portrayed as zones of violence, both in Brazil and internationally through film, photography and video games (Allen 2017). Perhaps most notable among the cultural imagery of favelas is the Academy Award nominated film *Cidade de Deus* (*City of God*), which portrays the development and conflict of trafficking gangs in the eponymous favela. As Rial y Costas (2011) argues, the favela is presented as remote and distant, separated both physically and culturally from the formal city. In the case of Vila Autódromo, this narrative of favelas as zones of violence, poverty and insecurity underpins two key claims about the space of the community promulgated by the municipal government: that people do not want to live there, and that the people who live there are unlawful invaders. These claims serve as *técnicas* defining the space of the favela, promoted by state actors and supported by a sympathetic mainstream media. I will address each of these claims in turn.

When Rio's Mayor Eduardo Paes announced that twenty families would be able to stay on the land in newly built housing, he argued that the aggressive campaign of pressure and evictions was necessary (Michaels 2016). This was, in his view, because people who didn't really want to stay were refusing to move in order to gain larger compensation packages. Paes explained that he 'had to keep [the rehousing plan] secret to avoid new arrivals in the Vila, looking for a chance to live in a just-upgraded neighbourhood' (Michaels 2016). He argued that this meant he had kept to his regularly repeated promise that whoever wanted to stay could stay in the community, despite evicting 97 per cent of the community. The narrative that residents wanted to leave was prominent in Brazilian media, which tends to view favelas as dirt to be removed from the city (Sánchez et al. 2016). Yet this belies everything I experienced in the community: the dedication of residents to remaining in their homes, even as they described the municipal government's 'psychological terrorism'. Many only left due to the pressures of living in the community as it was being demolished. One former resident told me that they regretted leaving, but explained that they had needed to for the good of their children, so they would not grow up in what was becoming an increasingly inhospitable location.

The accusation of being invaders was a common one faced by favela residents. In Luiz's speech before he presented the trophy at the football tournament, he touched on this, stating: 'we are not invaders, as the mainstream media sometimes describes us, *O Globo* in particular has already said this several times. We are a community that has been here for around fifty years, so it's very clear that the invaders are those who are arriving now.' The term 'invaders' was used by those seeking to evict residents, to frame the settlement as illegal, implying that the community's claim to the land was illegitimate. The land itself was owned by the State of Rio de Janeiro, but lay within the City of Rio de Janeiro. The community held a 99-year lease to the land from the State, gained in a previous fight against eviction in the 1990s, as well as other legal protections (as discussed in the previous chapter). This gave Vila Autódromo a solid legal entitlement to use the land, a far stronger legal position than many favelas enjoy. Paes described such legal protections, which thwarted his previous attempts to remove the favela, as the work of a 'political demagogue' (Vettorazzo 2016), suggesting that these rights were granted illegitimately by the State of Rio de Janeiro.

These two narratives about favela space stand in conflict, a contradiction which, I argue, runs through all favelas and, indeed, informal communities more generally. The conflict between the 'peaceful and orderly community' and the inhospitable slum inhabited by criminal invaders is played out in lived spaces. As Sánchez et al. (2016: 415) put it, 'the official narratives and the resistance narratives may be regarded as part of the symbolic and political struggle for the territory of Vila Autódromo'. In this same space, residents organised events like the football tournament to show that their community spirit exists. Simultaneously, the municipal government destroyed homes and disrupted services, such as bus routes, rubbish collection, mail delivery, even water and electricity, to emphasise the illegitimacy of the community. The conflicted understanding of the space of Vila Autódromo was at the centre of the struggle to stay in the favela, with residents seeking to gain (or maintain) the legitimacy of their community. Through the *Ocupa Vila Autódromo* events, residents and their supporters sought to reinforce their notion of the favela as a peaceful and orderly community through occupying the space with joy, creating a festive atmosphere.

As Larissa, a member of the Comitê Popular who was heavily involved in supporting the *Ocupa* events explained in 2018:

> The cultural occupations in Vila Autódromo, which we called *Ocupa Vila Autódromo*, was the final stretch of the struggle. The idea came when the community had already been heavily destroyed by demolitions of homes, and the fact that rubble was left behind – which is another of the violations committed by City Hall – made the situation even more sombre. As a way of trying to resignify the atmosphere, to lift the spirits of the families that still resisted there, we thought about doing cultural events among the rubble – and it worked! There were various kinds of activities, with lots of different groups involved, and we gained a lot of visibility.

Luiz, also speaking in 2018, agreed that this was one of the major contributions activists beyond the community brought to the struggle:

> These supporters, this network that we created here, was fundamental because from this network came a lot of tools of defence, the tactics of resistance. The cultural events were one of these: we had lots of cultural events here, all coming from our supporters, big events here … and that lifted our spirits a lot.

While lifting the spirits, to use Luiz's term, was important to the struggle, giving residents the energy and confidence to continue resisting eviction despite the ongoing threats, I argue that these events also served to mobilise the space of the favela to political ends. By inscribing a different sense of what a favela could be on the space, and celebrating that, activists contested the myth of marginality, thereby undermining the underlying logic of removal.

Contentious space

Occupying public space is a common tactic for social movements. A great deal has been written on this strategy, particularly following major occupations around the world in 2011, from Tahrir Square in Cairo to Zuccotti Park in New York (see Castells 2012; Gerbaudo 2012; Juris 2012; Kohn 2013; Frenzel et al. 2014). These movements all took place in iconic locations in city centres, using the highly visible and symbolic public space to gain attention for their political message. As Kohn (2013: 99) puts it, Occupy Wall Street sought 'to focus attention on growing levels of economic inequality by laying claim, physically and symbolically, to sites close to the nodal points of corporate power'. Proximity to these key sites of corporate power gave increased visibility to activists occupying the space. Such spaces are transformed into spaces of protest through occupation, inscribing critiques of capitalism onto urban space (Juris 2012). As such, occupations function as lived space, serving 'as markers of protest movements; both in the external and internal view' (Frenzel et al. 2014: 462) as conflicts between perceived and conceived space are played out.

Vila Autódromo, situated in a traditionally peripheral part of Rio de Janeiro became a highly visible space due to the construction of the Olympic Park adjacent to the community. The proximate political opportunity, the particular political climate this change engendered (see Tarrow 1996) is somewhat paradoxical; activists fighting against eviction were emboldened and given new opportunities by the same change of circumstances which emboldened the municipal government and made possible new opportunities for eviction. Importantly, with Vila Autódromo geographically peripheral, the increased visibility was contingent on things happening in the community. *Ocupa Vila Autódromo* events can therefore be seen as the community's attempt to engage with the world on their own terms, instead of on the municipal government's terms, as was the case when journalists travelled to the favela to report on demolitions. In the words of the *Remo(vidas)* player, *Ocupa Vila Autódromo* events served to show the lighter side of the community instead of the 'heavy' reality of evictions. While the Olympics brought new threats of eviction, the Games also brought significant interest to the community, from around the world. Through global attention, the stakes were raised regarding the resistance to evictions in Vila Autódromo, with the favela becoming a symbol for Brazil's treatment of favelas, and the urban poor more broadly, in Rio's mega-event years.

Despite the name *Ocupa Vila Autódromo*, this campaign did not share the enduring occupations of its namesake Occupy Wall Street, or any of the occupation-based movements which have been heavily analysed by social movement theorists (Frenzel et al. 2014). This was a campaign of single-day events in the favela: not an enduring occupation with people moving into the favela for weeks and months. The use of the term 'occupy' was a clear attempt to draw a link to the wider Occupy movement in order to generate support, both locally and internationally. Activists in Vila Autódromo used this protest brand to generate attention for their cause, but these events were not occupations in the sense used by the Occupy movement and discussed by Frenzel et al. (2014).

Social movement theory has historically ignored the spatial context in which contention occurs (Martin and Miller 2003). In particular, many social movement theorists have underplayed the importance of the construction of space and place, focusing on the pre-existing meanings attached to certain geographical locations (see Frenzel et al. 2014). The significance of space inherent in the occupations of Occupy Wall Street and the Arab Spring does apply in the case of Vila Autódromo; the symbolic meanings inscribed on the space give meaning to the events held there. What is different is that these meanings are not pre-existing connotations seized upon by activists: they have been actively constructed by residents and their supporters. In essence, the meanings inscribed on space become part of the performance of contentious politics. While contentious politics encompasses a wide spectrum of social movement organising, including aspects of quotidian social life, our focus here is on the public performances of claims through *Ocupa Vila Autódromo* events. Specifically, this section discusses how residents and activists inscribed the claim that Vila Autódromo was a friendly, welcoming community and a good place to live onto the space of the favela.

After the agreement for new homes was made with the municipal government, the *Ocupa Vila Autódromo* events did not stop, instead serving to pressure the government to keep their promises. In particular, the Museu das Remoções (which will be discussed in more detail in chapter 6) was organised, with eight exhibits dotted around the community dedicated to different buildings and spaces, including the Residents' Association, several residents' homes and the children's play area. One of these exhibits was dedicated to *Espaço Ocupa* or Occupy Space, with photos from these

Figure 3.2 *Espaço Ocupa* exhibit in the Museu das Remoções, May 2016.
(Image: author's own.)

events and the slogan *Urbaniza já*. This exhibit (Figure 3.2) refers to a site within the community where most of the *Ocupa Vila Autódromo* events occurred. Relatively central to the community, it included a slightly raised paved rectangle which served as a stage for performances in the community, as well as a significant amount of open space around it, relatively clear of rubble.

Figure 3.3 shows the *Espaço Ocupa* in full swing during a cultural festival in November 2015, as a band played to around a hundred people in the community. In the background, graffiti is scrawled across the walls of an abandoned building, saying 'my house' and 'this is our home'. Despite the cruel irony of such slogans written on an abandoned house, such messages served to construct the space of Vila Autódromo as a legitimate community to which people feel a sense of attachment. This is particularly illustrated by the use of the word *lar* (home) in place of the far more common but less emotive *casa* (house), adding connotations of belonging and community: this is perhaps even more telling than the English translation, as *lar* is rarely used in Brazil, where *casa* is the generic term used in day-to-day life. Returning to the case of the football tournament, we can see how Luiz's point about the sense of abandonment inherent to the community applies. Without the revellers, the *Espaço Ocupa* appears abandoned and neglected, with claims of residence in graffiti appearing outdated and meaningless. As a backdrop to the festivities of the cultural festival, however, such messages are more clearly statements of defiance, emphasising the legitimacy of the community.

Figure 3.3 *Espaço Ocupa* during the Cultural Festival, November 2015.
(Image: author's own.)

The banners visible in Figure 3.3, draped across the buildings, also serve to bolster the claim that Vila Autódromo is a legitimate community. One points out, for example, that the community gained the legal right to use of the land from the State in 1992, demanding that the Mayor respect the law. Similar messages were common in the community's omnipresent graffiti, detailing the various legal protections residents had won in previous struggles, as discussed in chapter 2. These messages, inscribed on the space of the community, challenged the notion that residents were 'invaders' in the same way that Luiz did in his speech. In inscribing the legitimacy of the community onto the space, activists are directly contesting the municipal government's conceptualisation of the space as an illegal settlement.

These events were often fronted and led predominantly by women, who played a crucial role in resisting evictions. This gendered dynamic is not unusual in urban land struggles, where land and home have long been perceived as the realm of women (Gusmão 1995). Developing this point based on ethnographic research in Salvador, Perry (2013: 161) argues that women's predominance in struggles over land is based on women seeing 'the collective community interests as coinciding with their own individual needs as poor black women – thus, women have sustained leadership over time and the neighbourhood movement has not been co-opted or dismantled by politicians'. Such gendered leadership does not rest upon men's work outside the home and women's work within the home, instead it rests on the understanding of the neighbourhood, unlike the workplace, as the key site for women's political struggle. As Larissa Lacerda (2016), one of the Comitê Popular activists who was heavily involved in organising *Ocupa Vila Autódromo* events notes, the leadership of women also creates a different type of politics, based in affective and emotional attachment to community and the city.

While Luiz ostensibly organised the football tournament described above, this event was atypical in having a man as the main resident organising the event and making speeches. Generally speaking, the *Ocupa Vila Autódromo* events involved speeches by women: usually both Penha and Amanda would speak, often followed by some combination of Yasmin, Ana and Carol. Augusto was the only man who frequently spoke at events, as the Residents' Association president, but he often restricted his speech to introducing others. Luiz could normally be found milling around, taking photos or recording videos, as in the event described in chapter 2, while another male resident, Guilherme, would often provide logistical support such as arranging loudspeaker systems or helping to build platforms. Guilherme was also the author of the majority of graffiti around the community, although many of the slogans written were quotes from other residents. While men were involved in the struggle, this was often therefore in support of women leaders such as Penha and Amanda, who, to borrow Perry's (2013) terms, kept their focus squarely on the collective community interests.

The spatial construction of Vila Autódromo was not only evident in the favela during the events of *Ocupa Vila Autódromo* but also in discussions of the events on social media, both before and after the event. An event page was created on Facebook inviting participants to the football tournament, stating that the event was being held because residents had recently renovated their pitch. This page included details for how to organise teams, but also made clear that people were welcome to come without a team and arrange a team in the favela: 'the objective is that everyone takes part', with all welcome to come for beers and *churrasco*. This event page served to choreograph assembly, to use Gerbaudo's (2012) term, not simply through the instructions regarding time, activity, team size and cost but also setting the scene for a welcoming, friendly event by emphasising the objective that everyone should participate. These event pages also served to set the scene for an inclusive space in gendered terms, using gender-inclusive language. As well as this, there were plans for 'cold beers to close 2015 in high spirits', aiding in 'the construction of an emotional narration' (Gerbaudo 2012: 12) to frame the event. This scene-setting, as Gerbaudo (2012) argues, is crucial in shaping the character of mobilisations and therefore the space of protest events.

Municipal government officials frequently denigrated those residents who resisted removal, suggesting they were merely seeking to increase the size of the compensation package they received. This was the justification Mayor Eduardo Paes offered when asked why he had refused to release details of his plan for the favela before March 2016. This argument not only serves to delegitimise those who were refusing to leave, it also implies that everyone wants to leave, that conditions in the favela are unfit for habitation. The Mayor's definition of those who wanted to leave included anyone who had begun negotiations for compensation. This included Carol, an Afro-Brazilian woman and Candomblé priestess, who had begun negotiating for compensation after her home had first been fenced off within the Olympic construction site, then destroyed. She planned to use her compensation to build a new home in the core of the community (the area which was not threatened by eminent domain). The suggestion by the municipal government that residents such as Carol were holding out simply for higher compensation packages entirely ignored the possibility that the municipal government's valuation of the land differed from that of residents. A common phrase attributed to Penha and scrawled across the favela in graffiti stated that 'not everybody has a price': for residents, there was a value in the community that could not be bought.

As the *Radical Contra* player told me when I asked why he had come to the football tournament, guests were well received in Vila Autódromo. I was repeatedly struck by the courteousness of residents to visitors, particularly journalists: they always made a point of thanking visitors to the favela and went out of their way to ensure visitors felt welcome and comfortable. The insistence by Luiz that I played football, despite my own reservations, is characteristic of the imperative to participate evident in *Ocupa Vila Autódromo*. Likewise, the enjoyable and convivial spirit of the day – the light mood which the *Remo(vidas)* player spoke of – was typical at these events, also visible in Penha heckling Luiz's exhaustive list of legal rights, wanting to move on to enjoying the *churrasco*.

As such, the struggle over evictions in Vila Autódromo was played out spatially, as a conflict over the meanings inscribed on the space. Activists realised that by contesting the nature of the space, they undermined the logic of removals. Residents emphasised the legitimacy and vibrancy of their community as part of a wider struggle against favela evictions, using the platform they were provided by the adjacent Olympic construction to argue for housing rights across the entire city, country, and indeed the world. Activists were fully aware that they had the opportunity to share their struggle internationally due to the favela's location directly next to the Olympic Park. *Ocupa Vila Autódromo*, then, was an attempt to exploit this proximate opportunity, recognising that, unlike the public spaces occupied during Occupy Wall Street and the Arab Spring, this space was in the periphery of the city. By attracting people to the favela, activists sought to draw press attention, to give themselves an opportunity to spread their message on their own terms, outside the context of victimisation.

Enforcing state conceptions

The spatial character of the favela was transformed when journalists travelled to the community to report on demolitions. On 24 February 2016, the Residents' Association was expected to be demolished and I spent the previous night in the favela in order to be there for the duration. At around 6 a.m., I made my way to the area around the association building, where residents and supporters were holding a vigil. They hung banners and posters on the walls demanding a 'social legacy' from the Olympic Games and thanking the international press for covering the story. A group of residents – their mouths gagged to represent the degree of influence they felt they had in reshaping their own community – stood holding banners for the gaggle of press photographers who had arrived. Residents talked to journalists with dictaphones about this demolition being unnecessary, questioning whether the association building was really in the way of the Olympic Park.

At 7 a.m., the space changed dramatically. The *Guarda Municipal* arrived in numbers, literally bussed in to the favela. There were at least a hundred of them, with armour and batons. Many activists seemed to disappear, leaving to defend another building that was thought to be under threat. Papers were handed to Augusto, the association president, who examined them as the *Guarda Municipal* cordoned off the building, slowly moving activists away, meeting little physical resistance. As residents were shepherded away from the building, Amanda shouted that 'the association is more than a building' in defiance, claiming that 'even when the buildings of Carlos Carvalho are here, we will remain'.[5] As a backhoe rolled in, a few activists linked hands and attempted to block its path, but they were too few and the backhoe simply drove around them. Nobody seemed to be really trying to stop the demolition. The building itself put up little resistance and was gone in under five minutes.

5 Carlos Carvalho is a real estate tycoon who owns much of the land around Vila Autódromo (see Watts 2015b).

Figure 3.4 *Espaço Ocupa* without an event, March 2016.
(Image: author's own.)

In this situation, residents and their supporters were seen to be power-less in contrast to the power of the state. The space of the favela was trans-formed: no longer safe and welcoming, it felt tense and dangerous. In this, the state was attempting to enforce its conception of the space on the com-munity. The demolition papers given to Augusto undermined residents' claims that the removals were illegitimate, clarifying that residents were not arguing that these demolitions were illegal; rather, they were arguing that the law is unjust. As such, the simplicity with which the building was destroyed lent credence to the accusation that the residents were illegal invaders. After the *Guarda Municipal* departed, the rubble was left in a heap, making the favela seem derelict and abandoned, undermining resi-dents' claims that this was a vibrant community. This is the standard mode of demolitions, with the government 'leaving a trail of cracked buildings, broken sewage and water pipes, exposed rebars, mounds of demolition debris and multiple foci attracting rodents and insects' (Sánchez et al. 2016: 419). The abandonment and neglect Luiz spoke of can be seen in Figure 3.4, a photograph of the *Espaço Ocupa* taken in March 2016, a few days before the Mayor announced his plans to rebuild the community, when no event was taking place and with no signs of conviviality and com-munity on display. This photo also illustrates the constantly shifting physi-cal space of Vila Autódromo, with the walls on which graffiti messages had been sprayed in Figure 3.3 long since demolished.

This taps into a wider degradation of the favela throughout the process of removals. Through cutting off various local services, such as transport links, mail delivery, rubbish collection and even electricity, the state created an inhospitable space for residents to live in. The *Guarda Municipal* often arrived unannounced to conduct demolitions or erect new walls in the community that isolated homes and extended the territory claimed for Olympic construction. This placed intense pressure on residents, who described not knowing whether their homes would still be standing day-to-day as 'psychological terrorism'. Residents and their supporters only had warning that the Residents' Association would be destroyed from the public defenders, who had been contesting the legality of the demolition order in court: the municipal government gave no advance notice. Several former residents who had left told me that they did so for their children. For them, the rubble and the threatening presence of the *Guarda Municipal* meant that the favela had become an inappropriate place to raise a child. Beyond this degradation of space, local elites envisioned a different future for the space on which the favela sat: real estate development. Real estate mogul Carlos Carvalho spoke openly of his desire to transform the area around the Olympic Park into 'a city of the elite … with noble housing, not housing for the poor' (Watts 2015b). In this, the elites recast the space as one of real estate speculation and opportunity for profit, not housing.

When press attention was attracted to the community because of an eviction, it was difficult for residents to explain the positive aspects of life in the favela. The questions journalists tended to ask were related to the anguish, pain and suffering of those who remained, leaving little room to talk lucidly about the value of community life in the favela. As such, *Ocupa Vila Autódromo* emphasised the legitimacy of the favela, and provided a platform for residents to share a positive vision of their community with journalists and activists. In particular, the space during *Ocupa Vila Autódromo* events was infused with inclusivity, friendliness and security. In this, activists' contestation of removals went beyond the public justification for removals, challenging what they saw as the underlying logic of favela evictions: the view that favelas are a form of pollution to be excised from the city.

This created a sense of place for Vila Autódromo, a process which is the focus of the following chapter. It allowed residents and activists to maintain a clear notion of the inclusive, safe, community place of Vila Autódromo, which was crucial in contesting evictions. As the Residents' Association was being demolished, residents and their supporters joined hands in a circle and chanted slogans against demolitions and the Olympic Games. Many around the circle, including myself, were crying as they did so. For me, I was thinking of happy memories of the football tournament held on the pitch behind the building. The friendly, inclusive community spirit was in my mind, despite the presence of a threatening number of *Guarda Municipal*. Here, as I will argue more comprehensively in the following chapter, the sense of place forged during *Ocupa Vila Autódromo* events effectively fixes the meanings inscribed on space in the imagination of those taking part. In the next chapter, I will explore this process and begin to consider how this allows ideas about Vila Autódromo and the legitimacy of favelas to be spread across geographical scales.

Conclusions

In this chapter we have seen how Lefebvre's conceptualisation of socially produced space holds specific complexities when considering favelas and informal communities. Lefebvre's analysis precludes the possibility that built space could be conceived and constructed by marginalised populations. By exploring the *técnicas* by which actors influence the space, we see how the social production of space is contested, revealing a conflict of ideas which underlies all favelas. On the one hand, favelas are home to populations who would otherwise be homeless, representing an innovative use of space for communities who built their own homes and a strong sense of community. On the other hand, favelas are marginal, dangerous places, illegal and illegitimate by their very nature, with poor infrastructure and endemic poverty, providing a haven for criminality. With these two narratives in dispute, the influence residents have in shaping the built space of the favela is crucial in this episode of contention. In Vila Autódromo, the conflict surfaced in the attempt to evict the community, enforcing the 'official' perspective on the space, which casts favelas as marginal. In short, the question at stake is the legitimacy of the favela as a form of housing and community.

In response to this, residents organised and resisted the attempt to remove their community. The contest is played out spatially, a battle fought over these conflicting meanings of space. Previous research on social movements has not fully appreciated the spatial dimension of contention. In the protest camps analysed by Frenzel et al. (2014), space was used as a tool for amplifying the movement's message: in the case of Vila Autódromo, space *was* the message. Residents and their supporters were not simply resisting in space, they were resisting through space. By constructing the space of the favela as welcoming, friendly and safe, residents undermined the municipal government's justifications for evictions. The government, however, sought to transform the space into an inhospitable environment through physical destruction as well as psychological pressure. *Ocupa Vila Autódromo* events became a crucial element of the movement through seizing the proximate political opportunity presented by the Olympic Games. These events, and their significance for building support for the resistance movement, will be discussed in more detail in the following chapter.

4

Espaço Ocupa: Liminal placemaking in the protestival

Ocupa Vila Autódromo events provided an opportunity for residents and activists to construct the space of the favela. In these moments, residents and activists were able to show a friendly, welcoming and safe version of Vila Autódromo free from contestation by the state. This was part of a wider contest over the nature of favelas in the Olympic city, with residents and activists contesting the justifications for regressive policies of removals and pacification. In this chapter, I will argue that the football tournament discussed in chapter 3, along with the rest of the *Ocupa Vila Autódromo* events, was liminal in character. The temporary inversion of social structures during these events created a temporally and spatially limited communitas, including anyone who came to support the community. As liminal events, these were bound up with a rupture in social structure known as anti-structure, where there exists the possibility to modify, transform or destroy existing social structures that serve to keep favelas marginal (Turner 1969). As such, these events served to generate radical alternative possibilities for relations between the state and favelas, engaging in what Crossley (1999) calls a working utopia (this will be discussed in more detail in chapter 6).

Furthermore, I will argue that these liminal events served to create a sense of the place of Vila Autódromo. As outlined in the previous chapter, space refers to the constantly changing and contested environment, whereas place refers to solidified understandings of a location built over time: place refers to space 'when it is caught in the ambiguity of an actualization' (de Certeau 1984: 117). Specifically, I argue that, in a constantly changing space, *Ocupa Vila Autódromo* events created a clear vision of a community that was safe and welcoming, serving the role identified by Santos (2006 [1996]: 25), where events serve to give places new meaning by unifying objects and actions. This was important in the continued mobilisation of both residents, who spoke of their feelings of hopelessness which these events addressed, and their supporters, who generated a clear sense of purpose and togetherness from their understanding of the favela. In particular, the liminal character of *Ocupa Vila Autódromo* meant this sense of place was bound up with anti-structure, infused with an implied radical transformation of Brazilian structures of power. This sense of place, as well as fixed a set of ideas about the favela in the minds of activists, could be spread to and understood by people who had never been to Vila Autódromo. I will discuss the use of social media in communicating this sense of place across Brazil, and the wider world in the latter part of this chapter, before discussing favelas and international media coverage in the following chapter.

Liminal protest

The festive events of *Ocupa Vila Autódromo* differ from traditional methods of protest such as marching with placards and banners. However, similar events have been used as political action in other contexts, such as the Reclaim the Streets movement against the car in the late 1990s, in what Carmo (2012) calls a 'protestival', a hybrid of protest and festival. St John (2008) traces the development of festive activism from the 1960s to the alterglobalisation movement of the early 21st century, drawing on Mikhail Bakhtin's notion of the carnivalesque. Bakhtin (1968) argues that in medieval folk festivals, for specific short periods of time, societal norms were inverted in a celebratory atmosphere. In these carnivalesque moments individuals experienced a unique sense of time and space, temporarily surrendering their individuality to become part of a collective whole. These temporary inversions of social structures actually served to strengthen those structures for Bakhtin (1968). In this sense, the carnivalesque festival serves a 'regulatory function performed by the licensing of deviant practices', reinforcing the deviant nature of such practices (Ravenscroft and Gilchrist 2009: 35). Thus, its usefulness for social movements to create change would appear limited. As I will argue here, however, the closely linked notion of liminality brings the potential to uproot and invert social structures permanently.

Some, including those involved in organising such activities, have expressed scepticism of the political impact of such protestivals, noting that 'it was easy for the street party to be seen as JUST fun, just a party with a hint of political action' (Carmo 2012: 113, emphasis in original). The argument I make here is that this did not occur in the case of *Ocupa Vila Autódromo* because this episode of contention was inscribed on the space of the community. I make this point by drawing on Victor Turner's (1969, 1970, 1979) conceptual triad of liminality, communitas and anti-structure, a theory of rituals often used interchangeably with the carnivalesque. However, while all carnivalesque events are liminal in character, not all liminal events are carnivalesque, as these liminal events simply provide a break in social structures, creating possibilities beyond reaffirming existing social structures. Specifically, I argue that Turner's (1969) concept of anti-structure is crucial to understanding these liminal forms of protest, and that Turner's (1969, 1970, 1979) theoretical approach to these temporary inversions of norms provides a more fruitful lens for social movement theorists than that of Bakhtin (1968).

The concept of liminality comes from the work of anthropologist Victor Turner (1969, 1970, 1979), who studied rituals. Turner noted that rites of passage involved a segregation from social structures followed by a period of liminality: an interstructural situation. This period on the threshold, momentarily outside the constraints of social structures, is full of 'potency and potentially ... experiment and play. There may be play of ideas, a play of words, a play of symbols, a play of metaphors' (Turner 1979: 466). As Blackshaw (2010: 91) notes, this concept, along with the related concepts of communitas (which I will discuss shortly) and anti-structure, has been applied outside Turner's specific field of religion to explain secular ritualistic events involving a 'spatial separation from the familiar and habitual'. We can see elements of this spatial separation in *Ocupa Vila Autódromo* events, in the celebration of the community, stepping outside the everyday social reality of a community living with the omnipresent threat of eviction.

Anti-structure is fundamental to Turner's (1969) approach to liminality. Turner (1969) argues that liminal moments are characterised by anti-structure, wherein the structures of society can be replaced, modified or abandoned. This is not to say that social structures are always transformed through these ritualistic experiences, merely that there is the potential for transformation for those involved. Bakhtin's (1968) notion of the carnivalesque, developed from the specific case of folk festivals, always serves to reinforce social structures (see Ravenscroft and Gilchrist 2009). Conversely, anti-structure provides the potential to change those structures. For Turner (1969), the transformation of social structures could radically alter the social world in a vast range of ways – including not changing anything at all. While carnivalesque moments serve to reinforce social structures, liminal moments encompass a range of possibilities, including reinforcing, destroying or modifying existing social structures. In this, Turner's (1969) approach to these ritualistic inversions of norms provides a more fruitful avenue for thinking about social movement organising than the Bakhtinian approach to the carnivalesque.

By examining the spatial meanings inscribed on the community, we have seen how these characteristics imbued the favela with particular political meanings. The *Ocupa Vila Autódromo* events provided a forum for communicating ideas about the community as a hospitable and secure location, not as a drag on real estate values. Revisiting Figure 3.1 from the previous chapter, we can see how football occurs in a politically charged space, with graffiti in the foreground attacking real estate developer Carlos Carvalho. Importantly, the dynamics of the favela were transformed for these events. Residents who lived day-to-day in fear of eviction were celebrated for their strength and resilience. Crowds came to hear them and share in the idolisation of the community. 'Idolisation' is a useful term for this, as in these moments residents transcended their own specific struggle to represent the struggle against evictions across the city. In this carnivalesque moment, Vila Autódromo became the focal point of the debate around the ongoing Olympic transformations in the city, in stark contrast to the everyday 'sense of abandonment' Luiz described.

In the liminal spirit, these events were inclusive, not spectacles to be observed, but festivals to be part of, as shown through Luiz's insistence that I play football with them. As is the case with previous examples of protestivals (St John 2008; Carmo 2012), this inclusive spirit pervaded all *Ocupa Vila Autódromo* events: when a clown troupe performed in the community in February 2016, I was reporting on the event for RioOnWatch and asked one of the clowns where he was from. He responded in riddles, making me (unwittingly) part of the act. When a band played at a cultural festival in November 2015, they paraded around the community surrounded by revellers, allowing others to play their instruments as they went. In this sense, through these activities, which Santos (2006 [1996]) would conceptualise as *técnicas*, unifying the physical object of the community with celebratory and inclusive actions served to give new meaning to the place of Vila Autódromo.

Through these events then, the norms of the community were transformed. Normally, the favela 'has a sense of abandonment, it has a sense of a community that already surrendered', according to Luiz, but during these events, the community was filled with vibrant energy of sometimes hundreds of people. As Penha explained in an interview in 2018:

> Those occupations with music, with dancing, with films, with everything, that culture sustained us. It gave us hope, because when someone left, we lost a neighbour, and when we would do those events with such joy and so much love, so many people from beyond the community coming and saying 'I'm with you'. For us it was as if Jesus was sending angels, angels to say 'oh, you're on the right path, you will get what you want because I am sending soldiers to fight with you and they are happy soldiers, full of life'.... It was wonderful and priceless.

In these moments, those who still lived in the favela and resisted eviction were almost revered, a clear inversion of the general disregard held for them by City Hall. These events brought crowds to the favela, often supported by elements of Rio's creative class who would perform there in support of residents, often groups associated with leftist causes. For example, the clowns mentioned earlier came from the Free School of Clowns, which seeks to promote human rights by bringing people together in dialogue. In this sense, the protestival was an arena of creative transformation (Carmo 2012) wherein spaces of hope were created, with artists from across the city contributing to the social production of space. In this liminal, in-between space, an alternative, utopian future could be imagined; an alternative idea of what the community could be was therefore celebrated.

A key element of the liminal experience is communitas. This refers to the social relations which exist in liminal moments, described by Turner (1969: 96) as a community that is 'unstructured or rudimentarily structured and relatively undifferentiated', in contrast to highly structured societies. *Ocupa Vila Autódromo* engendered this communitas, with the only distinctions made during events being between residents (including former residents) and their supporters. This is markedly more open than many kinds of social relations I encountered throughout my fieldwork: in Vila Autódromo, I was not treated as a *gringo* researcher but as a supporter of the community. As an illustrative example, after my first Comitê Popular meeting in November 2015, I headed to a bar nearby for a beer with several members of the group. As is the tradition in Brazil, someone ordered a few large bottles of ice-cold beer for the table and small glasses were brought for everyone. In Brazil, everyone shares from the same bottle and usually pours each other drinks. Larissa, a Comitê Popular activist heavily involved in Vila Autódromo, took the bottle and poured out glasses of beer for everyone sitting around the table except me, with my glass left standing empty. I was left to pour myself a beer, feeling excluded and unwelcome. A couple of months later, in Vila Autódromo, protesting against the demolition of the Residents' Association as analysed in detail later in this chapter, activists formed a circle, holding hands and chanting slogans against evictions and the Olympic Games. I found myself in two minds as to whether to join the circle or take photos of the ongoing demolition when Larissa stretched out her hand to me and invited me into the circle.

The differing reactions towards me suggest differing structures of classification: in Vila Autódromo I was part of the group and included in these activities, whereas in the formal city of everyday relations I was excluded. While this may simply be related to the amount of time I had been involved (time had passed between these events and Larissa knew more about who I was when she offered her hand, although we weren't close), it is but one example of the differing structure of classification in Vila Autódromo. In the favela, we belonged together in the temporally and spatially bounded communitas. At meetings of the Comitê Popular, I was a *gringo* researcher bringing little to the table (several established Western academics were already working with and writing about the Comitê Popular), whereas in Vila Autódromo I was another supporter of the community, there to support the community, part of the group.

The final element of Turner's triumvirate, anti-structure, is of crucial importance here. It is with anti-structure that Turner's work on rituals departs most clearly from Bakhtin's concept of the carnivalesque. Whereas the carnivalesque inverts norms temporarily, serving to strengthen social structures (Ravenscroft and Gilchrist 2009), Turner (1969) identifies the potential in the liminal threshold to create a moment of rupture in social structures: a moment of anti-structure. This anti-structure can be seen in the imagining of a new favela, most clearly given form in the *Plano Popular* as discussed in chapter 2. During these liminal moments, those who participated imagined a different social structure, where favelas could be celebrated for their qualities and supported, on their own terms, by the state, where favelas could be seen as simply another form of housing, not as a blight on the city.

Thus, the liminal periods of *Ocupa Vila Autódromo* events created moments of potential change, that challenged existing social and political structures, which occurred in a spatial context imbued with specific claims about the welcoming, friendly and secure nature of the favela. As such, these liminal festivals invoked a demand for a new social structure in which favelas are treated as viable, legitimate communities, as opposed to dangerous, poverty-stricken areas to be excised from the city. In short, these liminal events are demands for residents' rights to housing and to the city to be respected. *Ocupa Vila Autódromo* events, then, were characterised by a radical recasting of the favela as a safe and friendly community, challenging existing discourse about favelas, and the power structures which uphold this discourse. To be clear, social structures were not transformed directly through these events – those with the most ability to change the relations between the favela and the state (such as government officials) did not participate. However, the utopian vision of a different social structure that these events represented helped to sustain residents and activists in their struggle against evictions. As such, *Ocupa Vila Autódromo* was important in generating a fixed sense of place from the space of Vila Autódromo, the importance of which is discussed in the remainder of the chapter.

Placemaking

Place is fundamentally distinct from space, theoretically speaking. However, as Low (2017) notes, there is a considerable degree of semantic confusion around the terms. It is therefore worth elucidating here precisely how I conceptualise and use these terms. While space is constantly subject to (re) construction and contestation, with different meanings inscribed upon and played out across geographical locations, place is more fixed. If space refers to the constantly changing locations we experience in everyday life, place refers to our ideas about those locations: bound up with memories, they are less malleable, less subject to change. However, the two are indelibly linked, as de Certeau (1984: 117) argues: 'in relations to space, place is like the word when it is spoken, that is when it is caught in the ambiguity of an actualization'.[1] Places are often, although not always, bound up with a structure of feeling about localities (places) developed through embodied experience in those locations (spaces). Importantly, 'the sense of place need not be restricted to the locality' (Agnew 1987: 28), meaning people who have never been to the favela can still understand the sense of place. In this section, I will argue that the liminal events of *Ocupa Vila Autódromo* served to forge a strong sense of place for those who took part, bound up with anti-structure and challenging state treatment of favelas. This sense of place, as I will argue later in this chapter and the next, could then be spread across geographical scales.

Returning then to the *Espaço Ocupa* discussed in the previous chapter as a malleable and changing space, I will now explore the place of *Espaço Ocupa*. As a reminder, this was the central site for many of the *Ocupa Vila Autódromo* events, a flat platform providing something of a stage for performances while a tarpaulin rigged to nearby buildings protected revellers from the strong sun. Filled with vibrant energy during these events (see Figure 3.3) but derelict and abandoned outside these events (see Figure 3.4), this space was transformed through *Ocupa Vila Autódromo*. This transformed, vibrant space was 'caught in the ambiguity of an actualization' (de Certeau 1984: 117) to forge a sense of place. In this sense, generating a sense of place 'is a kind of imaginative experience ... a way of *appropriating* portions of the earth' (Basso 1996: 143, emphasis in original). In particular, this sense of place is formed through memories of a liminal experience in the politicised space of the favela. A shared conception of place helps diverse groups of activists feel connected to a larger whole, which I will discuss in more detail shortly. This sense of place then, is an appropriation of a particular understanding of Vila Autódromo based on the spatially inscribed meanings of *Ocupa Vila Autódromo* and the liminal rupture of social structures.

Primarily, this sense of place emphasises the continued presence and vibrancy of the community, emphasised by Luiz when he was handing over the trophy at the football tournament described in the previous chapter: 'This struggle encourages us, because we feel that we aren't here alone and we aren't

---

1 Following Gray (1999: 456), I have swapped the terms 'space' and 'place' in the quote from de Certeau, as he reversed the general usage of the terms in his writing.

abandoned.' The place of the *Espaço Ocupa*, then, is bound up with memories of the vibrant displays of community experienced there, giving those who took part a clear sense that the favela was still strongly resisting eviction. This sense of place being forged through liminal events creates a 'felt sense of quality of life' (Pred 1983: 58) bound up with anti-structure, the radical idea that the favela could coexist with the Olympic Games and didn't have to be demolished. Thus, the sense of place generated through *Ocupa Vila Autódromo* was bound up with contentious politics, having been forged through these liminal moments and complemented in other ways, such as the *Plano Popular da Vila Autódromo* (Associação de Moradores e Pescadores da Vila Autódromo 2016), which helped define the place as a legitimate, peaceful community.

This sense of place was therefore bound up with ideological critiques of top-down development, real estate speculation and, ultimately, global capitalism. The emphasis in the *Plano Popular* on the rights of residents to shape their own community is translated into a sense of place as residents showed how they wanted their community to be. This included graffiti asserting that 'Vila Autódromo is ours' and 'My house is made for living, not for negotiating', as well as the broader atmosphere of friendliness and security. Through this, residents are articulating a critique of the Olympic city from which their voice is excluded, most clearly expressed in the graffiti displayed in Figure 4.1, which states that 'the city is not what the Mayor wants ... it has to be how we want it to be. It is ours.' The omnipresent references in graffiti to real estate developer Carlos Carvalho and corruption serve as a reminder of how the favela is envisaged by elites: as a drag on land value. This image is contrasted with the vibrant and friendly community living on the land, starkly showing what would be lost for the material gain of a few.

This sense of place was relatively untouched by the constantly changing physical space of the community. When the *Espaço Ocupa* was destroyed in April to make space for new homes, it simply moved to another part of the community where the events could be hosted. The place endured even as the physical space was destroyed. The new *Espaço Ocupa* retained the sense of place associated with Vila Autódromo, as can be seen in the following description from a RioOnWatch event report, based on a traditional *festa junina* party in the new *Espaço Ocupa*:

> Under colourful flags and lights strung from a tent at the entrance to the community's one remaining street, residents of all ages ate, danced and chatted late into the evening, as children dressed in the plaid dresses and straw hats typical of such June celebrations dashed around, laughing and chasing their friends. (Southwick 2016)

As well as this transcendence of space, the place of *Espaço Ocupa* was commemorated in the Museu das Remoções (see Figure 3.2), which is discussed

Figure 4.1 Graffiti on the back of the community church states that 'the city is not what the Mayor wants, Mayors pass while the city stays, it has to be how we want it to be. It is ours. The Mayor is a public servant', April 2016.
(Image: author's own.)

in chapter 6. The exhibit included photographs of festivities mounted on the bricks of demolished homes, colourful paintings and a board with many handprints and the slogan '*Urbaniza já*', to which I will return to in the following section. The subtitle for the exhibit read 'Where resistance, permanence and struggle are united for a single ideal'. This ideal of the favela transcends time: it relates not only to what the favela is but also to what the favela was and what the favela could be. The valorisation of the favela as a safe, welcoming space may not be historically accurate, but it has been constructed in this way. Similarly, the ideal for what the favela could be has been laid out in the *Plano Popular da Vila Autódromo*, constructed through numerous meetings and deliberations. This possible future depends on the transformation of power structures in Brazil, placing value on the anti-structural rupture that *Ocupa Vila Autódromo* generated. The ideal held up in the Museu das Remoções, then, links directly to the sense of place generated through these events.

The diverse groups coming together in the space of Vila Autódromo affirmed the spatial characteristics of the favela to a wider group than just the residents. In this, the favela takes on meanings through affective bonds tied to place, based on shared experiences in the temporally bounded moments of *Ocupa Vila Autódromo*. The spatial meanings of the celebratory event are frozen in time as a sense of place, removed from the ever-shifting space where meanings change with the demolition of buildings. As such, the sense of place created in the liminal moments of *Ocupa Vila Autódromo* transcends the reality of destruction and demolition which characterised the space outside these moments. In this, the political meanings, as shaped by the residents, not the municipal government, are preserved in the imagination of those who participated in the events.

Diverse groups worked to support residents of Vila Autódromo in their fight against eviction (Sánchez et al. 2016). During *Ocupa Vila Autódromo* events they were referred to simply as supporters, distinct from residents but not from each other: what I have argued to be communitas. Away from these geographically and temporally bounded events, however, these supporters shared a sense of togetherness, a form of community based on their shared sense of place, forged through these events. These bonds facilitated organising both in Vila Autódromo and across the city, around other issues, by creating a shared narrative with which activists identified. This allowed support to transcend geographical scales through social media, as will be discussed in the following section.

Spreading place on social media

Social media is a source of great debate within social movement studies following the development of Web 2.0 technologies that allow for interactive communications free from mediation by traditional elites. Such technologies have become commonplace in recent years, including in favelas, particularly through smartphones (Nemer 2016). Some scholars have optimistically argued that this development presents new opportunities for social movements, which have historically been marginalised in media coverage by traditional media elites (Shirky 2008; Castells 2012). However, this belies the difficulty of building an audience for social movements and social media, generally speaking, have not been transformative in the ways Shirky (2008) and others predicted (Khondker 2011; Gerbaudo 2012). However, in the case of Vila Autódromo, the proximate political opportunity (see Tarrow 1996) brought by the Olympic Games stimulated global interest in the community, meaning the transformative potential of social media could be realised to spread this sense of place across geographical scales. The coverage of the event through social media, as well as alternative media sources (including but not limited to RioOnWatch) was another important contribution made by supporters beyond the community, as Luiz explained in an interview in 2018: there were many supporters 'that created materials and many, many alternative medias that shared our struggle'. I will discuss two examples of this at different geographical scales here: the *Urbaniza já* online video campaign (national) and RioOnWatch's live-tweeting from the favela (international). The designation of these as national and international is not clear-cut and is derived primarily from the different languages used in each case (Portuguese in the former, English in the latter). These, it should also be said, are simply two illustrative examples among many of the ways in which social media were used to spread this sense of place.

After months of intense pressure and a week of symbolically significant demolitions, residents and supporters had gathered for another *Ocupa Vila Autódromo* event, where they launched an updated version of the *Plano Popular* (described in chapter 2). Here, I focus on the events after this launch, when several residents recorded videos of themselves asking Rio's Mayor Eduardo Paes to stop the removals and instead provide upgrades to the community, often drawing on the sense of place created during these events. In particular, the videos responded to Paes's claim, frequently repeated to journalists, that whoever wished to stay in the community could stay. The common thread running through every video is the challenge to Mayor Eduardo Paes to implement the *Plano Popular*. These videos were uploaded online, primarily on Facebook, with each person inviting three others to record their own video and upload it with the hashtag #*UrbanizaJá*.

In the days that followed this event, these videos were ubiquitous on my Facebook feed, with many shared by the Vila Autódromo community Facebook page or other supporters of the community. The sense of place developed through *Ocupa Vila Autódromo* events is embedded in these videos, providing support for a narrative of favelas being safe, welcoming places. The videos came from a wide range of people: initially, many were people I knew or recognised, having seen them at events in the community or other protests around the city. As the days wore on, I began to see public figures posting videos as the campaign gained important elite allies for the community, including public intellectuals such as Raquel Rolnik and David Harvey, along with prominent politicians such as Jean Wyllys and Marcelo Freixo, both from the left-wing PSOL party. Brazilian celebrities associated with leftist causes, including actress Camila Pitanga – a household name in Brazil – and comedian Gregório Duvivier, also recorded videos. Pitanga's video alone was watched over 250,000 times and shared by over 2,500 people. The participation of celebrities in the movement drew significant mainstream press coverage, with an *O Globo* article explaining the campaign, one of the few Globo articles about the community written in a sympathetic tone. As Larissa explained in 2018, talking about this and other work supported by the Comitê Popular:

> Without doubt, one of the areas in which we were able to give the most support was in communication, in putting in place a network of journalists and communicators in Brazil and other countries to bring more visibility to the

violations that were happening, but also to the resistances that were surging from these.

This campaign lasted for just a couple of weeks, with momentum building rapidly from the relaunch of the *Plano Popular* on 27 February described in chapter 2, then largely dissipating once the Mayor announced his plan for upgrades on 8 March, despite this being markedly different from the *Plano Popular*. Residents wanted to keep the campaign going to ensure the Mayor kept his promises, but were unable to generate similar levels of support and momentum, although new videos would pop up occasionally. It's unclear what specific factors led to the involvement of elite actors, although it is worth noting that the vast majority of those who posted videos had links to left-wing groups, hinting at the importance of what Granovetter (1973) calls the strong power of weak ties. It is also unclear why the initial mobilisation gained traction, although there was a clear sense among activists that this was a crucial moment for influencing decision-making, giving the impression that a relatively small action could have significant consequences. This sense was fuelled by the looming deadline of the Olympic Games, then less than six months away, meaning the situation would need to be resolved soon, with the demolition of the official centre of the community (the Residents' Association) signalling the climax of City Hall's removal efforts. Despite quickly dissipating, the campaign was considered by activists to be a huge success, partly responsible for the announcement and subsequent (albeit partial) execution of an upgrading plan by a Mayor who had tried to destroy the favela for years. This campaign served to spread the sense of place, which itself was drawn from a space constructed as friendly, welcoming and safe, across Rio and Brazil. In essence, the #*UrbanizaJá* campaign spread the idea that Vila Autódromo's right to remain should be respected and the community was not an impurity to be excised.

RioOnWatch operated on a different geographical scale, beyond the borders of Brazil. Publishing about favelas in English, the organisation was concerned with taking local stories to an international (although primarily North American) audience. While there was a significant readership on RioOnWatch's Portuguese site, the English content was a key function of the site in this context. I will discuss the role of RioOnWatch in shaping international media coverage in the following chapter, but here I will focus on its live-tweeting of events in Vila Autódromo; that is, providing short snapshots of news from the favela to report on events. In this example, I was live-tweeting with other members of the RioOnWatch team from the favela as the Residents' Association building was being demolished. While it was not an *Ocupa Vila Autódromo* event, the sense of place forged was evident in the coverage of this demolition, with those who were tweeting about it having attended several earlier events. I use this as a case study because it was one of the most prominent examples of live-tweeting from Vila Autódromo. Being involved myself gives me the benefit of in-depth knowledge, although some might argue such involvement raises questions about the validity of using this vignette for analysis. There are three important points to note in this respect. First, taking an ethnographic approach means data is gathered by becoming immersed in the field: as such, influencing the field (and indeed being influenced by the field) is inevitable. Second, my involvement was as a volunteer with RioOnWatch and was not drastically different from that of other volunteers I observed on other occasions. Finally, I was following set guidelines for RioOnWatch volunteers on how to live-tweet: this guidance particularly recommended using common hashtags, posting photos and using quotes from favela residents.

When the Residents' Association was demolished, I was in Vila Autódromo with three others from RioOnWatch: Olivia, Charlotte and Emma. Olivia was a Western European student then studying abroad at one of Rio's universities. She wanted to be a camerawoman so her volunteer work with RioOnWatch tended to be filming events and creating videos. Charlotte and Emma both studied abroad in Rio in 2014, volunteering with RioOnWatch during the World Cup. Having now completed their studies, they were back in Rio to support the organisation in maximising its impact during the Olympic Games. Charlotte's focus tended to be on housing policy and its impacts on urban space, while Emma spent her time focused on the role of media in representing favelas.

We had travelled to Vila Autódromo as a group, planning to stay in Penha's house, along with around forty activists, in anticipation of action by the municipal government in the morning – City Hall could now legally demolish the Resident's Association and, following a legal decision late at night, Penha and Carol's homes. Penha's home was a large, square concrete building with two floors and a rooftop terrace which had wonderful views over the nearby lagoon. She and Luiz had built this home over twenty years before, when they moved from the huge South Zone favela of Rocinha to Vila Autódromo shortly after their daughter was born. It had been their family home ever since, with Penha's mother living there as well. There was a small courtyard enclosed by walls 8 foot high and containing a couple of trees which bore fruit in the springtime. Opposite the house was a garage and a covered walkway, which presented the only way to enter the courtyard, through a blue metal door with a sticker on the frame saying 'peace in Rio'. The couple had held their wedding on this covered walkway, but in recent weeks it had been used as a space where chairs and a table with food and drinks were provided for the many activists supporting the community, so they could refresh themselves and recharge.

Shortly after arriving late at night, we bumped into Penha sweeping the floor in the hallway. Emma asked Penha how she was and she replied 'good, strong'. She continued, with a grin, 'They can destroy my house, but they can't destroy me.' In the evening, there was an emotional meeting, with activists spilling out from Penha's lounge into corridors and listening through open windows, planning what should be done the following day when the shock troops of City Hall arrived. After explaining how people could help her move her belongings into the church if they came for her home, Penha expressed her gratitude to those who had come to support her and the community, telling the crowd overflowing from her lounge that 'It's ok, I'm very much at peace ... I'm very happy because I have so many friends, and how many people are loved like this? We just have to thank you, I am very happy for each one of you that is here with me.' After speaking, she shared a long hug with another resident, tears forming in both of their eyes.

We had stayed on the fringes of the meeting; unable to fit in the room, we had stood in the doorway to listen. We had our own little meeting afterwards: if demolitions occurred, Olivia would film while Charlotte would take photographs, documenting the event so that materials could be provided for journalists who were unable to attend, as well as for RioOnWatch's own publications. Emma and I would live-tweet events from RioOnWatch's dedicated live-tweeting account, using my phone's data connection. Essentially, we would provide short, real-time updates on what was happening, including photos and quotes from residents. The intention was to comprehensively document events from the perspective of residents of the community, in real time.

We began our actions before the *Guarda Municipal* had even arrived, sending out photographs of a candle-lit vigil at dawn and banners adorning the area around the Residents' Association building, with translations into English of what was said on the banners as captions for the photographs. Emma and I functioned like a well-oiled team, particularly considering we only had one functioning phone, with one of us going to get information and quotes while the other wrote tweets, and regularly swapping the phone between us. As the *Guarda Municipal* arrived with officials from the municipal government at 7 a.m., we tweeted photos and descriptions of them creating a cordon around the building and moving people away, even as these people shouted 'we are the association' in protest. The *Guarda Municipal*, most of whom were brown-skinned, surrounded the building while white municipal government officials in suits handed the demolition orders to Augusto. As the backhoe rolled in to demolish the building, I tweeted a couple of photos before joining a group of activists who stood holding hands, shouting their protestations over the crunching sounds of steel ripping down concrete. I gave my phone to Emma, who went to tweet quotes from the stage-like area that formed the *Espaço Ocupa*, where someone had set up a microphone and speakers, with Yasmin's cracked voice amplified across the favela, speaking of her shame that this could happen in Brazil.

A few minutes later, when I caught up with Emma, she told me what had been said. Amanda had been on fine form, she reported, having exclaimed that 'When the buildings of Carlos Carvalho are here, we will be here too', drawing the link between real estate speculation, capitalism and evictions. Emma was hesitant to tweet a remark made by one of the speakers. She told me that they had said 'we will continue to fight ... we will fight until the last house', but Emma questioned whether it would be helpful to tweet that. She felt that such a statement indicated resignation to every house being demolished, which was, in her view, a counter-productive message. She worried that the idea that every home could be destroyed could be interpreted as an admission of defeat, an admission that the municipal government had the right to remove the favela and transform the space. After much deliberation, she tweeted the quote, taking the view that her role was to promote residents' voices, not decide which voices to promote. Once the demolition was complete, we walked back to Penha's house, now the de facto centre of the community. The demolition had been surprisingly difficult to watch (I had cried watching the building being pulled down, as had many others in the circle of activists) but I was instantly reinvigorated when I laid eyes on Penha's house. The front of her house had previously been entirely clear of graffiti, which was unusual for a house in Vila Autódromo. Now, scrawled across the front of her home in big letters were the words 'Residents' Association'. Later, these words appeared across many homes in the community, reaffirming the assertion that 'we are the association'.

At the weekly Catalytic Communities meeting the following Monday, Theresa (RioOnWatch's founder and editor-in-chief) explained that she had received great feedback from journalists on this live-tweeting campaign, which had spanned the entire week of pressure in the community, with responsibility passed between volunteers on a rota system. Specifically, she told volunteers that journalists from all over the world were thankful for getting 'a window into the community'. That is, people around the world had gained insight into the place of Vila Autódromo and had come to understand the value of the community for its residents. She had been able to send out concise packages of information, including Charlotte's photos, Olivia's video, quotes Emma and I had collected, as well as previous RioOnWatch articles, as background information to help journalists who had never visited favelas write accurately about the demolition.

Online articles by *The Guardian* and a heavily picked-up agency piece specifically quoted tweets from the RioOnWatch live-tweeting account in reports about resistance to evictions in the favela, while other reports included quotes and materials provided by RioOnWatch. RioOnWatch deliberately sought to have such an impact, aiming to become a 'trusted source' for news on Rio's favelas, as one of the editors described it. Over several years, RioOnWatch had built up an audience that included journalists and researchers interested in Olympic development. As one of the editors described it, the audience for RioOnWatch was intended to reflect 'quality not quantity': the audience was small, but consisted of influential individuals who would learn from the materials posted and spread the ideas to a wider audience, a common tactic for social movements (see Escobar 2001). In particular, numerous journalists interested in the Olympic Games were included, as well as foreign correspondents based in Latin America. In the language of resource mobilisation theorists such as McCarthy and Zald (1977), RioOnWatch helped gain elite allies for several favela causes, particularly Vila Autódromo, a point I will develop further in the next chapter.

While the examples described above were not *Ocupa Vila Autódromo* events, the sense of place spread through these tweets was imbued with an understanding of the place of Vila Autódromo developed during the liminal moments of those events. RioOnWatch volunteers regularly attended *Ocupa Vila Autódromo* events in large numbers, with many understanding the place through their experiences in these moments. As such, even while different spatial meanings related to powerlessness and marginalisation were on show in the favela, the sense of place disseminated on social media remained related to the spatial values imbued in *Ocupa Vila Autódromo* events, with information strategically shared to promote the vision of a strong, vibrant community.

This use of social media was important in generating support for the favela's objectives. The heavily shared *Urbaniza já* videos, and the images and quotes tweeted from the favela, served to bolster a community of supporters that was not limited to the small geographical location of Vila Autódromo. This served to demonstrate the level of support the movement had beyond those who could attend events in the favela, giving residents and activists the sense that they were part of a larger whole, thus sustaining the movement. It also served to reinforce the weak ties which existed between the diverse groups involved, facilitating collaboration on a variety of issues beyond the case of Vila Autódromo, including contesting other aspects of mega-event led development and other cases of favela evictions.

It was by no means only RioOnWatch that spread this sense of place from Vila Autódromo. A video posted to YouTube documenting the football tournament discussed in the previous chapter portrayed a friendly, welcoming and enjoyable place through imagery of convivial chat around the *churrasco* and the smiles on the faces of those taking part, as well favourable testimony about the event. Social media content like this simultaneously serves different functions for different audiences. Those who were there, as discussed above, watch this video with a nostalgic recollection of their liminal experiences in the community, reinforcing their sense of place. Those who have not been to the favela see a welcoming and friendly community, disrupting the common stereotype of favelas. The competing understandings of favela-places are at the core of evictions and housing rights protests, not just in Vila Autódromo but also across Rio, Brazil and informal communities around the world. In essence, these conflicts become contests between these different senses of place, between the dangerous, poverty-ridden slums and the friendly, welcoming communities which inhabit the same space. By asserting Vila Autódromo to be the latter, residents and activists are challenging the logic guiding the policy of displacement: that anywhere is better than the marginal favela.

As such, spreading this sense of Vila Autódromo as a friendly and welcoming community is not parochial and unremarkable – it has important global implications. The particular sense of place spread from Vila Autódromo is bound up with issues of rights and social justice, with implicit critiques of housing policy, real estate development and the system of capitalism. Thus, by spreading this sense of place, activists are spreading a set of ideas designed to unsettle systems of capitalist governance and to guarantee rights for the marginalised. At a moment of heightened global interest in Rio de Janeiro, Vila Autódromo residents and their supporters were speaking up for the estimated quarter of the global population who reside in informal settlements, arguing for an inclusive approach to integrating these communities into cities.

However, it is important to note that spreading this sense of place through social media was only possible due to the extraordinary circumstances in which the evictions in Vila Autódromo took place. While there are those who argue that the easily accessible, real-time communication provided by social media has made organising collective action 'ridiculously easy' (Shirky 2008: 54), the reality is more complex. The proximate opportunity for mobilisation that the Olympic Games brought for Vila Autódromo attracted global attention to this small favela. Research by Catalytic Communities (2016) shows that Vila Autódromo was one of the favelas most frequently reported on in the lead-up to the Olympic Games, yet it was by no means the only favela to experience evictions linked to mega-events (see Comitê Popular 2015: 36). What marks Vila Autódromo out as different from many other cases is its geographical proximity to the Olympic Park that makes the connection to mega-events undeniable. Indeed, it is this clear link to the Olympic project that piqued my own interest in the community. Those who argue that the rise of social media means an increase in influence for marginalised groups seem to ignore that marginalised groups also remain marginalised online. The Olympics brought attention to Vila Autódromo, and activists used social media (as well as traditional media) to turn this in their favour. As such, while the example of Vila Autódromo shows that there is potential to effect changes through online activism, in many struggles, this potential remains unrealised due to the lack of attention afforded to marginalised populations.

Conclusions

The space constructed during *Ocupa Vila Autódromo* events was a liminal form of protest, temporarily transforming and inverting everyday norms of fear and pressure to joy and community. These events were separate and removed from everyday life for both residents and those who travelled to the favela for the festivities. This engendered a temporally and spatially limited communitas among those taking part, creating an inclusive atmosphere which helped define the community as safe and friendly, as opposed to the hostile stereotype of favelas. Unlike carnivalesque inversions of norms, which serve to reinforce existing social structures, liminal events are characterised by a rupture of social structures, known as anti-structure, a moment wherein social structures can be reinforced – but also modified, transformed or destroyed permanently. As such, these liminal events were characterised by a radical reimagining of power structures in Brazil, recasting the favela as a safe and friendly community.

Through this liminal experience, space is transformed into a sense of place, bound up with the radical potential of anti-structure and the implicit critique of power relations in Brazil. This placemaking draws on memories created in the favela during these events and is thus infused with the constructions of space from *Ocupa Vila Autódromo*. This sense of place emphasises the friendly community that legitimately resides in the favela, not the destructive power of the state evident during demolitions. Importantly, this sense of place is not necessarily linked to a precise physical location, most clearly seen in the moving of the *Espaço Ocupa* as the process of demolitions proceeded. The lack of scalar binding meant that activists were able to spread this sense of place to people who had never visited the favela, through social media and traditional media (the latter I will discuss in the following chapter).

The use of social media was dependent on the attention brought by the Olympic Games, which generated interest in the favela. A campaign of videos demanding an urbanisation plan for the community gained significant attention in Brazil, with well-known allies strongly publicising the favela's fight to remain. Internationally, RioOnWatch's live-tweeting gained the attention of numerous journalists writing about Rio and the Olympic Games. Both these forms emphasised the legitimacy and community in the place of Vila Autódromo, underpinned by a radical alternative to removals. This sense of place, spread via social media, was bound up with ideological critiques of top-down development, real estate speculation as housing policy and, ultimately, the global system of capitalism. In this, social media became a tool for spreading counter-hegemonic ideological messages across geographical scales.

However, this does not serve to fully endorse the optimism of scholars such as Shirky (2008) and Castells (2012) about the ability of social media to change the world. Rather, it serves to show that social media have that potential, but only in specific circumstances: Vila Autódromo, almost by pure chance, found itself in the international gaze due to the adjacent Olympic developments. While the potential to spread counter-hegemonic ideas to a wide audience through social media may exist, it requires a specific set of conditions to be fully realised. Part of these conditions relate to the interest of the international press, as will be discussed in the following chapter. Through these engagements with journalists, RioOnWatch created a unique role for itself to influence coverage of Rio de Janeiro's favela communities during the Olympic Games. Chapter 5 explores this role in shaping discourse in international media accounts of Vila Autódromo. Chapter 6 then explores the museum created in Vila Autódromo after the Olympic Games.

5

RioOnWatch: Spreading place through the press

After years of struggling, the twenty families of Vila Autódromo who agreed to the collective rehousing deal with the municipal government finally received the keys to their new homes on 29 July 2016, days before the Olympic Games began. They had been due to receive them a few days earlier but, after inspecting the buildings, residents had refused to accept the keys, arguing the work was not yet complete. They suspected that if they had accepted the keys, the additional work that was required would never be finished. A few days later, the municipal government was ready to try again, confident the work had been finished to a standard that residents could accept. I made my way out to Vila Autódromo early in the morning, with several proverbial hats on: I was planning to live-tweet the events for RioOnWatch, write an article for RioOnWatch, collaborate with a journalist for RioOnWatch, all on top of taking field notes for this ethnographic research.

In this chapter, I focus on RioOnWatch's work with international journalists and its attempts to shape the discourse around favelas. In the run-up to the Olympics, RioOnWatch arranged favela visits for a significant number of international journalists and provided information to many more. This chapter builds on the discussion of place in the previous chapter, in exploring how, by working with traditional media sources, RioOnWatch sought to amplify the understanding of favelas as places of community and security. While journalists drew on RioOnWatch's wide network of connections and deep knowledge of favelas, they were also plied with information on the positive aspects of life in favelas, dispelling the myth of marginality. In exchange for contacts, interviews and access, journalists were exposed to an understanding of favela-places that was contrary to generic media coverage, which focused on sensationalised violence, drug use and poverty (Catalytic Communities 2016). The sense of the place of Vila Autódromo discussed in the previous chapter was spread among journalists in the hope that their reporting would further spread the narratives associated with this understanding of place in their reporting on Rio. In doing this, RioOnWatch was explicitly attempting to transform the discourse around favelas, engaging in a discursive contest over the nature of favela-places and challenging the logic of removals.

The keys to the favela

For the first time in almost a year of fieldwork, I made my way along the road to the community through crowds of people. The Olympic Park was finally abuzz with activity, seven days before the start of the Games, filled with people in bright colour-coded uniforms – volunteers, broadcast teams and sponsor representatives, the olive-green uniforms of the soldiers providing security the only dull colour on show. Closer to the community, the crowds disappeared and I headed into the community towards the new *Espaço Ocupa*, passing the newly built homes as I walked. There were two rows of identical, whitewashed houses on either side of the newly tarmacked street, with a gap for access to the church. The new homes were surrounded by a wall, with gaps for the road at either end of the street: if they had installed gates it would be a gated community.

I met Penha, but there were few other residents around, as far as I could see. She was upbeat, seemingly excited to move into her new home. One of RioOnWatch's editors had put in me in touch with Paul, a cameraman from a major US network, who was preparing a story on Vila Autódromo and I had arranged to meet him here. I spotted him – a white guy with

Figure 5.1 The new homes of Vila Autódromo, July 2016.
(Image: author's own.)

close-cut hair and a soft American accent – recognisable by the official IOC press accreditation pass around his neck, filming some of the remaining favela houses. After I introduced myself, he asked when the exchange of keys would happen. Unsure, I asked Penha, who told me they were waiting for the legal team from the Public Defender's Office before they began. Paul and I chatted briefly as we waited, about the favela and my research, as well as what he needed for his story. He wanted to interview someone from the municipal government and film the keys being handed over. I explained that I was unable to help with this as I did not have the contacts with govern-ment, but that I could help him with speaking to residents and understand-ing the community.

Paul went back to filming parts of the favela, ensuring he had enough shots to create a good story. I chatted to the tall, well-built tanned white man who was accompanying him, who spoke good English but with a Brazilian accent. Without ever clarifying this, I assumed this guy, named Alex, was a translator and fixer for Paul, and we discussed a little of the history of the favela. He seemed to be sitting on the fence between the argument that these people needed to live somewhere and that the Olympics needed the space until I explained that the community had been here since 1967 and had legal rights to the land. Shocked, Alex called Paul back to make sure he under-stood that the people here should not have been forced to move, saying he now understood why residents resisted eviction so strongly.

City officials had arrived and were talking to Penha and Luiz, while the public defenders were arriving, meaning things would likely soon get under way. Another team of journalists, from Australia, was walking around the community and Luiz approached to ask them – in Portuguese – if they needed anything. When he realised the journalist was unable to speak Portuguese, he tried again, this time in broken English, so I headed over and offered to help translate, but the journalist returned to the rest of his team. A small group of the young white women activists supporting the favela from the Comitê Popular arrived, all of whom were graduate students of urban plan-ning or architecture. The residents, public defenders and members of the Comitê Popular headed into Penha's temporary house for a meeting. I was not allowed in, as the public defender at the door keeping out the press didn't know me, and none of the people I knew, neither residents nor Comitê Popular activists, were close to the door to vouch for me. After a short meet-ing of maybe ten minutes, they emerged and headed over to the new homes for an inspection. Before the inspections began, Amanda gathered the press around her and explained that, although 'we love the press', residents did not want journalists to enter the houses during the inspection process.

The houses were inspected individually and thoroughly by a small group of people, including the municipal government officials and architects, the public defenders, the Comitê Popular members and the residents whose home it would be. The young women activists had clipboards and checklists and were assiduously assessing the quality of the homes. Journalists and other supporters were respectful of Amanda's request, occasionally filming and taking photographs through doors and windows, but never entering the homes. The inspections were tortuously long and detailed, taking up to half an hour per house as the journalists and many other supporters of the community waited in the street, chatting in the cool winter sun.

The Australian journalists took the opportunity to interview Penha and she was as defiant as ever, telling them 'the fight goes on' because 'other communities are still suffering', and that 'we should all be equal and our rights should be respected'. I asked Paul if he wanted to interview her, but he explained that he would come back in a few days once his colleague had arrived from the USA. Instead of doing an interview now, he wanted to arrange another day to meet her along with his colleague, so I asked Penha if she would be available. She was hesitant and unsure, saying she would be moving things into her new home, but she agreed to meet Paul again on Sunday after I explained that he was from one of the major US networks.

I chatted briefly with Luiz, catching up on how life had been for him here over the past few weeks. He seemed relaxed, asking how the others at RioOnWatch were, and whether I would write an article for the site on today's events. I told him I would, adding that I would like to ask him a few questions once he had inspected his house. He cut our chat short, as Penha's mother's house was being inspected and he needed to join the inspection team. He returned afterwards saying that there were still a few little issues: the window didn't shut properly and there was rubbish left on the floor. Luiz asked Paul if he wants to ask any questions, keen to ensure that the journalists understood the residents' perspective. I explained to Luiz that Paul had already arranged with Penha to come back and interview her in a few days. Shortly afterwards, when Luiz and Penha had inspected their own home, they gave speeches to the small press pack that had assembled in the community. Luiz said 'it is a good home, but it is not the dream', a tear forming in his eye as he remembered the home that was destroyed just a few short months ago. He said that in the new home, they could continue their life and 'write a new page of their story'. Penha was happy that, finally, her 'rights have been respected', but 'the struggle still goes on'. She thanked God, along with all those who had come to Vila Autódromo over the years: activists, students and international journalists.

As we waited for the inspections to be completed, Paul and I chatted about what he would cover during his time here in Rio. His hands seemed to be tied by so many rules: he had been told he could not enter any favelas at all (it could be argued that Vila Autódromo was no longer a favela at this point, as it had been so transformed by the evictions). He also had to travel everywhere with Alex, who, Paul explained, wasn't a translator or fixer but a bodyguard. Paul was not allowed to leave his hotel alone. Alex came over as we chatted and we discussed favelas, specifically, how dangerous it is for journalists to report from favelas. I explained, in line with the editorial position of RioOnWatch line, that favelas aren't all bad and that violence is exaggerated, but Alex emphasised crime and danger. He told us about 'microwaving': a slang term for when traffickers kidnap reporters and put tyres around them before setting them on fire, so that no remains are left except teeth. When I try to assert that this was unusual, Alex asked another of the Brazilian journalists, who agreed that it does happen. At this point I lost hope of painting any kind of positive picture of favelas and just stopped talking about them. I felt somewhat inadequate: a white Western kid arguing against Brazilian adults about Brazil: white saviour syndrome in action. Later, when chatting with Alex, I realised he was from São Paulo and didn't actually have any experience of working in Rio's favelas.

After the inspections were finally completed, we all returned to the *Espaço Ocupa* where municipal government officials wrote the agreement in longhand to deliver the houses in negotiation with the public defenders. The public defenders pushed for commitments to further urbanisation – a second phase of construction for public spaces was due to be completed after the Olympics – and a shorter deadline for the city to finish the final repairs. Public defenders and city officials eventually signed the agreement before each resident signed in turn, receiving a key for their home. Paul filmed as Penha signed the contract: he had been waiting to get that footage before leaving. He thanked me for my help and gave me his card, in case I heard of anything interesting happening around the city during the Games, before heading back to his Copacabana hotel.

As this passage shows, members of RioOnWatch's team, in this case myself, had many opportunities to influence press coverage of favelas, from ensuring that journalists have access to residents' perspectives and give adequate space to their voices in coverage, to shaping journalists' understanding of the situations they were reporting on. This chapter explores the influencing of the press as a deliberate strategy for effecting change. To achieve this, access to information and contacts was given out, along with a particular understanding of favelas as places of community and innovation. In the case of Vila Autódromo, this was the same sense of the place forged in the liminal moments of *Ocupa Vila Autódromo*, shaped and spread through social media as discussed in the previous chapter. Through influencing press coverage of favelas, RioOnWatch sought to transform the common conception of favela-places as dangerous, poverty-stricken slums. In essence, the attempt to influence coverage was part of the wider contest to define the space and place of favelas, a theme that runs throughout this book.

RioOnWatch

RioOnWatch was initially set up in 2010 to provide detailed news in English and Portuguese on how Olympic developments affected favela communities from the perspective of residents. By providing focused attention on hyper-local issues and through Catalytic Communities' (the NGO which ran RioOnWatch) pre-existing connections with favela residents, RioOnWatch quickly became a trusted source for news from favelas. Indeed, as Theresa, RioOnWatch's editor-in-chief and founder of Catalytic Communities described it to new volunteers at one meeting: 'trust is our biggest asset'. From this trust, the organisation saw an opportunity to provide assistance to journalists reporting on favelas, providing background information, photographs, contacts and, in some cases, guided trips to favelas (such as Paul's visit to Vila Autódromo). Initially, these trips were only conducted by Theresa, but as demand grew in the months before the Olympics, other members of RioOnWatch's core team became involved, as did long-serving volunteers, including myself and a few others. Wrapped up in the details of the story provided to journalists is the understanding of favelas as places of community, security and home. In this way, this sense of place was spread to journalists and, to some extent, the readers, listeners, or viewers of their reporting.

I had identified RioOnWatch as an organisation of interest for the research through my internet research prior to travel, and I was able to get in touch with Theresa before I arrived in Rio, chatting via Skype about what I could bring to the organisation and what I wanted to research with them – essentially, negotiating access. We had agreed that I would contribute several articles focusing on the history of the Olympics, serving to make the point that the problems discussed on the site hadn't just popped up in Rio. She had put me in touch with Emma before I arrived and, through discussions with her, I had already started working on an article about gentrification in Olympic cities. Theresa also added me into RioOnWatch's Facebook groups, where much of the organisation's business is conducted, shortly prior to my arrival in the city. On arrival, that week's RioOnWatch meeting was my first engagement with my actual research subject (i.e. beyond general Carioca life and culture). The meeting was held in Theresa's house: a large, airy home with a small pool in the yard, hidden behind a high wall and gate in the bohemian neighbourhood of Santa Teresa.

Theresa herself is a tall, white woman with long brown hair. Born in the UK to a British father and Brazilian mother, she was raised in Washington, DC, where her parents both worked as economists. Her mother's love for Brazil meant Theresa grew up reading and talking about Brazil, particularly about inequality and economic development, given her parents' work. Her mother ensured she grew up speaking Portuguese and there were annual visits to family who remained in the country. Passionate about the environment, Theresa initially studied biology at university until, on a semester abroad in Madagascar studying lemurs, she realised that 'all the Lemurs are going to die and so are all the forests if you don't take care of the people'. This prompted a shift into anthropology and eventually to a PhD in city planning, which, combined with a desire to return to Brazil, led her to study favelas in the city. Out of this doctoral research Catalytic Communities was born, initially focused on using new internet technologies to share solutions among informal communities. She now lives in Rio with her daughter and is a strong, chatty woman who seemed to have endless demands on her time as Rio geared up to host the Olympic Games.

Weekly meetings for RioOnWatch almost always followed a standard format. We would sit in a circle in a large square room with green walls on the ground floor while someone (usually Emma or Theresa) typed minutes in English on a laptop that was set up to project onto the wall so we could all see. Going around the circle, everyone would say what they had been doing for the past week – usually a short, 2- or 3-minute update – but sometimes wider questions would be opened up that were discussed as needed. The vast majority of the meeting would be conducted in English, although occasionally some people chose to speak in Portuguese about certain things, seemingly depending on personal preference. On rare occasions, typically when Theresa was away and her Brazilian second-in-command, Carla, was chairing the meeting, whole meetings would be conducted in Portuguese, although if people were not comfortable speaking Portuguese they could still speak in English. As we sat and discussed things together, people would occasionally pop out to refill their drinks in the kitchen, or swat away the mosquitos which are common in this part of the city. Otherwise, reports would listened to intently by others.

With Olympic events attracting huge press interest, many journalists were dispatched from far-flung corners of the world to Rio de Janeiro to report on Olympic preparations. In April I spoke to a Canadian journalist who had officially taken time off from his newspaper job to spend more time in the city, choosing instead to be paid as a freelance. He got in touch with me for an interview and I agreed, on condition that I could ask him a few questions about his experience of reporting on the Olympic preparations. He explained, as we sat eating rice and beans in a bar downtown, that had he travelled on newspaper expenses, he would have spent a maximum of ten days in Rio, with much of that spent indoors writing articles. He knew that would not be sufficient to understand the complex issues associated with favelas and the Olympic Games. Hannerz (2004) calls these short-term reporters 'parachutists', travelling from one location to the next, following major stories. RioOnWatch sought to ensure these parachutists could get a deeper understanding of the complexities of the city, particularly favelas, despite the short periods they spent in the city. As MacDonald (2008) notes, such parachute journalists have historically struggled to gain access to marginalised views, often relying on local governments or easily accessible sources, including business and media elites.

RioOnWatch sought to make favela residents an easily accessible source for these journalists, always trying to make it as easy as possible for journalists to connect to favela residents. The rise of social media helped in this, with journalists often using Twitter in particular to research stories, allowing activists to connect with them online. Social media enabled numerous *favelados* to publicise their voices online (Nemer 2016), allowing them to gain worldwide attention through Portuguese-speaking journalists: many favela groups were included on a list of social media accounts that RioOnWatch encouraged journalists to follow. RioOnWatch's own live-tweeting and reporting aimed to put favela voices into the spaces journalists were paying attention to, removing the language barrier to the inclusion of favela perspectives in reporting.

Foreign correspondents had a markedly different relationship with RioOnWatch. Living in Rio, many having moved there when it was announced that the city would host the Olympics, these journalists had little need for the translation and context RioOnWatch provided to parachutists, having developed their own understandings of the city and its favelas over years on their beat. That said, my fieldwork occurred in the year leading up to the Olympics, when most foreign correspondents were already embedded in the fabric of carioca life: as Hannerz (2004) notes, such correspondents tend to require more local help in the early years of their assignment. Editors at RioOnWatch pointed out that there was more collaboration with foreign correspondents in the early years. RioOnWatch kept in contact with many foreign correspondents, providing assistance where possible, but with foreign correspondents less dependent on the NGO, there were diminished opportunities to influence their coverage of informal communities. However, as Theresa explained in an interview in 2018, many of these journalists were reporting in similar ways to RioOnWatch already:

> in the very beginning I think they thought a little bit, 'hmm, are these guys partisan?' but over time, because they were living here, a lot of these journalists were, what they were seeing was corroborating the narrative that we had shared with them. So then they started taking that narrative as their own because it was being verified through their research and their reporting.

Collaborations with mainstream press were not limited to the kind of face-to-face assistance I provided to Paul in Vila Autódromo. As one of RioOnWatch's editors explained to me, journalists regularly picked up themes discussed on RioOnWatch for their own reports. This was not seen as competition, but as part of the role – the organisation's interest is served by getting the information to as wide an audience as possible, not ensuring their own website has large numbers of visitors. This collaboration with journalists can be seen in the revelation that the Olympic media village was built on a former slave burial ground, initially reported by RioOnWatch, but then picked up by *The Guardian*'s Latin American correspondent.

The sense of favela-places that RioOnWatch sought to spread to journalists (and by extension, their audiences) often crystallised into what appears at first glance to be an innocuous issue: how to describe favelas to an English-speaking audience. Most commonly, the Portuguese word 'favela' is translated into the English terms 'slum' or 'shanty-town'. Such terms carry connotations of poverty and danger, contrary to the understanding of place promoted by RioOnWatch and residents of Vila Autódromo. Recognising this, RioOnWatch actively pressured journalists to 'call them favelas'. As the Catalytic Communities website points out, the terms 'slum' and 'shanty-town' are inaccurate characterisations of many favelas in Rio (and definitely for Vila Autódromo). By questioning the language used to describe these communities, RioOnWatch was able to open a discussion about the nature of favelas, framing that discussion to challenge associations with violence and poverty as inaccurate.

Most of the team at RioOnWatch privately acknowledge that to minimise crime and poverty and focus on community values is a somewhat rose-tinted view of favelas, diminishing the violence of everyday life experienced by many *favelados*. However, they would counter, the stereotype of favelas as dangerous and squalid is similarly inaccurate and far more common. Catalytic Communities also tracked how favelas were discussed in international media through a long-running research project, with regular articles published highlighting the 'best and worst' reports about favelas, critiquing and deconstructing articles which reinforced the 'poverty-and-danger' narrative. At least one journalist even approached RioOnWatch for help with their article in an attempt to avoid being highlighted as one of the worst reports.

Through this work, RioOnWatch promotes a narrative about favelas that views them as places of community, security, solidarity and cultural vibrancy. This sits in direct contrast to the view of favelas promoted as part of what Magalhães (2019) calls 'the repertoire of removal', whereby favelas are presented as the source of problems for the city, linked to crime, uncleanliness and poverty. This narrative, discussed in chapter 1, had been promoted by local media and politicians including Eduardo Paes, and leads to the apparent solution of favela removal, with residents of favelas frequently portrayed as deficient through either active criminality or passive acceptance of poverty. Even when a sympathetic view of favelas is presented, residents tend to be cast as passive, victims of circumstance, powerless to change their situation, waiting for the state to intervene and improve their lives.

In contrast, RioOnWatch's work presents favela residents as active, even while often portraying them as victims: that is, victims of neglect by the state who have organised and fought to improve their material conditions and who, by virtue of the same conditions by which they are neglected, have an empowering potential to create new forms of sustainable urban living. That is, having been neglected by formal state structures of urban planning, favelas present an opportunity for innovation in such landscapes. The same informality and lack of regulation that makes favelas ideal hubs for drug trafficking gangs also makes creative, vibrant and sustainable communities possible. RioOnWatch, then, seeks to promote an alternative narrative about favelas to international media, one which is based in the same alternative conceptualisation of place generated in the liminal moments of *Ocupa Vila Autódromo*. This narrative stressed the strong community bonds often found in favelas, the security and safety found in many communities, and the innovative forms of sustainable living found across the city.

This narrative wasn't promoted only by RioOnWatch: other activists worked to generate positive perceptions of favelas in the media. Residents of Vila Autódromo, for example, bent over backwards to help journalists, going out of their way to ensure the press got the story they needed. Always courteous, residents made a special point of thanking those who visited the community, in particular international journalists, as Penha did when she had inspected her new home. In December, at the football tournament discussed in chapter 3, I noticed myself understanding Portuguese relatively easily for the first time. In the months that followed, I consistently found it easier to understand Portuguese when spoken by residents, rather than by activists in other organisations across the city. Vila Autódromo residents seemed to speak more slowly and clearly than other cariocas. This may have been a deliberate attempt to ensure they were understood or an unconscious effect of regular contact with gringos, but it made reporting on the favela markedly easier for non-native speakers of Portuguese.

Spreading the narrative

RioOnWatch's network of contacts and readers, the editors often stressed, was powerful because of its 'quality, not quantity'. By this, they were referring to the large numbers of journalists, activists and researchers among the readership who could use their influence to spread these ideas further. Similarly, the organisation has built up a vast network of trusted contacts in favelas around the city. In seeking to influence journalistic coverage, RioOnWatch draws on what Castells (2011: 773) calls network power: 'the power resulting from the standards required to coordinate social interaction in the networks'. By being the arbiter of connections between international journalists and favela residents, RioOnWatch is able to shape the relations between these people. Through its involvement in making these connections, the NGO is able to influence not only who is connected to who but also the nature of the interpersonal relationships created. By making an understanding of favelas as places of community and security a condition of inclusion in the network, RioOnWatch is able to influence media coverage. However, where Castells (2011), who was writing about digital networks, sees this network in a relatively binary in-or-out way, as I will illustrate in this section, being inside or outside is contingent and negotiated through human relationships.

Using a network of contacts built up through Catalytic Communities' previous decade of work in Rio's favelas, RioOnWatch has access to many of the city's favela communities. Beyond these contacts, RioOnWatch has built up an impressive array of expertise on issues affecting Rio's informal communities, translating (both linguistically and culturally) this expertise for its global audience. This gave the team a unique position in supporting journalists to advocate for the rights of favelas like Vila Autódromo. While RioOnWatch had around fifteen volunteers based in Rio in the build-up to the Games, only a select few of these worked with journalists in the way described above. Initially only Theresa, then paid members of staff, took journalists on favela visits, but as the numbers of parachutists increased in early 2016, several long-serving volunteers, including myself, began to work with journalists in this way. Through the resources built up over years of work in Rio's informal communities, RioOnWatch was able to attract journalists to collaborate with the organisation, based on the offer of access to favelas. While it is clearly not the case that without RioOnWatch journalists would be unable to report on favelas, the organisation made such reporting significantly easier, providing contacts and context. This removed some of the barriers that effectively excluded the voices of *favelados* from media reporting, which in turn supported the myth of marginality. Paul was by no means unusual in having been told by his employer not to visit favelas – many journalists reported this was the case – but RioOnWatch was able to persuade some of them that it was both necessary and safe to report from favelas.

Beyond this, RioOnWatch was able to provide assistance with understanding issues in favelas, making reporting on these communities easier. As one journalist who had worked with RioOnWatch reported, the organisation 'offers media access to areas that would otherwise remain unseen' (quoted in Taylor 2018). Another journalist noted that it would have been 'nearly impossible' to report on favelas without help, as she experienced when she tried using a taxi driver as a translator in the Vidigal favela (Savchuk 2016). In the months leading up the Olympic Games, RioOnWatch dedicated a section of the website to resources for journalists, aiming 'to support informed and nuanced reporting through the Games'. What RioOnWatch referred to as 'informed' implicitly connotes 'informed about favelas as places of community', using a narrative which doesn't portray favelas as marginal. In particular, RioOnWatch sought to challenge ill-informed tropes of favelas through promoting the voice of favelas' residents, whose lived experiences showed these tropes to be inaccurate. This support also helped favela residents deal with press interest, as even the press teams that had translators were often poor at explaining what they were doing to residents. When a North American television crew was reporting on Vila Autódromo in February 2016, for example, they barely spoke to favela residents when the cameras weren't rolling, with Penha relying on Theresa's explanations to understand what was happening and when she would be interviewed.

By providing this assistance to journalists, then, RioOnWatch mobilises journalistic and favela contacts to promote coverage of favelas as places of community, as opposed to places of danger and poverty. This network power, Castells (2011: 773) asserts, 'is exercised not by exclusion from the networks but by the imposition of the rules of inclusion'. As I will show, this is not as simple as Castells (2011) seems to suggest: the rules of inclusion are not imposed by structures but negotiated by free agents. While the network power approach suggests that, by working with RioOnWatch, Paul's reporting would have included implicit or explicit reference to favelas as places of security and community, the reality is more complex. Journalists would not have accepted RioOnWatch explicitly dictating what could or could not be included in their reporting. However, through discussions and negotiations, members of RioOnWatch were able to influence coverage through subtler means, framing the issues facing communities as problems of state neglect and mistreatment, not as problems with favelas per se.

My discussion with Alex on the dangers (or otherwise) of reporting on favelas illustrates that it is not a simple matter of the 'imposition of the rules of inclusion' (Castells 2011: 773): these rules are negotiated based on the relational power and status of the actors parsing the issue. In Vila Autódromo, where Paul could see that there was no violence and hear from residents about the value they placed on their land, I was trying to persuade him that this favela was not vastly different from others: that while there may be issues, the strong community, affordability and sustainability of favelas holds value for *favelados* across the city. Alex, Paul's Brazilian bodyguard, disagreed, saying these are dangerous places and it is right that journalists are limited in their reporting on them. He brought another Brazilian reporter into the conversation to back up his point that violence is sometimes inflicted upon journalists in favelas. Feeling outnumbered, I gave up trying to convince them of the positive aspects of favelas. In this context, the power I draw from intellectual capital as an expert on favelas was limited by Alex's cultural capital as a native Brazilian, with whom I was unable and unwilling to argue to any great extent.

This was a symbolic struggle, in Bourdieu's (1989) terms, over the nature of favelas. In this discussion of favelas, power relations served to ensure Alex's understanding of favelas appeared to be correct. When I later learned that Alex was from São Paulo and had only limited knowledge of Rio's favelas, I became bolder in arguing my case against him; the importance of his Brazilian nationality was diminished in relation to my own experience and knowledge of Rio. As such, when we later discussed specific favelas, I was able to succeed in convincing Alex and Paul that certain communities are not as dangerous as they are often perceived to be, based on my intimate knowledge of Rio. Alex and I were clashing in a 'symbolic struggle for the production of common sense' (Bourdieu 1989: 21). As such, this was not a network imposing rules of inclusion as Castells (2011) suggests, rather the rules of inclusion were a product of power relations between social actors.

Comparing this discussion with Alex to a discussion I had with European journalists on the dangers of reporting from favelas reinforces this point. At the end of March, I spent a day with an all-white Eastern European television crew, showing them around Vila Autódromo and helping them to interview residents. Before we entered the community to talk to residents, I briefly explained the history of the favela, to help them understand the context. They asked questions about the safety and levels of crime in the community and I responded that Vila Autódromo was perfectly safe, as are many other favelas. The cameraman in particular was nervous about visiting favelas, thinking about his two children back home. Their translator, a woman who lived in Rio, was also sceptical about the safety of reporting on favelas and we briefly discussed this point. I argued that as long as you go with someone who lives there, who can vouch for you and guide you in how to behave, favelas are safe places, which she conceded.

With the European television crew, I felt confident in pushing the point that favelas are safe for journalists; I was able, in Castells' (2011: 773) terms, to impose 'the rules of inclusion'. Conversely, Alex was able to draw not only on his national identity but also on others with experience to back up his argument that favelas are dangerous. To provide another example, when a North American television crew visited the favela escorted by Theresa in

February, she took every opportunity to provide background to the evictions in the favela, drawing on her own experience. She would frequently preface these statements about what life used to be like with 'when I first visited here several years ago', emphasising her long-term knowledge about the community and its struggle. The point here is that this is a process of negotiation, not imposition, based on the power relations between the individuals involved. Requiring journalists to write articles sympathetic to favelas as a condition of collaboration could never have worked: good journalists would not accept conditions being imposed on what they were able to write. However, through processes of negotiation like those outlined above, RioOnWatch had an opportunity to influence coverage of favelas in the years preceding the Games.

In Vila Autódromo, common tropes and stereotypes about favelas were easily refutable: the houses were large and well-built, served by electricity and running water, residents had legal title to their land, and there was no criminal presence. The only squalor in the favela was a result of evictions, with debris from demolished homes scattered throughout the community, strengthening the framing that the issues in these places are a result of state neglect, not their nature as favelas. Residents even had an internationally award-winning plan for continued upgrading of the urban space, evidencing the flexibility and potential of favela communities. As such, in Vila Autódromo and many of the other communities in which the organisation worked, RioOnWatch was able to present a view of favelas as reality, not a matter of perspective.[1] This is crucial in the symbolic struggle over the power to define favelas. The efficacy of this power 'depends on the degree to which the vision proposed is founded in reality' (Bourdieu 1989: 23). If the most knowledgeable and renowned expert on favelas were to persuade a journalist that favelas are safe and the journalist then experienced violence during a visit to a favela, that understanding of favelas would be unlikely to hold sway. The space and place of Vila Autódromo were crucial in ensuring that these symbolic struggles are effective.

Of course, chief among the characteristics which made Vila Autódromo a useful case for RioOnWatch (and others) in presenting an alternative narrative for favelas was its location. Directly next to the main Olympic Park,

---

1 However, this is not the reason RioOnWatch placed strategic importance on the community – that was Theresa's view that 'if a favela with two titles gets evicted, any favela can get evicted'. In our interview in 2018 I asked whether the sympathetic framing of communities like Vila Autodromo was part of the rationale for taking journalists there. Theresa countered that it was not a deliberate decision, but a consequence of which communities wanted to work with RioOnWatch: 'the idea that we support communities just because they're positive examples is not right, it's just that the negatives tend to be state induced. There are communities with community-induced negatives, but those communities don't look to us and that's part of the reason they have these negative community elements, they're not communities that are looking for support or that see their own value.'

Vila Autódromo was the only favela the municipal government admitted was being removed because of a mega-event. For journalists looking to report on the dark side of hosting the Olympic Games, Vila Autódromo was the prime example. In this, the favela represented a unique political opportunity for social movements to challenge existing narratives about favelas. As Penha put it in an interview in 2018: 'A large part of the media, which was important, they came more for the fact of the Olympic Park, and that was fortunate for us, and I think this land is very blessed, because we were literally next to the Olympic Park.'

In addition to the location, Vila Autódromo gained worldwide notoriety on 3 June 2015 when *Guarda Municipal* beat residents during an attempted eviction. Photos and videos of the violence rapidly spread around the world, particularly Penha's bloodied face. As she explained in 2018:

> After the third of June, the coverage increased, because when my photo was put in all the newspapers, my face bleeding and all that stuff, that created a big impact. Because how can you do that? How can the Olympics mistreat a community? That was when we got an expansion of coverage so big we didn't really understand the level of visibility we had gained. This was super important for the struggle, because people came, you know, disgrace sells! After that people became curious, foreign press, many people came, from Germany, from Switzerland, Japan, everywhere. From all of these places came people who wanted to know why? Why this violence?

For RioOnWatch and other social movements, Vila Autódromo also represented an important precedent. Given the community's strong legal rights, lack of drug trafficking or militia gangs, well-organised resistance to eviction and international visibility, removing the favela was not straightforward. As one of RioOnWatch's editors explained at one of the regular team meetings, Vila Autódromo was seen as a landmark case: 'if they can remove them, they can remove any favela'. From this stemmed the widely held belief that by fighting evictions in Vila Autódromo, activists were fighting against evictions in other parts of the city, not to mention the wider country and indeed across the world.

As such, by using network power to influence coverage of Vila Autódromo's resistance to eviction, RioOnWatch was implicitly challenging wider conceptualisations of informal communities as dirty, dangerous places, challenging what Magalhães (2019) calls 'the repertoire of removal', itself founded on the myth of marginality (Perlman 1976). Castells' (2011) concept of network power provides a useful lens to understand how RioOnWatch was able to influence journalistic coverage of favelas, translating its experience and knowledge into leverage over parachutists unfamiliar with the city. However, Castells (2011) gives too little attention to the social practices involved in the exercise of network power. The negotiations involved in leveraging RioOnWatch's power into sympathetic press coverage are more complex than his theorisation suggests. These individual negotiations with journalists formed part of a wider strategy to transform reporting on favelas during the Rio 2016 Olympic Games by changing the discourse surrounding such communities.

Changing the narrative

As I have argued elsewhere (see Talbot 2018), the application of network power served as a discourse intervention for Rio's favelas. Through this negotiated network power, RioOnWatch sought to change the way favelas are thought and spoken about, particularly targeting international media accounts of favelas. Those involved saw the attention brought to the city by the 2016 Olympic Games as both a threat and an opportunity for favelas. As Theresa explained in an interview in 2018:

> So it was like, on the one hand, dealing with all of those [threats], it was, what's the word, damage control, to try to reduce the damage the city was doing, and on the other hand it was trying to take advantage of a moment of incredible visibility to shift the narrative and work on the narrative. So you know, those two things came together, and nobody would want to have one for the other, but if you had the first then at least you had the second and you could do something productive with that so that was what we were always trying to do. We're always trying to figure out what in the moment we can do to further our mission [of supporting sustainable development in favelas].

RioOnWatch used the privileged position it had carved out for itself through its English-speaking experts on favelas to influence press coverage of these communities in the media spotlight that the Olympics brought to Rio de Janeiro. This discourse intervention, as Karlberg (2005) would describe it, was deliberately intended to effect a change in policy towards favelas, targeting the justification for removals and heavy policing.

Discourse intervention, as Karlberg (2005: 1) explains, is 'an effort to change our social reality by altering the discourses that help constitute it'. This draws on the notion that how people talk about a particular phenomenon affects how they think and act in relation to it. In essence, power relations influence society by generating a regime of truth: 'that is, the type of discourse it accepts and makes function as true' (Foucault 1980: 131). In attempting to change this discourse, RioOnWatch is part of a wider framing contest about favelas, intending to change the nature of decisions made about them by challenging the understanding of them as places of criminality and poverty. If favelas can only be thought about as marginal slums, ghettos, and havens of crime and poverty, the preferred action towards them will logically be to remove these blights on our cities. Within this regime of truth, *favelados* are thought of as uneducated criminals and their power to make claims about favelas is limited. RioOnWatch's work with journalists, then, was an attempt to promote an alternative discourse about favelas, whereby these communities are celebrated for their contributions to the city, transforming how favelas and their residents are treated as a result.

It would be inaccurate to suggest RioOnWatch didn't try to influence coverage by the Brazilian national and local media, but with these media it lacked the privileged position it held in relation to the international media. The focus on favelas from the perspective of those who live there was in direct contradiction to mainstream Brazilian media: as one of the editors described it, part of RioOnWatch's role was 'showing that [Globo] was saying something different from Vila Autódromo' residents. The marginalisation of favela perspectives in mainstream Brazilian media is well-established (Rosas-Moreno and Straubhaar 2015) and, by focusing on favelas, RioOnWatch was exploiting a niche in mainstream coverage. However, this focus on favelas was not unique to RioOnWatch: it was one of many small organisations writing about developments in favelas, meaning the Portuguese-language output was one voice among many. The English-language reporting landscape on favelas, conversely, was irregular and often ill-informed, written in some cases by journalists who had never visited the community which they discussed, giving RioOnWatch a fairly dominant position. Alongside this, given part of the rationale for hosting the Olympics was to showcase Rio and Brazil to the world, international media coverage was able to exert pressure on the authorities to change their behaviour in Vila Autódromo at least, as Luiz explained in an interview in 2018:

> I used to always say that it's a big coming together of factors [that enabled Vila Autódromo to resist removal] and the international media is for sure one of these factors. It was an incredible weight that it brought to our struggle from so many other countries, for sure this weighed heavily and made the authorities reflect on what they were doing in that period.

In the months prior to the Olympic Games, this discourse intervention crystallised into a specific strand of RioOnWatch's work. The NGO attempted to create an online campaign with the title 'Stop Favela Stigma' to explicitly challenge stigmatised representations of favelas during the Olympic Games. The title was specifically chosen to be understandable to both English and Portuguese speakers. On 3 August, RioOnWatch's social media accounts posted various stigma-busting articles and videos as well as commissioned articles from favela journalists. Several favela activists had been involved in the planning of the campaign and posted photos or descriptions tackling the issue of favela stigma. The intention was to create a moment in which favela residents' voices could be heard, which could then be collated, translated and handed to journalists who arrived to cover the Olympic city.

More generally, this discourse intervention can be seen in RioOnWatch's specific push to get journalists to 'call them favelas'. This focus proved an effective opening gambit, drawing in the various issues related to the misrepresentation of Rio's favelas from a single issue. RioOnWatch editors lobbied foreign correspondents to avoid using terms such as 'slum' and 'shanty town'. Theresa tells a story of discussing the issue with a *New York Times* correspondent in Brazil. In the days that followed, the correspondent asked his Twitter followers how best to translate the word favela. In his next report on the issue, he avoided using terms like 'slum' or 'shanty town', instead physically describing favelas as if no name existed, writing of a vast maze of cinder-block homes, for example. Others were less receptive. The Associated Press, for example, argued that journalists needed to use language which could be easily understood by all and, as such, 'favela' was not an acceptable term, according to one RioOnWatch editor. In my own work publishing about Vila Autódromo for small media outlets, editors have attempted to change the word 'favela' for 'slum' or 'shanty town', but backed down on my insisting that those terms were inaccurate in relation to this favela. These terms matter: they signify wider understandings of favelas as places of either poverty and criminality or culture and innovation. RioOnWatch, in short, was engaged in a symbolic struggle to define favelas.

In the months leading up to the Games, RioOnWatch helped a steady stream of journalists report on the Olympic city, attempting to subtly influence their coverage. As Hannerz (2004: 154) notes, 'the critical importance of local helpers in foreign news work tends not to be acknowledged', meaning RioOnWatch's contribution to discourses surrounding favelas in the international media remains in the background. While RioOnWatch's own content analysis of international media coverage highlights a variety of shifts in the discourse, hailed as 'a truly positive legacy of the 2014 World Cup and 2016 Olympics' (Catalytic Communities 2016: 63), the picture remains complex. 'Slum' remains the most common translation of 'favela' (although use of the word 'favela' itself increased over time), violence or drugs remain the most common topic, and a plurality of articles still give an overwhelmingly negative impression of favelas (Catalytic Communities 2016).

Rio's informal communities remain stigmatised in media coverage, however, drawing on popular culture representations such as the film *Cidade de Deus* (Allen 2017). This perhaps explains the municipal government's desire to hide favelas from view, to avoid negative press coverage. Harris's (2016a) excellent mini-documentary for US website Vox, supported by RioOnWatch, explores this policy, noting the wall along the highway in the North Zone which ensures 'that people who leave the airport to the South Zone don't catch a glimpse of the reality of this city'. After visiting Vila Autódromo, Harris perceptively concludes that the new houses were being built to hide the favela; 'lest, heaven forbid, the international community catch a glimpse of the real Rio'. A strikingly similar conclusion had been published on RioOnWatch's website a few months earlier – another example of media picking up themes from the site and sharing them with a wider audience. The second part of Harris's (2016b) mini-documentary provides a comprehensive overview of the insurgent narrative on favelas which RioOnWatch promotes. Visiting several favelas, he documents the creativity and innovation which spring from informality, while perceptively observing that the same unregulated environment is what allows some favelas to fall into the grip of trafficking gangs. This alternative narrative celebrates favelas as places of community and sources of culture: the place we see described in the *Plano Popular da Vila Autódromo* (Associação de Moradores e Pescadores da Vila Autódromo 2016) and drawn from *Ocupa Vila Autódromo* events. By promoting this insurgent narrative RioOnWatch is building on the sense of place developed through the events held in the favela, transmitting this sense of place across geographical scales to the other side of the world.

Paul's report included references to this sense of place, with Vila Autódromo described as a 'calm, working-class community', with residents noting that 'we miss our community, it was beautiful', directly contradicting the common view of favelas as dirty slums. Having established that Vila Autódromo was a pleasant community for residents, the report compared what had been built to replace the community, with one resident bemoaning that 'a parking lot has more value than my house' (referring to their original home). The salience of this point relies on RioOnWatch's alternative narrative about favelas, on the audience's understanding that the house was valuable due to its location in a 'beautiful' community, as opposed to a poverty-stricken slum. The report closes by reminding viewers of the attachment residents have for the place, quoting a resident: 'if I had left this community, I would have lost all sense of my life, because I am happy here'.

While RioOnWatch was able to shift discourses in the international media slightly through the application of network power, there is limited evidence of this change influencing policy shifts. In the weeks leading up to the Olympic Games, Brazilian media outlets *O Globo* and *Veja* produced reports on police violence that were uncharacteristically sympathetic to favela residents, perhaps suggesting that the tone of international coverage was influencing national discourse. However, such progress appears to have been transient, as Brazil's political discourse since has increasingly come to view favelas and the urban poor through a criminal lens, particularly during the presidency of Jair Bolsonaro (2019–2023). Even the gains made through working with foreign correspondents seem to have been lost, as bureaus moved away from Rio to São Paulo or Brasília after the Games, shifting both expertise and attention away from the city. However, the removal of the Olympic Games as a stimulus for urban transformation has at least also removed one significant threatening factor.

Conclusions

The sense of place generated in the liminal moments of *Ocupa Vila Autódromo* held a radical potential for changing the way we think and talk about favelas. Confined to the few hundred people who attended these events, however, this sense of place served little purpose. The value of this commonly held understanding of the place of Vila Autódromo lay in its ability to convey a radical critique of top-down development, and ultimately capitalist accumulation, through talking about a location. This provided an effective counter to the authority of the state to define favelas and the associated discourse. By welcoming press to the favela, this sense of place could be spread across geographical scales, even as journalists portrayed both sides of the argument. Residents embraced journalists, going out of their way to help them understand the community, as the example of Luiz approaching the Australian journalists illustrates. Journalists, particularly international journalists, were always thanked for visiting the community in the knowledge that international exposure would help pressure Rio's government into treating Vila Autódromo with greater respect. Brazilian mainstream media were also welcomed, but covered the story far less, in part due to the biases which exist within the national press (Rosas-Moreno and Straubhaar 2015).

With the influx of international press, RioOnWatch served as a middle-man between journalists and favela residents. In doing so, the NGO sought to promote an alternative way of understanding favelas, as places of innovation and community instead of sites of violence and poverty. While this approach could be criticised for minimising the everyday violence of favela life, RioOnWatch was an effective counterweight to an overwhelmingly stigmatising public discourse around favelas. Through publishing on the RioOnWatch website as well as collaborations with visiting journalists, the NGO disseminated this different understanding of favelas to an international audience. In this, RioOnWatch was exercising a form of network power, as journalists reaped the benefit of access to the network of contacts and the organisation gave them. The NGO had the opportunity, in Castells'

(2011) terms, to impose the rules of inclusion in order to promote sympathetic coverage for favelas and their residents. However, such network power cannot be seen as operating in a mechanical way: sympathetic coverage was generated through complex negotiations between individuals, not a simplistic imposition of rules.

6

Memória não se remove: Heterotopia in the Museu das Remoções

On 18 May 2016, International Museum Day, the Museu das Remoções was inaugurated with a special event to mark the opening. The museum itself is an open-air museum, with exhibits dotted around the community. While preparing to leave home, I followed a conversation on the WhatsApp group of Vila Autódromo supporters, where there was some debate about whether to go ahead with the launch that day as the forecast was for heavy rain. Eventually one of the residents wrote authoritatively that it would go ahead and they were waiting to receive guests. I headed out to meet a couple of friends from RioOnWatch and we made our way out to the community together as the rain began to fall.

We arrived early and met Penha and Luiz and the few supporters who had already arrived, including Larissa. As we prepared for the arrival of more guests, opening the church for shelter and laying out cups for water, they told us there were eight installations around the favela, describing their locations for us. These had been created by university students in collaboration with the community and sought to convey the social memory of the community and thereby denounce the violent process of evictions (Bogado 2017). Along with the two other RioOnWatch volunteers, I made my way around the exhibits before the rain got any worse, taking photos so that we could illustrate the RioOnWatch article on the inauguration of the museum. The exhibits were positioned around important (some long since demolished) parts of the favela, representing a link to what previously stood there. We started at the installation by the church, a mock Olympic torch made of rubble with a quote saying 'even on the ground, the light is not completely out'. Further installations were dedicated to Penha's home (a large foam ♀, highlighting the demolition of the house which occurred on International Women's Day) and the Residents' Association building. Alongside each exhibit was a small placard with a quote and a QR code which could be scanned with a mobile phone, providing more information about the part of the community the installation represented. As we walked around I was shocked to see a pile of rubble where a home had been, still inhabited, just a few weeks ago. The move to temporary homes, creating space for the construction of new homes, had already begun.

We stopped at the exhibit for the *Espaço Ocupa* (Figure 3.2). Rubble from demolished homes had been adorned with photos of the events, allowing us to reminisce about the cultural festival we had attended in November and agonise that we had missed the capoeira performance at another event. The installation was backed by a white board with the slogan *Urbaniza já* surrounded by handprints in different coloured paints, representing the coming together of different groups in *Ocupa Vila Autódromo* events, while the colours of the exhibit represented the vibrancy of events which took place in the *Espaço Ocupa*. As we headed back to the church, a large group arrived: these were the students who had helped create the installation as part of a university project, headed by their professor, Rosa. Others had arrived as well, including Thainã, a human rights defender who initially came up with the idea for a museum, and Mario, a museologist who had taught Thainã at university and helped develop the project. A journalist who had been working with RioOnWatch also arrived – we had instructions to help him conduct an interview later.

Rosa began the speeches to the assembled crowd outside the church, explaining the process of building the museum's installations. There were around forty people gathered to listen, mostly students with a smattering of supporters, residents and former residents mixed in. Luiz then spoke about the history of the community, remarking that while twenty families had been successful in their struggle to remain this was not the end: 'We went through a lot to reach this point and it's not right that all of that could be forgotten.' When Luiz finished, Thainã spoke about the idea behind the museum before one of the former residents spoke about her experience of being evicted and removed from the community where she had made her home. With the speeches over, there was a tour of each installation led by Amanda and Rosa, with an explanation of the meaning behind each of the sculptures. At the installation for the Residents' Association, for example, Amanda explained that: 'We talked a lot when they were demolishing the building about how the Residents' Association isn't the building, it's the organisation of the residents. While residents are still organised, united, having meetings and fighting together, we know that the Residents' Association still lives.'

The idea for a museum focused on evictions emerged when the community's future remained uncertain, in late 2015. Thainã de Medeiros, who studied museology at university before working as an activist with transparency NGO Meu Rio, saw the opportunity to use museology as a tool of resistance. He had attended numerous evictions across the city in the build-up to the Olympic Games, including in Metro-Mangueira and Santa Marta as well as in Vila Autódromo, and had become frustrated with only being able to reactively document the eviction process. He wanted to do something more constructive. Alongside this came a realisation that the history of the city and its institutions were linked to evictions: whole swathes of the city are built where people had been evicted, particularly in the periods of intensive evictions under Pereira Passos (1902–1906) and Carlos Lacerda (1960–1965). When he had attended evictions in Metro-Mangueira, some of the residents had fled to the nearby State University of Rio de Janeiro and been chased by police. The ensuing mêlée caused some minor damage to the university, and Thainã found himself with little sympathy for students inconvenienced by people being evicted. When he later learned that the university itself was built on land where the Favela de Esqueleto had been removed he realised that there should be an institution to record this aspect of Rio's history. Alongside this, Thainã had been conducting research into strategies for resisting evictions and realised that Vila Autódromo could be a useful example, as he explained in an interview in 2018:

> I thought, it'd be great if Vila Autódromo, if they're able to resist eviction, which hasn't really been seen before, then how can we make sure that other communities here in Rio, or in other events, won't suffer eviction again, because many others are threatened with eviction? And how can we build a tool, you know, something that those people who are under threat of eviction can go to, to study this phenomenon and create their own tools to resist this shit.

With this idea in mind, Thainã spoke to Mario Chagas, who had taught him when he was a student of museology at UNIRIO (the Federal University of the State of Rio de Janeiro). Mario has a long history of involvement, both as an academic and an activist, with social museology and had worked with the Museu da Maré and the Museu da Favela, among others, to put museology to work in favelas. When I interviewed him he explained that Thainã came to meet with him, along with a resident of the community, to explore the idea for an museum of evictions and the very same day they drew up a plan of action. Thainã had already spoken to several residents who were excited by the idea and, soon afterwards, Mario and Thainã travelled to Vila Autódromo to discuss the idea with Amanda and Penha. As they walked around the community discussing the idea for a museum, Mario recalled in an interview in 2018:

> They [Amanda and Penha] said to me, 'here was the home of Seu Adão, here was the home ...', and as they showed me and they could see the home, but I didn't, because they had the memory of the home. They would say, there was a family home here, and I only saw decimated land.... It was in this moment talking with them we realised, look, one of the easiest initiatives we can do is to identify the houses, let's create signs to identify each house, let's mark the homes here, a sign for the Residents' Association, a sign for the house. And then we started to think also about using the rubble, to use this rubble as an archive.

Over several collaborative events, a plan for the museum was put in place and work began to develop an archive of materials, based around three themes: sustainability, community and *saudades* (a notoriously difficult to translate Portuguese word that refers to a sense of nostalgic longing), with activists, residents and students from Rosa's class collaborating to create the museum. The museum itself draws on the notion of the ecomuseum, where social relations are seen as a crucial part of the archive (see Rivière 1985). Drawing on this, 'the Museu das Remoções was created with two main aims: to preserve the memory of the people evicted along with their stories; and to serve as a tool of struggle, not just for us, but for all who are under threat of eviction' (Museu das Remoções 2017: 4).

Fundamentally, the museum exists to serve as a tool of resistance. When it was created and developed, nobody involved knew how the struggle over Vila Autódromo would end. According to Thainã, part of the reason for developing the Museu das Remoções in Vila Autódromo was that 'if the Evictions Museum is evicted, man, that'd make for a great headline ... that's part of the strategy, thinking about what will create a good headline to generate political pressure'. More broadly, the museum was set up to 'present another view, another memory of the Olympics whose point of departure is the memory of the eviction of Vila Autódromo' (Bogado 2017: 5). The motto of the museum, '*memória não se remove*' (memory can't be evicted) points to this attempt to preserve the place of Vila Autódromo, to avoid the soul of the community being forgotten under the whitewashed homes the government was building for the residents who remained.[1] The museum sought to make good on the promise Amanda shouted as tractors tore down the Residents' Association building, that 'even when the buildings of Carlos Carvalho are here, we will remain', even as memory. Now, the museum hosts events in the community as well as participating in events hosted by others around the city and beyond. In doing so, it 'gives visibility and stops the wiping away of the memory of all the injustices that occurred' (Venancio et al. 2018: 108) in the community. As one resident put it: 'from rescuing these memories, we could do more than preserve them, we can use them to reaffirm our rights and not allow them to be forgotten or ignored' (Teixeira 2017: 162).

In some respects then, the Museu das Remoções can be seen as a continuation of the *Ocupa Vila Autódromo* events discussed in previous chapters. As one of the supporters, Luiza de Andrade, explained in an interview in 2018:

---

1 This motto could also be translated as 'memory is not erased'. I prefer the translation 'can't be evicted' as this better captures the way the slogan is used to refer to the ways in which memory can be preserved as part of a struggle for housing rights in informal communities.

We have had activities for the preservation of memory, a wide range of cultural activities, so [we have helped with] the organisation of expositions, organisation of events and film exhibitions, participated in panels. Ultimately, from the collective of the Museu das Remoções, Vila Autodrómo continues to have visibility.

In explaining the creation of the museum in an academic paper, the museologists involved in the Museu das Remoções also make the link to the *Ocupa Vila Autódromo* events clear:

The resistance of Vila Autódromo was developed by means of cultural and artistic actions, always counting on the support and collaboration of many people from different places and varied types of work. With these supporters, who are moved by and concerned with the processes of construction and history of our city, and from the rubble of Vila Autódromo, the museum was built. (Venancio et al. 2018: 108)

The organisation of regular events, such as documentary screenings and panel discussions, continued to bring visitors to the community, allowing an opportunity for the residents to share their story and gain a sense of the broader support that exists for them. The museum is organised by a team that includes both residents and supporters, while key parts of the initial museological plan aimed to keep the community on the map, through campaigning for new signage, for example, and adding details of the museum to online maps, showing that a vibrant community still exists in Vila Autódromo (Museu das Remoções 2017).

Heterotopia – from Lefebvre to Foucault

While performing its role in providing continuity, the museum also seeks to develop a new form of resistance beyond that of the *Ocupa Vila Autódromo* events. I have argued in previous chapters that these events and the spreading of the sense of place linked the case of Vila Autódromo to broader debates about housing rights and the right to the city around the world, but this was not their primary purpose. *Ocupa Vila Autódromo* was about the defence of the community: the broader discourse of housing rights which it contributed to was a (deliberate) side-effect of the attempt to support residents in their struggle in the face of eviction. The museum, inaugurated after the community had come to an agreement with the municipal government for rehousing, is less focused on the specifics of Vila Autódromo's permanence: it is an explicit attempt to engage with the question of evictions and housing rights more generally. As a result, the idea that this is spreading a sense of a specific place that carries political connotations related to that specific community, as explained in previous chapters, doesn't fully explain what is happening in the

Museu das Remoções. Now, with the threat of Olympic evictions withdrawn, those who remain in the community are more secure (although not entirely secure). The museum is about history, but also about the future and therefore a different way of thinking about its significance is needed.

The idea that utopian thinking is important for social movements is nothing new. Scholars have long emphasised the importance of imagining other possible futures in order to deconstruct and challenge hegemonic power (Maeckelbergh 2009; Pinder 2015). As such, the creation and dissemination of utopias through everyday practices, story-telling and education opens up possibilities for action (Pötz 2019). Movements tend to attempt to bring these utopian visions into reality to provide a safe space as well as a wider discursive resource in what Nick Crossley (1999) calls a working utopia. The occupations of Zuccotti Park and other spaces as part of the Occupy movement are an excellent example of this working utopia, putting in place the kind of social relations activists argue for more widely (Howard and Pratt Boyden 2013; Webb 2013). The Museu das Remoções seeks to play this role by making the utopia concrete: to present Vila Autódromo as a microcosm of what might be possible if housing rights and the right to the city were respected. In this sense, Penha reflected in 2018, Vila Autódromo can be an effective example for others:

> I think that what we have shown is that we are capable of changing this country, I think that [other communities under threat] come here strengthening themselves to have this voice to say no to power. I think that Vila Autódromo is an example, it leaves a mark, these twenty families that stayed, it enters into the history of evictions and it will continue, we are continuing to fight against evictions.

As such, the Museu das Remoções can be conceptualised as a heterotopia. Heterotopia, etymologically, refers to other (*hetero*) space (*topoi*), therefore referring to locations that are in some way different or distinct. Foucault (1986: 24), in his notoriously brief and frustrating lecture 'Of other spaces', defines heterotopias as 'a kind of effectively enacted utopia', thereby distinct from utopias which are, by definition, imagined. This is not to say that the utopia enacted in the Museu das Remoções is not socially constructed, as will be discussed shortly, but that it clearly asserts that it can be found in that specific portion of the earth which we call Vila Autódromo. For Foucault (1986), heterotopias can serve two diametrically opposed functions: they either expose the illusion of 'real' spaces or, as I contend the Museu das Remoções does, 'their role is to create a space that is other, another real space, as perfect, as meticulous, as well arranged as ours is messy, ill constructed, and jumbled' (Foucault 1986: 27). In essence, the museum presents a community existing and respected on its own terms, with self-defined rights, removed from the complex and messy relations with the Brazilian state. In doing so, the Museu das Remoções seeks to make Vila Autódromo a reference point for housing struggles globally, as an example of the world we should seek to create.

Lefebvre's notion of heterotopia, as Harvey (2013) notes, has frequently been seen as radically different from Foucault's. Through the Museu das Remoções though, we can trace a line between Foucauldian and Lefebvrian conceptions of heterotopias. For Lefebvre, heterotopias are perceived spaces – those spaces where clandestine meanings come to the fore, despite the meanings inscribed by the dominant social order, thereby making these heterotopias (Sacco et al. 2019). While this may at first glance appear to be at odds with the critique, expounded in chapter 3, that Lefebvre's theoretical lens rests on a false privileging of official conceptions of space over clandestine meanings in the context of favelas, this is not the case. Bearing this critique in mind, it could be argued that informal communities themselves represent heterotopias in the sense used by Lefebvre. But that would commit the opposite error. While the state does not physically construct favelas, setting in stone certain spatial meanings, the state remains an important actor in shaping the space of favelas, whether through community upgrading programmes or the violence of repression and removals.

However, when favelas are defined on their own terms, free from significant interference from the state, they are heterotopian spaces (in Lefebvre's terms). This is a rare occurrence. While favelas generally emerged in a context of state neglect, they are heavily regulated (Perlman 2010; Robb Larkins 2015). More importantly, for the purposes of the right to the city, when favelas are neglected the ideas and understandings of these communities remain peripheral, the myth of marginality is bolstered. This is why the *Ocupa Vila Autódromo* events were so powerful – they allowed residents to speak on their own terms about the community they lived in. In other instances, either state action shaped the space of the community, or neglect meant that very few people heard about it. The confluence of a community speaking on its own terms and the attention brought by the Olympic Games created a unique juncture, which the *Ocupa Vila Autódromo* events took advantage of.

Therefore, what the Museu das Remoções seeks to do is preserve this (Lefebvrian) heterotopia and expand it, making the case for informal communities across the city, country and globe to be able to speak on their own terms in this way. It does this by depicting Vila Autódromo as a Foucauldian heterotopia in that it illustrates a space that is 'as perfect, as meticulous, as well arranged as ours is messy, ill constructed and jumbled' (Foucault 1986: 27). As such, Lefebvrian and Foucauldian heterotopias are not as different as they may appear. They are merely steps on the same journey to urban revolution. Foucault sees in heterotopias the possibility of using examples of spaces where clandestine meanings have upended official meanings to expand the revolutionary trajectories which are inscribed on these spaces. In essence, the Foucauldian heterotopia is a stepping stone between Lefebvre's heterotopia and the realisation of utopia.

This Foucauldian heterotopia is the role the Museu das Remoções seeks to play in the fight for housing rights. By constructing an image of the community that demonstrates the utopian ideals of housing for all, free from threats of eviction, the museum intends to illustrate the revolutionary trajectory by which these rights can be claimed for informal communities across Rio, Brazil and the world. As Thainã intended, the Museu das Remoções shows how resistance can be successful, playing the role of a working utopia (Crossley 1999). However, as Pötz (2019) notes, imagining and creating a utopian vision is one step, but putting it into practice more broadly remains challenging. To share their working utopia, residents now host tours of the community as well as regular events, including online events during the Covid-19 pandemic. At live events, boards of photographs are placed around the community and residents have a regular route to show groups around, explaining the community's history. At online events, different speakers tell their stories of the community and/ or eviction processes.

The Museu das Remoções as a tool of resistance

On 5 August 2018, two years to the day since the beginning of the Olympic Games, residents and their supporters gathered in the community for an event titled 'The right to housing: struggle and resistance', jointly organised by the Public Defender's Office and the Museu das Remoções. A full afternoon schedule included an exposition of Luiz's photos, a guided tour of the museum, screenings of two documentaries and a panel discussion featuring Regina Beinenstein and Carlos Vainer, the academics behind the *Plano Popular*, and Penha, chaired by one of the public defenders who had supported the community's legal struggle. As I walked into the community, banners were hung on the fences outside homes denouncing 'more than 650 families disappropriated just here in Vila Autódromo' and '69 thousand people removed in Rio: 22 thousand families whose histories were interrupted'. Outside the church, boards had been erected and one of the supporters of the community who helps organise the museum was pinning up photos from the years of struggle.

It was a busy day and the church was full, mostly with students, but there were other faces I recognised from my visits here in the earlier period of fieldwork. In the panel discussion, Beinenstein explained that 'Vila Autódromo is an emblematic case of resistance' in the struggle for housing rights and, for this reason, 'we need to give visibility to this struggle'. Vainer's speech bordered on the philosophical, making the point that we are here to celebrate the community's continued existence, explaining that here, 'we construct the present from our past, and open possibilities in the future'. By doing so, he explained, 'we can think about, and change, the future, creating the possibility of a different future'. Penha spoke of her happiness at seeing the church full again – looking back I saw that people were spilling out onto the street, so large was the assembled crowd. Characteristically, she spoke fast and passionately, bringing a tear to my eye in parts, particularly when she talked about the fear for her life during the most intense period of struggle. 'Yes, I could have died', she stated plainly, 'but so what?', implying that her rights and her land were worth dying for. 'The beauty', she explained talking about her community 'is priceless.' These speeches were followed by questions and comments, including one community leader from the nearby Vila União favela thanking residents for supporting their struggle, saying 'my house would no longer be standing' without the support of residents of Vila Autódromo.

After the panel discussion and questions, Luiz led a tour of the community. He began by saying that when people come to the Museu das Remoções, they expect to see a museum, and ask where it is. Luiz replies to these people, 'you're in it', as the community itself is the museum. It was hard to hear him – there were some fifty people trying to take this tour and Luiz didn't have a microphone, so at the back of the crowd it was hard to make out his words. There were boards of photos placed along the street, each documenting a different aspect of the community's history: Luiz stopped at each and spoke for a few minutes, explaining the photographs. Some document community life, such as a board dedicated to 'social and leisure', while others focus on aspects of the struggle for resistance, including the *Plano Popular* and the barricades created to stop construction traffic passing through the community. With large numbers present, only about half of the people were listening to him intently, with the other half meandering along behind, looking at things, some taking pictures, others chatting to each other – these tend to be people who are already familiar with the community. At the end of the street, Luiz gathered everyone around the one sculpture of those initially constructed for the museum that still remains as a permanent feature, dedicated to the children's play area. He told everyone that there were eight sculptures, listing the different parts of the community that were remembered. He struggled to remember what the final sculpture was dedicated to, and Luiza, one of the museum's supporters, had shout from the back to remind him – 'your house!'

After a short walk around the empty ground where homes once stood, we returned to the entrance of the community and Luiz pointed out the new sign, which includes photographs of the community before and after the evictions. To end the tour, he moved on into the empty space between the community and the hotel which housed the International Olympic Committee and other VIPs during the Games, stopping for a minute or so to have a conversation with one guy, the whole tour waiting patiently for the conversation to end. Luiz stopped at a tree, picked fruit and ate it, talking about the importance of these trees, which previously covered the whole community. He explained that the person he was conversing with a moment ago, who had now left, was a resident of a condominium nearby, who barely knew the history of this place, which brought home to him how important the museum is. As he stood eating fruit, a few of the students picked fruit from the tree as well, listening as Luiz lamented what had happened. Passionate about sport, he felt that the Olympics 'missed a great opportunity' here, to have a genuine social legacy. He would have liked to see the community upgraded as an Olympic legacy project, showing the world what could be done in favelas when City Hall works with residents to improve urban space. Unfortunately, he said wistfully, that opportunity was lost.

Through events like this one, the Museu das Remoções presents Vila Autódromo as always having been a strong community, where people look out for each other, where children can play safely, where there is no threat from organised crime. The emphasis on social and leisure activities in the community, and on the importance of trees and green space, help visitors to understand the kind of community Vila Autódromo was and is. Other parts of the event reaffirm the community's rights, with references to specific laws frequently appearing in both speeches and written information, while the community is always displayed as unified and strong, brushing over historical conflicts. This is also clearly not just about this single community: one banner explaining the *Plano Popular*, for example, stated that 'The *Plano Popular* is part of the struggle of all communities in the city of Rio de Janeiro, the state and the country against the violation of the right to housing.'

This use of the space of the favela draws on the emerging trend for favela tourism. Resulting from the development of new forms of tourism based on understanding authentic urban life, as well as the global spread of favelas as part of Rio's city brand, favela tourism has grown, particularly in the touristic South Zone, where favelas sprawl above the beaches providing picturesque views (Freire-Medeiros 2009). While Vila Autódromo's peripheral geographic location in the city limits its appeal for tourists, its niche attractions bring student groups alongside more determined tourist visitors. Favela tourism takes on contrasting forms, characterised by Freire-Medeiros (2009) on the one hand as social tourism, which benefits the community, and on the other as dark tourism, which commodifies poverty. While these forms often coexist in favela tourism, the Museu das Remoções clearly tends towards the social, actively pushing back on the myth of marginality that underpins dark tourism in favelas.

The veracity of some of the claims made in Luiz's tour of the museum can be disputed, particularly the notion that the community always acted together: in 2013, some residents, allegedly organised by the municipal government, attended a small protest in favour of their own eviction. This event does not appear on the boards of photographs that are displayed around the community for museum visitors and is not mentioned when residents explain their history as part of the museum tours. Such imperfections are removed from the heterotopia of Vila Autódromo, hidden away and left unacknowledged. The 'effectively enacted utopia' (Foucault 1986: 24) preserved in the Museu das Remoções therefore is not necessarily based upon a wholly accurate history but a constructed version of events. Of course, this is not unique to this museum: all histories in all museums are constructed (Kaplan 1994).

The museum also places great importance on the *Plano Popular*, discussed in chapter 2. In the museological plan, planned actions include replanting of trees in the area and the construction of communal spaces, including a sports pitch and a new Residents' Association building (Museu das Remoções 2017). The plan itself plays an important role in the construction of the heterotopia, being the ideal future towards which the community is striving: collaboratively and deliberately planned through an inclusive process, with significant communal space. The Museu das Remoções thereby provides a platform to illustrate the (constructed) past, present and future of Vila Autódromo as a community whose self-determination is respected. In doing so, the museum provides an illustrative example that another world is possible. This is, of course, removed from the messy and complex reality, whereby even in 2018, residents were still struggling to cajole City Hall to fulfil the promises they made prior to the Olympic Games in 2016, specifically the construction of communal spaces and the delivery of individual deeds.

The museum is engaged in a series of actions to make true its motto: memory can't be evicted. These actions are focused on the community of Vila Autódromo specifically and generally seek to pressure City Hall into completing what residents refer to as the second phase of upgrading. The rehousing deal struck with City Hall in April 2016 included the delivery of homes before the Olympics as its first phase, but also the construction of communal spaces as a second phase, with a deadline of sixty days after the first phase. As Luiz explained in 2018:

> [I want to see] the works of the second phase and our documents, our title deeds, that still haven't been given, they're stalling us. They think we're fools, but we're not, we know that City Hall must be at a minimum be having second thoughts because they have not given us that document. Having in view

the contract that was signed with the Mayor who left [Eduardo Paes, who left office at the end of 2016], the public defenders and us residents, the section on delivery of documents gives sixty days after the Olympics, already we are two years and a month, and they've not delivered.

Residents also seek to pressure City Hall to release the formal deeds and proof of ownership, which should have been delivered with the keys, but were not. The actions to ensure memory can't be evicted, to reinforce Vila Autódromo's position, also go beyond what was agreed in the rehousing agreement. The museum has sought to be included on digital maps, inserting Vila Autódromo into a wider contestation over how informal communities should be included in maps of cities (see Ferraz et al. 2018). According the museological plan, this serves to 'reclaim, in a virtual form, the physically lost territory', and has been applied in other communities (Museu das Remoções 2017: 20).

Alongside the reclaiming of digital space, actions have also included putting up signs in the area around the community to help visitors find their way, as well as a new sign at the entrance of the community reclaiming the physical space (Figure 6.1). A significant victory was achieved in October 2019, when a proposal made by PSOL councillors Renato Cinco, Tarcíscio Motta and Babá to change the name of the nearby BRT station was passed in the council chamber.[2] The terminal, which is part of the TransOlímpica line linking Recreio with Deodoro, had previously been known as Centro Olímpico and had served as a key terminal for the Olympic Park. Construction of the terminal had been one of the reasons given by City Hall for the need for evictions in Vila Autódromo. The renaming followed an occupation of the terminal on 9 February 2019, along similar lines to the *Ocupa Vila Autódromo* events discussed in chapter 3, which demanded the name change along with the completion of upgrades in the community. Further successes included recognition as a point of memory by the Brazilian Institute of Museums in June 2023 and the opening of a new football pitch in July 2023 (seven years later than promised). The pitch was inaugurated the following month by the fifth edition of the *Taça Libertadores* football tournament, the first edition of which is described in chapter 3. Through actions and successes such as these, Vila Autódromo's residents and supporters are continuing to stamp their version of the space into the public discourse about the community.

The museum though, is not only concerned with the reaffirming the rights and permanence of Vila Autódromo. Indeed, the mission of the museum speaks to the wider struggle against evictions, intending 'to participate in struggles against evictions, preserving the symbolic connection, emotional memory and social practices of evicted communities'. As such, the work of

2 Law 6659/2019.

Figure 6.1 The new sign at the entrance to Vila Autódromo. It shows two aerial photographs of the community, before and after the evictions, along with captions in Portuguese, Spanish and English. July 2018.
(Image: author's own.)

the museum goes beyond the specific case of Vila Autódromo. In particular, the museum has strong links with the Conselho Popular, a group supported by the Catholic Church through its Pastoral de Favelas, which seeks to build links and organise favela residents across the city to mobilise on behalf of favelas. Along with the Public Defender's Office, these groups formed what Magalhães (2019) called a 'web of resistance', contesting evictions earlier in Eduardo Paes's period in office, particularly between 2010 and 2014. However, effective state action to disrupt these groups, particularly the public defenders and the Pastoral de Favelas, significantly interrupted this work, meaning that during the initial period of fieldwork for this research, the Conselho Popular was relatively inactive and largely superseded by the Comitê Popular, which was specifically focused on mega-events.

By 2018, with the Comitê Popular having disbanded in the aftermath of the Olympics, the Conselho Popular was a resurgent force, organising communities across the city to defend against a range of eviction threats, particularly in Horto, Barrinha and Rádio Sonda, among others. Residents of Vila Autódromo attended meetings of the Conselho Popular and contributed their experience to panel discussions, helping to adapt tools they had developed in their own struggle to resist evictions elsewhere. Alongside this, residents used social media and the internet to voice their support for communities facing eviction beyond Rio de Janeiro. When I visited Luiz and Penha to conduct interviews in 2018, they were organising a video to show support for Banhado, a community in São Paulo facing eviction due to alleged environmental damage. As Penha explained in the interview, supporting other communities under threat of eviction is an important function of the museum:

> In truth, we come together with other communities because if a community is being threatened, we are all together, we are all sharing, we are complaining, we are fighting, we are making videos. So we are together. And this is what we need, to unite every time the strength that we can say 'enough!' to evictions.

These videos of support and solidarity extended beyond the borders of Brazil even. In 2019 residents recorded a video voicing their support for homeless people in Tokyo being evicted from their encampments in public parks in preparation for Tokyo 2020, to coincide with a meeting of anti-Olympic activists from Los Angeles, Tokyo, Paris and Pyeongchang in Tokyo. Through these actions, residents are able to present their struggle as a success story, providing hope and inspiration to those currently fighting evictions across Rio, Brazil and the world. In this sense, the Museu das Remoções serves the role of an actually localisable utopia for these social movements, a concrete idealisation of what they seek to achieve.

Through the Museu das Remoções residents have also gained access to a range of institutional spaces from which they might otherwise have been excluded. They have been invited to speak on panel discussions in museums and universities, bringing their knowledge into these elite spaces, which have often excluded voices from favelas. While museums, and particularly universities, in Brazil are making positive strides to include favela residents in debates about informal communities more broadly, speaking on behalf of a museum confers a degree of respectability to the knowledge that residents bring to these events. Instead of speaking from a subjective, partisan position as a favela resident under threat of eviction, being associated with the museum as an institution allows residents' knowledge to be treated as authoritative instead of anecdotal. The quality of their contributions shifts in the eyes of audiences: instead of speaking about their experience, they are seen as speaking about history, as Penha affirmed:

> The museum comes to show that you don't need to go to university to possess this culture, to learn. So the museum brings this, social museology brings this cultural side to show that poor people, from favelas, that we are capable of understanding that it is a culture, and that is the struggle, to appreciate this, this culture being a tool for struggle, and that's what the museum is.

Mario, who as an academic has travelled further afield to speak about the museum, agreed:

> By affirming the museum, and affirming this tool of struggle, it's curious, because they now they are an institution and an institution has a power, so when they come to talk somewhere, they represent an institution. So they go to a university and they say 'we are the Museu das Remoções', and this resonates.... I've had the opportunity to talk about the Museu das Remoções in various places, I've spoken in São Paulo, I've spoken in Bogotá, I gave classes in the Louvre.

On the first anniversary of the opening of the Museu das Remoções in 2017, residents and their supporters celebrated by delivering a series of artefacts to the Museu Histórico Nacional (National History Museum) in downtown Rio.[3] Founded in 1922 to commemorate the centenary of Brazilian independence, the Museu Histórico Nacional seeks to present the history of Brazil through a traditional archive, contemporary pieces and multimedia resources, according to its website. As Santos (2006) observes, the museum was created to provide institutional and scientific legitimacy to the Brazilian nation. This is not unique: museums, and national history museums in particular, have long played an important role in the symbolic construction of nations (Kaplan 1994). Of course, in the process of constructing these national histories, through the archives of such museums, certain voices tend to be excluded: the non-white, women, indigenous groups and communities deemed 'other'. Campaigns around the world have sought to rectify these issues and argued for the repatriation of exhibits, particularly those held in the national museums of former colonial powers, such as the British Museum. Brazil's museums have traditionally been regarded as elite spaces, not only in relation to what is collected and exhibited, but also in who visits and uses museums, and therefore exhibit a tendency to be distant from social life (Chagas and Bogado 2017; Venancio et al. 2018). While there has not been a prominent public conversation about this issue in Brazil, Brazilian museologists have sought to tackle this issue in recent years (see Chagas 2012), as the then director of the Museu Histórico Nacional, Paulo Knauss de Mendonça, explained in an interview in 2018:

> One of the problems of the collection we have, although we are an historic museum, a history museum, our collection is mostly, I would say, elitist, in a way, and in another way, its anonymous – which means everyday life objects, that have no special meaning. That's the general identity of the collection.

---

3 Not to be confused with the National Museum of Brazil in São Cristóvão, which was devastated by fire in September 2018.

As such, while we can view the Museu Histórico Nacional as a documentation of Brazilian history, 'we must approach it as a contingent document that may be constituent of multiple, discontinuous historical series' (Lord 2006: 2). Indeed, in this sense, the Museu Histórico Nacional is continually evolving as it adds to its archive of over a quarter of a million pieces, all of which help to construct the story of Brazil, with a particular emphasis currently on expanding this beyond the history of the elite. The addition of pieces collected by the Museu das Remoções to this archive then, can be seen as accepting that Vila Autódromo's story has something important to contribute to what Brazil represents as a nation, and should therefore be preserved. As Paulo explained:

> The problem with the social museums [such as the Museu das Remoções] is that they don't build collections, so they can be very effective in the cause they have, which is contextualised historically in the moment, but they don't produce the memory, they use the memory for present effect, but there's no memory for the future generations.

Mario, a leading scholar on social museums, agrees:

> Social museums don't intend to exist forever, they are museums that can be created and can stop existing, I know this is a big problem. Conversely, the Museu Histórico Nacional has the intention to be forever – we know it is isn't forever, but it intends to be – so this is interesting because the archive of a favela is in the Museu Histórico Nacional.

When I visited the archives and interviewed the director of the Museu Histórico Nacional in 2018, they were still categorising and processing the donation. However, he explained that their intention was to display some of the pieces as part of the permanent exhibition (see Figure 6.2). In particular, these would be coupled with some pieces already in the archive from the demolition of the Morro do Castelo in the early 1920s – indeed, the presence of these pieces in the archive was part of the reason for offering the collection from Vila Autódromo to the Museu Histórico Nacional instead of another museum.

The Fortaleza de São Sebastião was built in 1567, just two years after the city, officially named São Sebastião de Rio de Janeiro, had been officially founded on 1 March 1565. The hill upon which it sat, the Morro do Castelo, sat at the centre of Rio de Janeiro for the length of its history, up to its demolition in the early 1920s to create space for the international exhibition that would be held to celebrate the centenary of Brazil's independence in 1922. The demolition of the hill also involved the eviction and demolition of working-class housing (in that period, *cortiços*) to clear space for a transitory mega-event. With the Museu Histórico Nacional also founded to commemorate the centenary, some pieces from the Morro do Castelo were included in its initial archive.

Figure 6.2 Remains of homes from Vila Autódromo on display in the Museu Histórico Nacional, alongside a painting of the Morro do Castelo. (*Source:* Museu Histórico Nacional.)

By linking this demolition to the evictions in Vila Autódromo, and for sporting mega-events in 21st-century Rio more broadly, the Museu Histórico Nacional seeks to show how history of Brazil tends to be built on spaces formerly occupied by working-class housing, one of Thainã's initial ideas for what a museum dedicated to evictions could do. As Mario explained:

> In 1922, for the occasion of the centenary of independence, the Museu Histórico Nacional is founded and the Morro do Castelo is destroyed. So there was a favela, a *cortiço*, and they had there [in the Museu Histórico Nacional] some materials, some remains. So nothing fairer than, in 2016, the year of the Cup and the Olympics, the eviction of Vila Autódromo, another side to the city, nothing fairer than to take this material there.

It remains the case, however, that what is collected in the archives of the Museu Histórico Nacional regarding evictions of working-class people does not quite match what is written in history books. As detailed in chapter 1, the history of evictions in Rio tends to emphasise three key periods of intense evictions associated with three mayors: Francisco Pereira Passos (1902–1906), Carlos Lacerda (1960–1965), and Eduardo Paes (2008–2016), although these are by no means the only evictions in the city's history. In particular, these were often the starting points for broad swathes of evictions that sometimes continued beyond their mandates. Passos oversaw a large-scale beautification project known as *bota-abaixo* (see Benchimol 1992: 235–276), particularly including the widening of boulevards, explicitly drawing inspiration from Haussmann's reforms in Paris (Benchimol 1992). Lacerda oversaw wide-ranging evictions, particularly in the touristic South Zone, and the removal of marginalised groups to Rio's West Zone (Gonçalves and Amoroso 2014). Paes, Rio's Olympic Mayor, rehabilitated eviction as a legitimate public policy that had not been pursued since the end of the military dictatorship in the 1980s and oversaw wide-ranging evictions, particularly in touristic Olympic areas, and the removal of marginalised groups to Rio's far West Zone (Faulhaber and Azevedo 2015; Magalhaes 2019).

While it would be fair to say that the demolition of the Morro do Castelo was inspired by the same ideas as *bota-abaixo*, it was not really part of that period; as Bechimol (1992: 319) puts it: 'the destruction of the Morro do Castelo ... in 1922, constituted an extension of that which was initiated by Passos'. Yet the reason these remains were deemed worthy of inclusion in the archives of the museum was the significance of the Morro do Castelo in the history of the city (and by extension Brazil) – the inclusion of artefacts and records of working-class Brazilians who lived there was incidental. Artefacts from the demolitions during Lacerda's tenure, particularly around the Lagoa de Rodrigo Freitas in Rio's South Zone and associated with the creation of Cidade de Deus, do not feature in the archives of the Museu Histórico Nacional. That the remains of homes from Vila Autódromo have been included here is relevant then, as it marks the first time that this elite Brazilian museum has actively sought to incorporate the history of the evicted into its archive. Such a landmark would not have occurred without the Museu das Remoções.

Conclusions

Struggles over memory and how history is etched onto urban space have been prominent around the world in recent years, including debate over confederate monuments in the US and the Rhodes Must Fall campaign in South Africa and at Oxford University, among others. The Museu das Remoções represents the other side of this coin by seeking to promote and preserve the otherwise marginalised history of the evicted. Such memory, or 'counter-memory', as Bogado (2017: 5) puts it, can play an important role in challenging hegemonic understandings of the past, present and future. In particular, the counter-memories of the Museu das Remoções challenge policies of favela removal, showing a past where life in the favela was positive, a present where the community is engaged in upgrading itself, and a possible future of integration with the formal city based a respect for housing rights.

The museum can be seen in some respects as a continuation of the *Ocupa Vila Autódromo* events discussed in chapter 3, preserving the connections built between residents and activists across the city as well as providing a forum for events in the community. Beyond this, however, it plays an important role as a totemic exemplar of what can be achieved and uses this success to inspire others struggling for housing rights, whether locally through participation with the Conselho Popular, or nationally and internationally through solidarity videos sharing residents' experience. In this sense, the Museu das Remoções can be seen as an attempt to create a heterotopia, an actually localisable utopia of what can be achieved when a community stands up for their right to housing.

Thainã, when asked about the importance of Vila Autódromo, noted that 'to work with human rights is to have a large chance of defeat all the time', and therefore the victories should be celebrated in order to preserve morale through the numerous defeats. While celebrating such victories is important in this way, there is also a broader importance to drawing the lessons from localised struggles. The victory won by the remaining residents of Vila Autódromo holds potential for other communities, whether through the concrete precedent for negotiating rehousing settlements with a community instead of individually, or through the clear vision of what success can look like. By preserving and promoting these lessons, the Museu das Remoções seeks to ensure that this victory is not meaningful solely for those families who were able to stay in the community, but that it reverberates around the world for other communities under threat of eviction.

Conclusion

'Rio', Theresa Williamson (2016b) predicted in the months before the Olympic Games, 'will host a trouble-free Olympics by doing what it does best: covering up the damage and showing its artificial face.' The treatment of Vila Autódromo is a perfect example of this, with the messy, informal charm of the favela gone, replaced by twenty small, identical houses, white-washed to ensure a uniformly inoffensive image. The municipal government's policy towards favelas in the Olympic city was been starkly reminiscent of the military dictatorship: removing these communities from wealthy areas and moving them westward to more sparsely populated, isolated parts of the city. Yet this process has not gone uncontested. As this book has documented, residents of Vila Autódromo, supported by activists across the city, mounted a fierce campaign resisting evictions.

In Vila Autódromo, this resistance was embedded in and inscribed upon the space of the favela. Beyond merely being a site of protests, or an area of land under dispute, the space of the community was mobilised in defence of housing rights. Such an approach paints a picture of the community that sits in contrast to the myths of marginality, described by Perlman (1976) decades ago, whereby favelas are seen as marginal and separate from the city. Based on this logic, removal is viewed positively, as it allows residents to relocate into housing that is connected to the urban resources of the broader city. In reality though, favelas are interwoven with the formal city, meaning removal has deleterious impacts on residents' ability to access urban resources: they find themselves in a new area with which they are unfamiliar, with limited support networks in the local area. Ultimately, by transforming the space of the community to show its vibrancy and connections to the city, residents sought to undermine the justification for removal.

It is important to note though that this justification of helping residents was not (necessarily) the true motive behind removals. Residents repeatedly claimed the real reason they were facing eviction was for real estate development. Comments made by Carlos Carvalho, the owner of the company which manages the Olympic Park, to the *Guardian* newspaper back this up, in which he boasted of his plans to build 'a city of the elite ... noble housing, not housing for the poor' (Watts 2015b). Further evidence can be found in the way the dispute was resolved: despite conceding that some residents could remain, as part of the agreement with twenty families, the municipal government insisted on demolishing their homes and rebuilding identical, whitewashed homes. Aesthetically speaking, the favela was transformed into a low-rise condominium community, including walls around the community. Such expenditure to demolish and rebuild homes only makes sense if the motive was to remove the effective drag the favela placed on nearby land values.

The municipal government spent over R$200 million (US$50 million) on evicting and removing the community, while the estimated cost of implementing the *Plano Popular* developed by residents and urban planners was just R$13.5 million (US$3.275 million). This plan firmly repudiated the myth of marginality, serving as a manifesto for developing the community based on residents' priorities. The plan makes the case that residents have a right to remain in their community, based on several legal frameworks, including the 1988 constitution, the City Statute and concessions won from the State of Rio de Janeiro in the 1990s. In making claims under these human rights frameworks, activists sought to claim what Holston (2008) calls 'insurgent citizenship', emphasising the importance of text-based rights. However, despite these claims to insurgent citizenship, evictions persisted, suggesting the expansive egalitarianism Holston (2008) identified in the early years of Lula's presidency was being pushed back, even before the removal of the PT (Workers' Party) from the presidency in 2016. While the *Plano Popular* was not implemented, the municipal government eventually accepted residents' right to participate in the planning of their community, albeit in a piecemeal way. This represents a tacit acknowledgement of the right to the city, made all the more meaningful by it coming from the sovereign power which forced evictions through.

The success of those families that were able to remain through the contentious evictions process was due in part to the way they mobilised the space of the favela as a form of resistance. The process of evictions in Vila Autódromo is symptomatic of a larger spatial conflict that lies at the heart of all informal communities. On the one hand, favelas are home to populations who would otherwise be homeless, representing an innovative use of space for communities who built their own homes and a strong sense of community. On the other hand, favelas are dangerous places, illegal and illegitimate by their very nature, with poor infrastructure and endemic poverty, providing a haven for criminals. The contention over evictions in Vila Autódromo is a manifestation of this conflict, with different groups actively trying to enforce their conception of the space. At stake then, is the legitimacy of favelas as a form of housing and as a community.

In this context, residents and their supporters sought to (re)construct the favela as a friendly, communal space through *Ocupa Vila Autódromo* events. Outside these events, the favela was a desolate place, with rubble strewn across the community, seeming more like a construction site than a residential area. The tactics of the municipal government physically degraded the favela in this way, as well as removing access to services in an attempt to make Vila Autódromo an inhospitable space. *Ocupa Vila Autódromo* pushed back against this, inviting people to the favela for a wide variety of events, from football tournaments and documentary screenings to live performances and book launches. In doing so, residents and their supporters presented an idealised vision of the favela as a safe space where people enjoy living in a tight-knit community. By bringing people from across the city to the community, they showed that the favela was not marginal, but an integral part of the city.

These events occurred in liminal spaces, as the favela was temporarily transformed, inverting the normal sense of abandonment and fear to a joyous celebration of community. The inclusive, welcoming atmosphere challenged the stereotypical narrative of favelas as dangerous, no-go areas, instead presenting a pleasant, culturally vibrant community. These liminal events were charged with anti-structure, allowing for radical re-imaginings of social structures which can stimulate transformations beyond the liminal moment. In this, *Ocupa Vila Autódromo* was a direct challenge to existing power structures in Brazil which marginalise and degrade informal communities. In these liminal moments, space was transformed into place for those participating. A concrete notion of Vila Autódromo as a place was formed, based on the spatial values of community, safety and friendliness inscribed on the space of *Ocupa Vila Autódromo* and bound up with the radical reimagining of Brazilian society associated with anti-structure.

Importantly, this sense of place endures, despite physical changes to the space: even as more houses were torn down, the notion of a friendly, welcoming community endured in the imagination of residents and their supporters, reinforced by regular events. In essence, Vila Autódromo became an idea, transcending the physical space. This allowed for the place to be spread across geographical scales, around the world, through stories told about the place via social and traditional media. This strategy was heavily reliant on the attention brought to the favela by the Olympic Games, which makes it a unique case. Social media campaigns, liveblogging and alternative media like RioOnWatch showed the friendly, communal and safe place of Vila Autódromo, emphasising the legitimacy of the favela, and its community spirit, challenging the dominant narrative of favelas which underpinned the logic of removals. Spreading this sense of place was not merely about Vila Autódromo but was also wrapped up with ideological critiques of capitalist principles of accumulation, particularly real estate development.

Catalytic Communities went beyond social media in its attempts to shape perceptions of favelas, seeking to influence international media coverage through both direct collaboration with journalists and publishing stories on the website that served as background research for journalists. RioOnWatch sought to challenge the dominant narrative of favelas as sites of violence and poverty through reporting on resistance and innovation in favelas. In doing so, the organisation challenged the logic behind various negligent or harmful state policies in favelas, including gentrification and police violence, as well as forced evictions. In its work with journalists, RioOnWatch attempted to influence coverage to provide greater insight into positive aspects of life in favelas, including affordability, culture, sustainability and community spirit. Having built up a reputation for its English-speaking experts on favelas, the NGO was frequently contacted by journalists for assistance in reporting on these communities. RioOnWatch was able to exercise a negotiated form of network power (Castells 2011), setting the rules of inclusion with these journalists through a process of negotiation.

This contributed to a larger discourse intervention in the run-up to the Olympic Games, as I have elaborated elsewhere (Talbot 2018). RioOnWatch saw the opportunity to effect a lasting change in the discourse around favelas through influencing media coverage during Rio de Janeiro's moment in the global media spotlight. Often, the organisation framed these issues in terms of accuracy, appealing to journalists' desire to precisely describe issues in the city. In doing so, it was engaged in what Bourdieu (1989) would call a symbolic struggle over the power to define what favelas are. In this, the sense of place generated in *Ocupa Vila Autódromo* was valuable in showing that RioOnWatch's version of favelas corresponded to the real world, at least to some degree.

In the run-up to the Olympics, residents formed the Museu das Remoções as an additional tool to resist evictions. Post-Games, the museum plays a similar role for the community as the events did, albeit on a smaller scale. It functions as a tool of resistance for the present, enabling residents to have a platform to continue making claims on the government for further upgrades to their own community, as well as to support other communities facing eviction, particularly through the reinvigorated Conselho Popular. The preservation of what Bogado (2017) calls 'counter-memory' through the museum also represents an attempt to provide a more accurate history of Rio, one that includes the poor, working-class communities that have frequently been evicted to make way for marquee developments. The organisation of the Museu das Remoções enables this to be formalised, particularly through the creation of an archive for the Museu Histórico Nacional. Access to elite spaces such as this is facilitated through the name of the museum, enabling residents to spread these ideas further.

Beyond this, the Museu das Remoções functions as a heterotopian space, an other space. In presenting an idealised version of the community whereby rights are respected, residents are seeking to create an actually localisable utopia, a kind of working utopia in Crossley's (1999) terms. In this sense, the museum remains, at heart, a tool for resistance to evictions, working with communities across the city that face similar threats of eviction. This remains based on the alternative conception of favelas contained within the *Plano Popular* that was actualised through *Ocupa Vila Autódromo*. In essence, the Museu das Remoções presents a community existing and respected on its own terms, thereby challenging the myth of marginality. By constructing an image of a community free from threats of eviction, the museum intends to illustrate the revolutionary trajectory by which these rights can be claimed for informal communities across Rio, Brazil and the world.

Through resisting Olympic evictions, Vila Autódromo challenged what Perlman (1976) identified as the myth of marginality, the idea of favelas as separate from the city. While a great deal of academic work has examined the consequences of the myth of marginality for favelas and informal communities more broadly, this book provides a theorisation of resistance to that myth. The myth of marginality underpinned what Magalhães (2019) called 'the repertoire of removal', a new logic to justify the return of favela removals in the 21st century. Through mobilising the space of the favela, *Ocupa Vila Autódromo* demonstrated that the myth of marginality was just that: a myth. Concretising a sense of place through liminal events in the community enabled residents to speak on their own terms and to spread an alternative way of thinking about the favela, using the global spotlight of the Olympic Games. Whether such challenges to the myth of marginality remain possible without the spotlight of the mega-event however, remains unclear.

A legacy unfulfilled?

In the immediate aftermath of the Rio 2016 Olympic and Paralympic Games, mayoral elections were held. Incumbent Eduardo Paes, who had overseen the bidding, preparation and delivery of the Olympic Games, was term-limited, unable to run for a third consecutive term. His chosen successor, Pedro Paulo, was eliminated in the first round, which was widely seen as a condemnation of Paes's administration. PSOL's Marcelo Freixo ran on a platform of citizen engagement to develop the right to the city, supported by many of the activists mentioned in this book, but was defeated by Marcelo Crivella, who ran on a programme of smaller government. Previously a Senator for the State of Rio de Janeiro, Crivella was an evangelical bishop and nephew of the founder of the Universal Church of the Kingdom of God. In 2018, when I returned to Rio for the second period of fieldwork, two years into his mandate, I found it difficult to find people with a good word to say about him (although this may have been hampered by my main social and research circles being firmly on the left). Even some residents of Vila Autódromo, whose homes had been destroyed by Paes's administration, suggested that Paes was a better mayor than Crivella, such was his reputation for incompetence. In particular, residents were angered by City Hall's lack of engagement on the second phase of the upgrading agreement reached in March 2016. The first phase, the building of homes, was to be completed before the Olympic Games, with the second phase, the construction of community amenities, following before the end of 2016. In 2018, work had still not even started. For his part, Crivella blamed the situation on the poor state of the public finances he inherited, explaining that 'we found the government broke. The Olympic legacy was a real Olympic abandonment, a herd of white elephants that left only debts' (Cerqueira and Guimarães 2018). Indeed, the Portuguese term *largado*, translated as 'abandonment' in this quote, had become a common slang to talk about the Olympic Games, given its linguistic similarities to the word *legado* (legacy). Despite this, Magalhães' (2013) prediction that the major legacy of the Games would be the renewed legitimacy of favela removal as public policy was borne out, with ongoing evictions in numerous favelas across the city under Crivella, including Horto, Rádio Sonda, and Barrinha.

Two years after the event, the Olympic Games had receded from the public imagination. In part this may have been due to neglect by Crivella, but it was also surely due to the broader political context of Dilma Rousseff's impeachment, the conviction of former President Lula (which has since been quashed) and the rise of Jair Bolsonaro. As Thainã summarised in 2018, 'everyone is talking about this subject, the rise of fascism, Bolsonaro, these things ... [of the] World Cup and Olympics, I hardly hear anything'. In 2018, the federal government had announced a military intervention in Rio de Janeiro, particularly focused on favelas, deploying armed forces to support the beleaguered and under-fire pacification project. This intervention, based on the idea that favelas needed to be controlled and made legible to the state and the market, played on the myth of marginality in a similar way to the logic underpinning evictions. As Robb Larkins (2015: 139) points out, the pre-Olympic policy of pacification used a kinder face to mask the 'same old variety of oppressive state action in the favela', doing little to actually ensure security for many residents. Since the Games, the mask has slipped, especially under Bolsonaro and his ally Wilson Witzel as Governor of the State of Rio de Janeiro, with the military actively targeting favela residents.

Many on the left were highly critical of the military intervention, which they saw as leading to increased police brutality and extra-judicial killings. On 14 March 2018, Marielle Franco, a black PSOL councilwoman from a favela and a strident critic of the intervention, was assassinated. Bolsonaro was the only presidential candidate not to offer condolences to the family and, while it has not been determined who ordered the murder of Marielle, Bolsonaro's family have been linked to the case. Bolsonaro, dubbed by the international press as the Trump of the tropics, rose to power on a platform of crime control that involved the persecution of marginalised populations in Brazil. His policy platform included reforms to ensure military police (who killed thousands of predominantly young, black, *favelados*, in the run-up to the Olympic Games) were able to kill with even greater impunity. Bolsonaro's campaign, along with those of his allies in the media, promulgated discourses which served to dehumanise and criminalise these groups in the run-up to the election and beyond (Cavalcanti 2022). In doing so, Bolsonaro played on the myth of marginality to present favelas as other, to be dealt with through state violence. Actively supported by the Universal Church of the Kingdom of God, Bolsonaro won the 2018 election, beating the Worker's Party candidate Fernando Haddad by 55 per cent to 45 per cent in the second round. Former president Lula had initially led in the opinion polls, but was banned from running for office due to his conviction on corruption charges, which was later quashed on the basis of judicial bias. Sergio Moro, the judge who convicted Lula, was made Justice Minister in Bolsonaro's government.

Bolsonaro was in office when the Covid-19 pandemic arrived in Brazil in 2020. The government's response was poor, with Bolsonaro railing against any public health interventions and a series of health ministers resigning in frustration. He promoted conspiracy theories for treating the virus and passed up on chances to buy vaccines, meaning Brazil's world-leading vaccination infrastructure got off to a very slow start. Brazil had the second highest death total, behind only the United States. Covid-19 presented specific problems for favelas, but limited support was provided, either by the federal government or City Hall. In the early phases of the crisis, the main public message asked Brazilians to regularly wash their hands – but many favela residents did not have consistent access to clean running water to be able to do so due to issues that had not been addressed for months before the pandemic arrived. Expectations to quarantine at home were also challenging in relatively small homes in these densely populated communities. Luiz, writing for RioOnWatch in April 2020, summarised the situation:

> Our day-to-day consists of everyone being inside their homes. We talk to each other less than normal. We know very well that if we become sick we will be left to our own luck. We thank God that, as of yet, we have no suspected cases of coronavirus. This is because we are taking care of each other to keep it this way, and because through of our resistance and struggle, we have managed to obtain adequate sanitation, water, and paving. We have no doubt that if the hard-won services we have achieved here became a reality in all of the favelas of Brazil and the world, the risk of contagion would decrease. (Silva 2020)

Crivella lost his bid for re-election as mayor in 2020, defeated 64 per cent to 36 per cent in the second round by Eduardo Paes, who had unsuccessfully run for governor in 2018. Under Paes, City Hall continued to seek to remove favela communities, announcing new removals in the South Zone favela of Estradinha in August 2021 (successfully resisted by residents with the support of public defenders). As was the case with Vila Autódromo, this was not the first time Paes had attempted to remove the favela, which also faced threats of eviction in the early years of Paes's first period in office. More broadly, the myth of marginality continues to guide policy-making. The latest iteration in a long-running attempt to make favelas legible to the state, which appears largely based on the Olympic-era pacification policy (see Robb Larkins 2015), bears the slogan 'Integrated City', clearly implying that favelas are not currently integrated, a key tenet of the myth of marginality.

Informal communities are not perfect: there are myriad problems in Rio's favelas, and in similar communities around the world. Yet these communities exist because housing is unaffordable and unavailable for large sections of the population of major cities. Any solution to these problems must respect these people, not push them further towards the periphery through evictions and violence, but by tackling the issues which exist in informal communities through working with residents. This can be difficult, but the *Plano Popular da Vila Autódromo* provides a workable roadmap for delivering upgrades to favelas while placing the needs and desires of communities at the heart of the planning process. This kind of participatory planning will address the issues associated with informal communities. Evictions and violent repression only serve to sweep the problems under the carpet and save up greater problems for the future.

With Paes back in City Hall, however, there has finally been action on the second phase of upgrading in Vila Autódromo. Work is ongoing at the time of writing in 2023, seven years after it was due to be completed, but residents are clearly pleased to it is finally taking place, posting videos on social media to show off the new facilities and enjoying them as they are opened. This is one of a number of projects linked to the Olympic Games that lay dormant during Crivella's time as Mayor that have been taken up again by Paes. The handball arena for the Games – widely praised at the time of the event – is another, with its nomadic architecture enabling the structure to be recycled into four schools, although at the time of writing it has only just begun to be dismantled, let alone reconstructed. Clearly, Paes prioritises these projects more than his predecessor did, possibly because of his previous involvement with them. It seems clear though, that Paes's ambitions extend beyond the City Hall and he will likely use the management of the Olympic Games as part of his platform if he runs for higher office. As such, the renewed engagement with legacy projects is likely best explained through his desire to extract maximum political capital from the event, rather than any charitable feeling towards Vila Autódromo.

Resisting the Olympics

The Rio 2016 Olympics were among the most obviously problematic editions of the event in recent years.[1] Where normally the closing ceremony is accompanied by celebration and commemoration by the press, for Rio there was an additional question: was it worth it? This question doesn't just apply to Rio, but to any prospective host city – many of the issues that faced the Olympic Games in Rio, while of course having their own, Brazilian flavour, are issues associated with the event wherever it is hosted. Put bluntly, the Olympic Games has become too big for a single city to host. There is too much construction needed for it to be a sustainable event, economically, environmentally, and socially. Indeed, the trajectory is for the Games to become less sustainable with each iteration (Müller et al. 2021), despite increasing attention being paid to trying to ensure their sustainability. The Rio 2016 Olympic Games served as a juggernaut to force through a radical transformation of the city with limited democratic engagement. Changing the event itself is crucial to spare communities in future host cities the turmoil seen in Vila Autódromo.

Arguably, Rio's example has been an indirect driver of change. In 2017, the IOC conducted a bidding process for the 2024 Olympic Games. After local resistance in Boston, Rome, Budapest and Hamburg, the remaining

---

1 Clearly, there were serious human rights and sustainability issues at many other Olympic events, particularly the Beijing 2008 Summer Games and the Sochi 2014 Winter Games. However, the lack of a free press in China and Russia means that the scale of issues associated with these events is not as widely known as in the case with Rio's Games.

cities were Paris and Los Angeles, both of which had hosted the event twice previously. To avoid the risk of having no possible host in 2028, the IOC took the unprecedented step of awarding both contenders the right to host: Paris in 2024 and Los Angeles in 2028. The problems of securing willing hosts are magnified for the Winter Olympics, with a contest between Almaty and Beijing for the 2022 event, both with poor records on human rights. At the time of writing, there are no willing bidders for the 2030 Winter Games, with cities such as Sapporo and Vancouver unwilling to bid due to concerns around sustainability. The Olympic Games cannot take place without a host and history suggests that when there are few hosts there are opportunities for change in the hosting model – Los Angeles was the only bidding city for the 1984 Games and its proposal embraced capitalist professionalised sport to present a radically different event, which has been the case ever since.

In the case of Los Angeles 1984, the IOC found itself forced to accept Los Angeles' proposals in order to secure a host. In an attempt to avoid a repeat of that situation, an internal reform process was put forward under the presidency of Thomas Bach. Known as Agenda 2020, this placed significant importance on youth, credibility and sustainability. The sustainability reforms were intended to bring about a more inclusive approach to hosting that would avoid the violations of rights such as those seen in Vila Autódromo. Perhaps most eye-catchingly, the host city contract now includes a stipulation that hosts respect human rights. As I have argued elsewhere, however (Talbot 2023), these reforms will have little practical impact on the ground for a number of reasons, including that they rely on national laws and that there is little recognition of the unique legal arrangements for hosting an Olympic Games. Most concerningly, there is no new recourse to remedy for those whose rights are infringed, as the clause is part of contract law and can only be challenged by either the IOC or the host city. For Vila Autódromo, at best this clause would have made their rhetorical argument slightly stronger. At worst, the existence of the so-called safeguards could have whitewashed their plight altogether.

The Agenda 2020 reforms have been planned since 2014, but have largely not yet been enacted in practice. The signs from Paris, the first Olympics to take place fully under a reformed model, are not promising. Many of the common problems of the event remain present in the city, including evictions and gentrification, environmental damage and militarisation of the city. As Wolfe (2023) convincingly demonstrates, if the reforms have had any impact it is merely to shift responsibility for changes onto the host city, while failing to address the neoliberal development logics underpinning the urban transformation that comes with the event. Ultimately, he concludes, the very notion of reform is a Potemkin mirage, a convincing act intended to give the appearance of change without engaging in meaningful reform.

More radical changes to the Olympic model have been pushed for by activists in host cities around the world, including forceful calls for the Olympic Games to be abolished. Vila Autódromo continues to serve as an inspiration for activists in future host cities resisting the Olympic juggernaut, as one of the few examples where it has been possible to force change. The community has been involved in this new transnational mobilisation, having recorded videos in solidarity with groups facing evictions in the shadows of Olympic stadiums in Tokyo and Los Angeles. Their struggle continues to serve as inspiration, not only to favela residents across Rio and Brazil but also to activists facing down mega-event-led development all over the world.

Defining success

Vila Autódromo's success in fighting eviction stands out as a true David and Goliath story, the tiny favela which took on the Olympics and won. But is this really accurate? The community was reduced from six hundred families to just twenty. I say 'community' deliberately in this case because Vila Autódromo today lacks several fundamental features of a favela: it is not self-built (with the exception of the church and one house) and the neighbourhood was professionally planned. The whitewashed homes are exactly that: whitewashed of any trace of the uniqueness and personality that characterised the old favela buildings. The favela no longer exists. Penha and Luiz's home, full of joy and love, is but a memory, like the homes of all their neighbours. When those twenty families were granted the right to remain, other residents who had been forcibly removed and had planned to rebuild their homes were not allowed to return to the community. As Penha summarised, writing in the *Guardian* after the Games:

> All that remains of our old community is one house, a Catholic church, and a handful of trees that we fought to protect. The rest has been completely demolished. The area where most of our homes once stood is now a large concrete car park that is usually empty and insufferably hot. It is sad. There used to be 650 families here. Today, there are 20. (Penha Macena 2017)

Even if we count twenty families remaining in the favela as a success, it was won through sheer grit in the face of severe violations of human rights. While (most) residents were removed legally, as compensation – either financial or in the form of alternative housing – was offered, many argued that the broader treatment of residents constitutes abuse of human rights (see Comitê Popular 2015: 38–39). Negotiations over compensation were conducted in an atmosphere of coercion and 'psychological terrorism', with residents told 'if you don't leave with love you'll leave in pain' by city officials, suggesting that if they refused to negotiate they would get nothing. Residents were often given no warning when their homes were demolished, waking up in the morning to find *Guarda Municipal* outside their home with demolition papers. In some cases, they were not even at home: one woman's home was demolished while she was at a medical appointment, unaware her home was under threat. Residents' desires and plans for their community were completely disregarded as they were excluded from the planning process.

Yet, despite all this, Vila Autódromo was one of the lucky ones. More evictions occurred under Eduardo Paes than under any other mayor in Rio's history, including the years of military dictatorship (Faulhaber and Azevedo 2015). Across Rio, over 22,000 families were evicted from favelas between Rio winning the right to host the Games and 2015 (Comitê Popular 2015: 36). As Magalhães (2019) argues, this is a worrying trend. In the decades since re-democratisation, favelas have not faced major threats of eviction (Perlman 2010), yet the Olympics inspired a return to policies not seen since the military dictatorship. The post-Olympic municipal government has not backed away from evictions now the pressure to prepare the city for mega-events has receded. At the national level, the federal government created an atmosphere of impunity for violent state action in favelas. While the return of Lula to the presidency after the 2022 election may offer some hope, it is worth remembering that all of the 77,209 people evicted in the run-up to the Olympic Games were evicted while the Worker's Party was in control of the presidency.

Perhaps the most depressing point is that it was all for nothing. The evictions, which residents perceptively blamed on real estate speculation, created space for new buildings. According to the upgrading plan agreed between the residents and the municipal government, community amenities including schools and a community centre should have been built. According to the planned timetable, these should have been completed in the months following the Games. But, with international attention turning away from Rio after the Olympic Games, residents' ability to pressure the government was significantly diminished, although the amenities are now finally being completed, as discussed above. However, this still leaves considerable vacant space around the community, with residents presuming condominiums will be constructed – apparently confirmed by a report in the *O Globo* newspaper shortly after the Games, showing plans to build multiple apartment blocks on the Olympic site. At the time of writing, nothing has been built, or even started. The homes were destroyed for private profit, yet no profit has even been made. The climate of real estate speculation engendered by mega-events in the city dissipated in the broader economic woes post-Games. The evictions were utterly pointless, as many predicted at the time.

The twenty families who still live in Vila Autódromo represent a tiny light of success in a sea of darkness for housing rights activists and favela advocates. The outlook appears dark as Rio struggles to cope with an Olympic legacy of debt, and economic and political crises unfold across the country. Even if Lula's return marks a ray of hope for those on the left, the headwinds he faces, both internally and externally, are immense. However, there are reasons to be optimistic despite this gloomy outlook. The tiny light of success that Vila Autódromo represents threatens to grow stronger for a variety of reasons. Perhaps most importantly, Rio is no longer preparing to host the Olympic Games. There is no strong justification for evictions, especially as real estate development is no longer booming in the city. With limited money due to the Olympic debt and economic crisis, it seems unlikely that Rio's government will seek to transform the urban landscape so dramatically again in the near future.

In a variety of ways, Vila Autódromo residents were better placed than most to resist evictions. Unlike many other favelas, it had strong, clearly established legal rights from previous struggles against eviction. These struggles had also left a legacy of organisation: residents in Vila Autódromo knew what they were doing and were well organised. The quality of life in the favela, with no history of violence and good access to local amenities, made residents more determined to fight against eviction. Further, it was directly next to the Olympic Park, with the municipal government unable to deny the eviction was linked to the mega-event and thus making it a point of interest to international journalists. Because of all this, the community garnered significant support from other sectors of Rio's civil society; I have particularly highlighted RioOnWatch and activists from the Comitê Popular in this book, but there were many other groups involved in various ways as well.

Against this was an array of powerful interests, first and foremost the Olympic Games organisers, who sought the removal of the favela to remove a potential blight from the perfect image they would project through the Games. Backed by the IOC and their who's who of corporate royalty as sponsors, the government had no shortage of reasons to remove the favela. Carlos Carvalho, Brazil's twelfth richest man and a generous donor to Eduardo Paes's political career, coveted the land for real estate development. Paes himself had personal history with the favela, which had resisted his previous attempts at eviction in the 1990s. Construction companies had the ear of a great number of Brazilian politicians, as the *Lava Jato* corruption scandal showed, and had an economic interest in the removal of the community. In this context, Vila Autódromo's struggle for permanence became about much more than one favela: it became a struggle of the people against the powerful over who decides on the future of Brazil. In this, the inability of the state to fully evict the community appears as a failure, with the campaign to stay appearing to be a great victory for social movements. As Thainã put it, reflecting in 2018:

> To work with human rights is to have high chances of defeat all the time, especially in Brazil, you will be fucked in many things. So some of the victories feel so good, they are so gratifying. Look at Vila Autódromo, you can say only 3

per cent of it survived and that's sad, but fuck, 3 per cent is there, it's fighting, it's engaged, they do great things there, you know, so they continue fighting proud for their community, continue fighting for the pride to say 'I live in Vila Autódromo', you know? That is so gratifying!

The success of those twenty families sets some important precedents, as discussed in chapter 3. The upgrading agreement reached between residents and the municipal government is the first deal of its kind in history. Previously, and throughout process of removals in Vila Autódromo, the state insisted on negotiating with individual families, refusing to recognise collective bargaining rights. These individual negotiations often meant residents were unaware of what neighbours were offered and made their decisions without important information. This agreement marks a break with that, which other favelas facing eviction will be able to point to when they argue that the government should be negotiating with them collectively. Further, as I argued in chapter 3, the modifications residents were able to make to the municipal government's plan, albeit small, represent a de facto recognition of favela residents' right to the city.

Vila Autódromo's success in resisting eviction provides some illustrative examples of what favelas can do. While, as I argued in chapter 4, the lightning rod for mobilisation and attention that the Olympic Games provided in Vila Autódromo means various tactics of resistance will be difficult to replicate, there are some aspects which could be used by others. Primary among these is the *Plano Popular*, which provided irrefutable evidence for residents' claim that they didn't need to leave, that 'permanence is possible' (Associação de Moradores e Pescadores da Vila Autódromo 2016: 16). Other favelas have explored the possibility of creating a *Plano Popular* in a similar mould, not only to resist evictions but also to exert pressure on the municipal government to support ongoing development. Alongside the *Plano Popular*, the community's contestation of space in the favela to undermine the justification for eviction, as discussed in this book, can also be replicated by others. That said, the spreading of place across scales, as discussed in chapters 4 and 5, will be more challenging without the political opportunity brought by the Olympic Games.

Finally, in Penha's words, 'the fight goes on', even though Vila Autódromo have their victory, 'because other communities are still suffering'. Vila Autódromo residents continue to be involved in promoting housing rights through the Museu das Remoções, with some speaking with human rights groups in Geneva and others participating in the UN Habitat III conference in Quito. While some allies, particularly those international groups which work on issues associated with mega-events, may have moved on, residents still retain some valuable allies in Rio's universities, left-wing political parties and civil society. Vila Autódromo's struggle, memorialised in the Museu das Remoções, continues to provide inspiration for favelas facing eviction. The incorporation of artifacts from the favela in the archives of Brazil's Museu Histórico Nacional marks a recognition that this episode of contention will not be forgotten, that favelas are recognised as an important part of the Brazilian nation, and maybe, just maybe, the myth of marginality is beginning to break down.

Six hundred families were reduced to just twenty over the course of evictions, leading some to question, legitimately, whether the fact that twenty families remain really constitutes success. From my observations and conversations with people involved, it is a huge victory. Yes, the number of families living in the community was massively reduced by state violence. But it is a remarkable triumph that, thanks to a strong campaign of resistance, it was not cut to zero.

References

Note: All URLs were checked on 5 December 2023 unless otherwise stated.

Agamben, G. (1998). *Homo Sacer: Sovereign Power and Bare Life*. Stanford, CA: Stanford University Press.

Agamben, G. (2005). *State of Exception*. Chicago, IL: University of Chicago Press.

Agnew, J. (1987). *Place and Politics: The Geographical Mediation of State and Society*. Boston, MA: Allen and Unwin.

Allen, A. L. (2017). *Shifting Horizons: Urban Space and Social Difference in Contemporary Brazilian Documentary and Photography*. Oxford: Wiley.

Alves, J. A. (2018). *The Anti-Black City: Police Terror and Black Urban Life in Brazil*. Minneapolis, MN: University of Minnesota Press.

Arendt, H. (1958 [1951]). *The Origins of Totalitarianism*. Cleveland, OH: Meridian.

Associação de Moradores e Pescadores da Vila Autódromo [Association of Residents and Fishers of Vila Autódromo] (2012). *Plano Popular da Vila Autódromo: Plano de desenvolvimento urbano, econômico, social e cultural [Popular Plan of Vila Autódromo: Plan of urban, economic, social and cultural development]*. Available online at: https://comitepopulario.files.wordpress.com/2012/08/planopopularvilaautodromo.pdf

Associação de Moradores e Pescadores da Vila Autódromo [Association of Residents and Fishers of Vila Autódromo] (2016). *Plano Popular da Vila Autodromo 2016: Plano de desenvolvimento urbano, econômico, social e cultural [Popular Plan of Vila Autódromo: Plan of urban, economic, social and cultural development]*. Available online at: https://vivaavilaautodromo.files.wordpress.com/2016/02/ppva_2016web.pdf

Bakhtin, M. (1968). *Rabelais and His World*. Cambridge, MA: MIT Press.

Basso, K. H. (1996). *Wisdom Sits in Places: Landscape and Language among the Western Apache*. Albuquerque, NM: University of New Mexico Press.

Becker, H. (1967). Whose side are we on? *Social Problems*, 14 (3), 239–247.

Benchimol, J. L. (1992). *Pereira Passos, um Haussmann tropical: A renovação urbana da cidade do Rio de Janeiro no início do século XX [Pereira Passos, a tropical Haussmann: The urban renewal of the city of Rio de Janeiro in the beginning of the 20th century]*. Rio de Janeiro: Prefeitura da Cidade do Rio de Janeiro.

Blackshaw, T. (2010). *Key Concepts in Community Studies*. London: Sage.

Bogado, D. (2017). Museu das Remoções da Vila Autódromo: Resistência creative à construção da cidade neoliberal [The Museum of Evictions of Vila Autódromo: Creative resistance to the construction of the neoliberal city]. *Cadernos de Sociomuseologia*, 54 (10), 3–27.

Borneman, J. and Hammoudi, A. (2009). The Fieldwork Encounter, Experience, and the Making of Truth: An Introduction. In: Borneman, J. and Hammoudi, A. (Eds.) *Being There: The Fieldwork Encounter and the Making of Truth*. Berkeley, CA: University of California Press, 1–24.

Bourdieu, P. (1989). Social space and symbolic power. *Sociological Theory*, 7 (1), 14–25.

Boykoff, J. (2014a). *Celebration Capitalism and the Olympic Games*. London: Routledge.

Boykoff, J. (2014b). *Activism and the Olympics: Dissent at the Games in Vancouver and London*. New Brunswick, NJ: Rutgers University Press.

Boykoff, J. (2016). *Power Games: A Political History of the Olympics*. London: Verso.

Boykoff, J. and Mascarenhas, G. (2016). The Olympics, sustainability, and greenwashing: The Rio 2016 Summer Games. *Capitalism Nature Socialism*, 27 (2), 1–11.

Boyle, P. and Haggerty, K. (2009). Spectacular security: Mega-events and the security complex. *International Political Sociology*, 3 (3), 257–274.

Caldeira, T. and Holston, J. (2015). Participatory urban planning in Brazil. *Urban Studies*, 52 (11), 2001–2017.

Carmo, A. (2012). Reclaim the Streets, the protestival and the creative transformation of the city. *Finisterra*, 47 (94), 103–118.

Carvalho, B. (2013). *Porous City: A Cultural History of Rio de Janeiro*. Liverpool: Liverpool University Press.

Carvalho, B. (2016). Occupy All Streets: Protesting a Right to the Future. In: Carvalho, B., Cavalcanti, M. and Venuturupalli, V. R. (Eds.) *Occupy All Streets: Olympic Urbanism and Contested Futures in Rio de Janeiro*. New York, NY: Terreform, 90–108.

Castells, M. (2011). A network theory of power. *International Journal of Communication*, 5, 773–787.

Castells, M. (2012). *Networks of Outrage and Hope: Social Movements in the Internet Age*. Cambridge: Polity.

Castro, D. G., Gaffney, C., Novaes, P. R. and Rodrigues, J. M. (2015). O Projeto Olímpico da Cidade do Rio de Janeiro: Reflexões sobre os impactos dos megaeventos esportivos na perspectiva do direito à cidade [The Olympic Project of the City of Rio de Janeiro: Reflections about the impacts of sporting mega-events in the perspective of the right to the city]. In: Santos Junior, O. A. D., Gaffney, C. and Ribeiro, L. C. D. Q. (Eds.) *Brasil: Os impactos da copa do mundo 2014 e das olimpíadas 2016 [Brazil: The impacts of the 2014 World Cup and the 2016 Olympics]*. Rio de Janeiro: Observatório das Metrópoles, 409–436.

Catalytic Communities (2016). *Favelas in the Media: How the Global Narrative on Favelas Changed During Rio's Mega-event Years*. Available online at: http://catcomm.org/wp-content/uploads/2016/12/Favelas-in-the-Media-Report-Cat Comm.pdf

Cavalcanti, M., O'Donnell, J. and Sampaio, L. (2016). Futures and Ruins of an Olympic City. In: Carvalho, B., Cavalcanti, M. and Venuturupalli, V. R. (Eds.) *Occupy All Streets: Olympic Urbanism and Contested Futures in Rio de Janeiro*. New York, NY: Terreform, 60–89.

Cavalcanti, R. P. (2022). The pursuit of the 'dead bandit': A decolonial analysis of the persecution of the marginalized in Brazil. *Critical Criminology*, 30 (3), 757–775.

Centre on Housing Rights and Evictions (2007). *Fair Play for Housing Rights: Mega-events, Olympic Games and Housing Rights*. Geneva: COHRE.

Cerqueira, S. and Guimarães, S. P. (2018). Marcelo Crivella tem maior índice de rejeição na prefeitura em 25 anos [Marcelo Crivella has the highest unfavorability rating in City Hall for 25 years]. *VejaRio*. Available online at: https://vejario.abril.com.br/cidades/marcelo-crivella-indice-de-rejeicao-prefeitura/

Chagas, M. (2012). Museus, memórias e movimentos sociais [Museums, memories and social movements]. *Cadernos de Sociomuseologia*, 41, 5–15.

Chagas, M. and Bogado, D. (2017). A museologia que não serve para a vida, não serve para nada: O Museu das Remoções como potência criativa e potência de resistência [Museology that doesn't serve life doesn't serve anything: The Museum of Evictions as creative potential and potential of resistance]. In: Calabre, L., Cabral, E. D. T. and Siqueira, M. (Eds.) *Memória das Olimpíadas no Brasil: Diálogos e olhares [Memory of the Olympics in Brazil: Dialogues and views]*. Rio de Janeiro: Fundação Casa de Rui Barbosa, 139–146.

Chalhoub, S. (1993). The politics of disease control: yellow fever and race in nineteenth-century Rio de Janeiro. *Journal of Latin American Studies*, 25 (3), 441–463.

Coaffee, J. (2015). The uneven geographies of the Olympic carceral: from exceptionalism to normalisation. *The Geographical Journal*, 181 (3), 199–211.

Cocco, G. (2016). As favelas entre o balaio de gatos e o mito da marginalidade [The favelas between the basket of cats and the myth of marginality]. In: Mendes, A. F. and Cocco, G. (Eds.) *A resistência à remoção de favelas no Rio de Janeiro [The resistance to favela removals in Rio de Janeiro]*. Rio de Janeiro: Editora Revan, 25–41.

Comitê Popular (2014). Map shows hundreds of Vila Autódromo residents want to remain. *RioOnWatch*. Available online at: https://rioonwatch.org/?p=15503

Comitê Popular (2015). *Olimpíada Rio 2016, os jogos da exclusão: Megaeventos e violações dos direitos humanos no Rio de Janeiro [Rio 2016 Olympics, the exclusion games: Mega-events and human rights violations in Rio de Janeiro]*. Rio de Janeiro: Comitê Popular da Copa e Olimpíadas do Rio de Janeiro.

Constitução Federal (1988). Available online at: www.planalto.gov.br/ccivil_03/constituicao/constituicaocompilado.htm

Costa Vargas, J. H. (2006). When a favela dared to become a gated condominium: The politics of race and urban space in Rio de Janeiro. *Latin American Perspectives*, 33 (4), 49–81.

Crossley, N. (1999). Working utopias and social movements: An investigation using case study materials from radical mental health movements in Britain. *Sociology*, 33 (4), 809–830.

Davies, A. (2019). Milton Santos: The conceptual geographer and the philosophy of technics. *Progress in Human Geography*, 43 (3), 584–591.

Dean, J. (2017). *Doing Reflexivity*. Bristol: Policy Press.

Dembour, M. (2010). What are human rights? Four schools of thought. *Human Rights Quarterly*, 32 (1), 1–20.

de Certeau, M. (1984). *The Practice of Everyday Life*. Berkeley, CA: University of California Press.

Douglas, M. (1966). *Purity and Danger*. Abingdon: Routledge.

Earle, L. (2012). From insurgent to transgressive citizenship: Housing, social movements and the politics of rights in São Paulo. *Journal of Latin American Studies*, 44 (1), 97–126.

Emerson, R. M., Fretz, R. I. and Shaw, L. L. (2011). *Writing Ethnographic Fieldnotes*. 2nd edn. Chicago, IL: University of Chicago Press.

Escobar, A. (2001). Culture sits in places: Reflections on globalism and subaltern strategies of localization. *Political Geography*, 20 (2), 139–174.

Faulhaber, L. and Azevedo, L. (2015). *SMH 2016: Remoções no Rio de Janeiro Olímpico [SMH 2016: Removals in Olympic Rio de Janeiro]*. Rio de Janeiro: Mórula Editorial.

Ferraz, N. S., Leme, F. B. P. and Maia, F. N. (2018). Histórico da representação das favelas cariocas em mapas [A history of the representation of Rio de Janeiro's favelas in maps]. *Arquiteturarevista*, 14 (1), 59–72.

Ferreira, O. A. V. A. and Fernandes, R. P. (2000). O direito constitucional à moradia e os efeitos da Emenda Constitucional 26/00 [The constitutional right to housing and the effects of Constitutional Amendment 26/00]. *Jus.com.br*. Available online at: https://jus.com.br/artigos/579/o-direito-constitucional-a-moradia-e-os-efeitos-da-emenda-constitucional-26-00

Fischer, B. (2008). *A Poverty of Rights: Citizenship and Inequality in Twentieth-century Rio de Janeiro*. Stanford, CA: Stanford University Press.

Foucault, M. (1980). *Power/Knowledge: Selected Interviews and Other Writings 1972–1977*. New York, NY: Pantheon.

Foucault, M. (1986). Of other spaces. *Diacritics*, 16 (1), 22–27.

Freire-Medeiros, B. (2009). The favela and its touristic transits. *Geoforum*, 40 (4), 580–588.

Frenzel, F., Feigenbaum, A. and McCurdy, P. (2014). Protest camps: An emerging field of social movement research. *The Sociological Review*, 62 (3), 457–474.

Gaffney, C. (2016). An Anatomy of Resistance: The Popular Committees of the FIFA World Cup in Brazil. In: Dart, J. and Wagg, S. (Eds.) *Sport, Protest and Globalisation: Stopping Play*. London: Palgrave Macmillan, 335–364.

Geertz, C. (1988). *Works and Lives: The Anthropologist as Author*. Stanford, CA: Stanford University Press.

Gerbaudo, P. (2012). *Tweets and the Streets: Social Media and Contemporary Activism*. London: Pluto Press.

Gibb, R. and Danero Iglesias, J. (2017). Breaking the silence (again): On language learning and levels of fluency in ethnographic research. *The Sociological Review*, 65 (1), 134–149.

Gillan, K. and Pickerill, J. (2012). The difficult and hopeful ethics of research on, and with, social movements. *Social Movement Studies*, 11 (2), 133–143.

Giulianotti, R. and Brownell, S. (2012). Olympic and world sport: Making transnational society? *British Journal of Sociology*, 63 (2), 199–215.

Gohn, M. G. (2009). Social Movements in Brazil: Characteristics and Research. In: Denis, A. and Kalekin-Fishman, D. (Eds.) *The ISA Handbook in Contemporary Sociology*. London: Sage, 336–350.

Gonçalves, R. S. and Amoroso, M. (2014). Golpe militar e remoções das favelas cariocas: Revisitando um passado ainda atual [Military coup and evictions in Rio's favelas: Revisiting a past still present]. *Acervo*, 27 (1), 209–226.

Gouldner, A. (1968). The sociologist as partisan: Sociology and the welfare state. *American Sociologist*, 3 (2), 103–116.

Gouldner, A. (1973). *For Sociology: Renewal and Critique in Sociology Today.* London: Allen Lane.

Granovetter, M. S. (1973). The strength of weak ties. *American Journal of Sociology*, 78 (6), 1360–1380.

Gray, J. (1999). Open spaces and dwelling places: Being at home on hill farms in the Scottish borders. *American Ethnologist*, 26 (2), 440–460.

Gray, N. and Porter, L. (2015). By any means necessary: Urban regeneration and the 'state of exception' in Glasgow's Commonwealth Games 2014. *Antipode*, 47 (2), 281–556.

Gusmão, N. M. M. (1995). *Terra de pretos, terra de mulheres: Terra, mulher e raça num barrio rural negro [Land of blacks, land of women: Land, women and race in a rural black neighbourhood].* Brasília: Fundação Cultural Palmares.

Gutterres, A. d. S. (2014). 'It's not easy, I ask for public mobility and the government sends *Skull* against me': An intimate account of the political protests in Rio de Janeiro (June & July, 2013). *Anthropological Quarterly*, 87 (3), 901–918.

Hannerz, U. (2004). *Foreign News: Exploring the World of Foreign Correspondents.* Chicago, IL: University of Chicago Press.

Harris, J. (2016a). 2016 Olympics: What Rio doesn't want the world to see. *Vox.* Available online at: www.vox.com/2016/6/27/12026098/rio-olympics-2016-removals-eviction

Harris, J. (2016b). Inside Rio's favelas, the city's impoverished, neglected neighborhoods. *Vox.* Available online at: www.vox.com/2016/8/1/12322566/rio-favela-olympics-brazil

Harvey, D. (2004). *The New Imperialism.* Oxford: Oxford University Press.

Harvey, D. (2008). The right to the city. *New Left Review*, 53 (Sept.–Oct.), 23–40.

Harvey, D. (2013). *Rebel Cities: From the Right to the City to the Urban Revolution.* London: Verso.

Holston, J. (1991). Autoconstruction in working-class Brazil. *Cultural Anthropology*, 6 (4), 447–465.

Holston, J. (2008). *Insurgent Citizenship: Disjunctions of Democracy and Modernity in Brazil.* Princeton, NJ: Princeton University Press.

Hoover, J. (2015). The human right to housing and community empowerment: Home occupation, eviction defence and community land trusts. *Third World Quarterly*, 36 (6), 1092–1109.

Howard, N. and Pratt Boyden, K. (2013). Occupy London as pre-figurative political action. *Development in Practice*, 23 (5–6), 729–741.

Juris, J. S. (2012). Reflections on #Occupy Everywhere: Social media, public space, and emerging logics of aggregation. *American Ethnologist*, 39 (2), 259–279.

Kaplan, F. S. (1994). *Museums and the Making of 'Ourselves': The Role of Objects in National Identity.* Leicester: Leicester University Press.

Karlberg, M. (2005). The power of discourse and the discourse of power: Pursuing peace through discourse intervention. *International Journal of Peace Studies*, 10 (1), 1–23.

Kennelly, J. and Watt, P. (2011). Sanitizing public space in Olympic host cities: The spatial experiences of marginalized youth in 2010 Vancouver and 2012 London. *Sociology*, 45 (5), 765–781.

Khondker, H. H. (2011). Role of the new media in the Arab Spring. *Globalizations*, 8 (5), 675–679.

Kohn, M. (2013). Privatization and protest: Occupy Wall Street, Occupy Toronto, and the occupation of public space in a democracy. *Perspectives on Politics*, 11 (1), 99–110.

Lacerda, L. (2016). Mulheres na frente da resistência aos Jogos da Exclusão [Women in the forefront of resistance to the Games of Exclusion]. In: Mendes, T. (Ed.) *Atingidas: Histórias de vida de mulheres na cidade olímpica [Affected women: The life stories of women in the Olympic city]*. Rio de Janeiro: Instituto PACS, 17–20.

Lauermann, J. (2019). The urban politics of mega-events: Grand promises meet local resistance. *Environment and Society*, 10 (1), 48–62.

La Barre, J. (2016). Future shock: Mega-events in Rio de Janeiro. *Leisure Studies*, 35 (3), 352–368.

Lefebvre, H. (1991). *The Production of Space*. Oxford: Blackwell.

Lefebvre, H. (1996 [1968]). *Writings on Cities*. Oxford: Blackwell.

Lefebvre, H. (2009 [1979]). Space: Social Product and Use Value. In: Brenner, N. and Elden, S. (Eds.) *State, Space, World: Selected Essays*. Minneapolis, MN: University of Minnesota Press.

Lenskyj, H. (2000). *Inside the Olympic Industry: Power, Politics, and Activism*. Albany, NY: State University of New York Press.

Lenskyj, H. (2008). *Olympic Industry Resistance: Challenging Olympic Power and Propaganda*. Albany, NY: State University of New York Press.

Lord, B. (2006). Foucault's museum: Difference, representation, and genealogy. *Museum and Society*, 4 (1), 1–14.

Low, S. (2017). *Spatializing Culture: The Ethnography of Space and Place*. Abingdon: Routledge.

Macdonald, I. (2008). 'Parachute journalism' in Haiti: Media sourcing in the 2003–2004 political crisis. *Canadian Journal of Communication*, 33 (2), 213–232.

Maeckelbergh, M. (2009). *The Will of the Many: How the Alterglobalisation Movement is Changing the Face of Democracy*. London: Pluto Press.

Magalhães, A. A. (2013). O 'legado' dos megaeventos esportivos: A reatualização da remoção de favelas no Rio de Janeiro [The 'legacy' of sporting mega-events: The revival of the removal of favelas in Rio de Janeiro]. *Horizontes Antropológicos*, 19 (40), 89–118.

Magalhães, A. A. (2019). *Remoções de favelas no Rio de Janeiro: Entre formas de controle e resistências [Evictions of favelas in Rio de Janeiro: Between forms of control and resistances]*. Curitiba: Appris Editora.

Manzenreiter, W. (2010). The Beijing Games in the Western imagination of China: The weak power of soft power. *Journal of Sport and Social Issues*, 34 (1), 29–48.

Maricato, E. (1982). Autoconstução, a arquitetura possível [Autoconstruction, the possible architecture]. In: Maricato, E. (Ed.) *A produção capitalista da casa (e da cidade) [The capitalist production of the house (and of the city)]*, 2nd edn. São Paulo: Alfa-Omega.

Martin, D. G. and Miller, B. (2003). Space and contentious politics. *Mobilization*, 8 (2), 143–156.

Massey, D. (2005). *For Space*. London: Sage.

McCarthy, J. D. and Zald, M. N. (1977). Resource mobilization and social movements: A partial theory. *American Journal of Sociology*, 82 (6), 1212–1241.

McDonald, I. (2002). Critical Social Research and Political Intervention: Moralistic versus Radical Approaches. In: Sugden, J. and Tomlinson, A. (Eds.) *Power Games: A Critical Sociology of Sport*. London: Routledge, 100–116.

Medeiros, M. (2019). *Parque Olímpico contra Vila Autódromo: O papel das parcerias público–privadas no empreendedorismo urbano [Olympic Park against Vila Autódromo: The role of public–private partnerships in urban entrepreneurship]*. Rio de Janeiro: Editora Lumen Juris.

Mendes, A. F. (2016a). O Núcleo de Terras e Habitação no enfrentamento de um novo ciclo de remoções no Rio de Janeiro: O ano do 2009 [The Nucleus of Land and Housing confronting a new cycle of evictions in Rio de Janeiro: The year of 2009]. In: Mendes, A. F. and Cocco, G. (Eds.) *A resistência à remoção de favelas no Rio de Janeiro [The resistance to favela removals in Rio de Janeiro]*. Rio de Janeiro: Editora Revan, 147–163.

Mendes, A. F. (2016b). O debate em torno de risco, da moradia e das remoções em um ano de tragédias [The debate around risk, housing and evictions in a year of tragedies]. In: Mendes, A. F. and Cocco, G. (Eds.) *A resistência à remoção de favelas no Rio de Janeiro [The resistance to favela removals in Rio de Janeiro]*. Rio de Janeiro: Editora Revan, 181–207.

Mendes, A. F. and Cocco, G. (2016). *A resistência à remoção de favelas no Rio de Janeiro [The resistance to favela removals in Rio de Janeiro]*. Rio de Janeiro: Editora Revan.

Merrifield, A. (1993). Place and space: A Lefebvrian reconciliation. *Transactions of the British Institute of Geographers*, 18 (4), 516–531.

Michaels, J. (2016). Mayor at last presents upgrade plan for Vila Autódromo. *Rio Real blog*. Available online at: https://riorealblog.com/2016/03/09/mayor-at-last-presents-urban-upgrade-plan-for-vila-autodromo/

Müller, C. (2016). As remoções na cidade do Rio de Janeiro a partir de uma visão crítica do direitos humanos [Evictions in the city of Rio de Janeiro from a critical point of view on human rights]. In: Mendes, A. F. and Cocco, G. (Eds.) *A resistência à remoção de favelas no Rio de Janeiro [The resistance to favela removals in Rio de Janeiro]*. Rio de Janeiro: Editora Revan, 79–87.

Müller, M., Wolfe, S. D., Gaffney, C., Gogishvili, D., Hug, M. and Leick, A. (2021). An evaluation of the sustainability of the Olympic Games. *Nature Sustainability*, 4 (4), 340–348.

Museu das Remoções (2017). *Plano Museológico [Museological Plan]*. Available online at: https://museudasremocoes.com/ (accessed 1 August 2018).

Nemer, D. (2016). Online favela: The use of social media by the marginalised in Brazil. *Information Technology for Development*, 22 (3), 364–379.

NEPLAC/ETTERN (2016). *Arroio Pavuna e Vila Autódromo: Histórias*. Rio de Janeiro: NEPLAC/ETTERN.

Omena, E. (2015). Não foi só por 20 centavos: a 'copa das manifestações' e as transformações socioeconômicas recentes nas metrópoles brasileiras [It wasn't just about 20 cents: The 'World Cup of protests' and the recent socio-economic transformations in Brazilian metropolises]. In: Santos Junior, O. A. D., Gaffney, C. and Ribeiro, L. C. D. Q. (Eds.) *Brasil: Os impactos da Copa do Mundo 2014 e das Olimpíadas 2016 [Brazil: The impacts of the 2014 World Cup and the 2016 Olympics]*. Rio de Janeiro: Observatório das Metrópoles, 203–218.

Ost, S. and Fleury, S. (2013). O mercado sobe o morro: A cidadania desce? Efeitos socioeconômicos da pacificação no Santa Marta [The market goes to the favela: Does citizenship come back? Socio-economic effects of pacification in Santa Marta]. *Dados: Revista de Ciêcias Sociais*, 56 (3), 635–671.

Park, R. (1967). *On Social Control and Collective Behaviour*. Chicago, IL: University of Chicago Press.

Parkin, B. (2015). Mayor announces eminent domain in Vila Autódromo as MIT report criticizes city policy. *RioOnWatch*. Available online at: https://rioonwatch.org/?p=20983

Penglase, R. B. (2014). *Living with Insecurity in a Brazilian Favela: Urban Violence and Daily Life*. New Brunswick, NJ: Rutgers University Press.

Penha Macena, M. (2017). They smashed my face and demolished my home – all for the Rio Olympics. *The Guardian*. Available online at: www.theguardian.com/global-development/2017/may/18/smashed-my-face-demolished-my-home-rio-olympic-games-maria-da-penha-macena

Perlman, J. (1976). *The Myth of Marginality: Urban Poverty and Politics in Rio de Janeiro*. Berkeley, CA: University of California Press.

Perlman, J. (2010). *Favela: Four Decades of Living on the Edge in Rio de Janeiro*. Oxford: Oxford University Press.

Perry, K. K. Y. (2013). *Black Women against the Land Grab: The Fight for Racial Justice in Brazil*. Minneapolis, MN: University of Minnesota Press.

Pinder, D. (2015). Reconstituting the possible: Lefebvre, utopia and the urban question. *International Journal of Urban and Regional Research*, 39 (1), 28–45.

Portes, A. (1979). Housing policy, urban poverty, and the state: The favelas of Rio de Janeiro, 1972–1976. *Latin American Research Review*, 14 (2), 3–24.

Pötz, M. (2019). Utopian imagination in activism: Making the case for social dreaming in change from the grassroots. *Interface*, 11 (1), 123–146.

Pred, A. (1983). Structuration and place: On the becoming of sense of place and structure of feeling. *Journal for the Theory of Social Behaviour*, 13 (1), 45–68.

Ravenscroft, N. and Gilchrist, P. (2009). Spaces of transgression: Governance, discipline and reworking the carnivalesque. *Leisure Studies*, 28 (1), 35–49.

Resende, C. A. R. (2010). O esporte na política externa do governo Lula: O importante é competir? [Sport in the foreign policy of the Lula government: The important thing is to compete?]. *Meridiano* 47, 11 (122), 35–41.

Rial y Costas, G. (2011). Spaces of insecurity? The 'favelas' of Rio de Janeiro between stigmatization and glorification. *Iberoamericana*, 11 (41), 115–128.

RioOnWatch (2013). Victory for Vila Autódromo! Rio's Mayor commits to permanence, urbanization, and fair compensation. *RioOnWatch*. Available online at: https://rioonwatch.org/?p=10734

Rivière, G. H. (1985). The ecomuseum: An evolutive definition. *Museum International*, 37 (4), 182–183.

Robb Larkins, E. (2015). *The Spectacular Favela: Violence in Modern Brazil*. Oakland, CA: University of California Press.

Rocha, D. (2015). Moradores protestam contra desocupação na Vila Autódromo [Residents protest against removal in Vila Autódromo]. *R7*. Available online at: http://noticias.r7.com/rio-de-janeiro/rj-no-ar/videos/moradores-protestam-contra-desocupacao-na-vila-autodromo-30112015

Roche, M. (2000). *Mega-events and Modernity: Olympics and Expos in the Growth of Consumer Culture*. London: Routledge.

Rolnik, R. (2013). Later neoliberalism: The financialization of homeownership and housing rights. *International Journal of Urban and Regional Research*, 37 (3), 1058–1066.

Rolnik, R. (2015). *Guerra dos lugares: A colonização da terra e da moradia na era das finanças [War of places: The colonisation of land and housing in the era of finance]*. São Paulo: Boitempo.

Rosas-Moreno, T. C. and Straubhaar, J. D. (2015). When the marginalized enter the national spotlight: The framing of Brazilian favelas and favelados. *Global Media and Communication*, 11 (1), 61–80.

Sacco, P. L., Ghirardi, S., Tartari, M. and Trimarchi, M. (2019). Two versions of heterotopia: The role of art practices in participative urban renewal processes. *Cities*, 89, 199–208.

Sánchez, F., Oliveira, F. L. and Monteiro, P. G. (2016). Vila Autódromo in dispute: Subjects, instruments and strategies to reinvent the space. *Revista Brasiliera de Estudos Urbanos e Regionais*, 18 (3), 408–427.

Santos, M. (2006 [1996]). *A natureza do espaço* [The nature of space]. 4th edn. São Paulo: Editora da Universidade de São Paulo.

Santos, M. S. (2006). *A escrita do passado em museus históricos [The writing of the past in historical museums]*. Rio de Janeiro: Garamond.

Santos Junior, O. A., Gaffney, C. and Ribeiro, L. C. Q. (2015). *Brasil: Os impactos da Copa do Mundo 2014 e das Olimpíadas 2016 [Brazil: The impacts of the 2014 World Cup and the 2016 Olympics]*. Rio de Janeiro: Observatório das Metrópoles,.

Savchuk, K. (2016). The tiny NGO that changed reporting on Rio's favelas during the Olympics. *Bright Magazine*. Available online at: https://brightthemag.com/the-tiny-ngo-that-changed-reporting-on-rios-favelas-during-the-olympics-8fd24e623f22

Scheper-Hughes, N. (1992). *Death without Weeping: The Violence of Everyday Life in Brazil*. Berkeley, CA: University of California Press.

Schmitt, C. (1985 [1922]). *Political Theology: Four Chapters on the Concept of Sovereignty*. Cambridge, MA: MIT Press.

Shirky, C. (2008). *Here Comes Everybody: The Power of Organizing without Organizations*. New York, NY: Penguin.

Silva, L. C. (2020). Coronavirus in the daily life of favelas, part 1: An inside look at Vila Autódromo. *RioOnWatch*. Available online at: https://rioonwatch.org/?p=58759

Soja, E. (1996). *Thirdspace: Journeys to Los Angeles and Other Real-and-imagined Places*. Oxford: Blackwell.

Southwick, N. (2016). With traditional June cultural festivities, Vila Autódromo celebrates memory and hope. *RioOnWatch*. Available online at: www.rioonwatch.org/?p=29976

Stammers, N. (2009). *Human Rights and Social Movements*. London: Pluto Press.

St John, G. (2008). Protestival: Global days of action and carnivalized politics in the present. *Social Movement Studies*, 7 (2), 167–190.

Tagliarina, D. (2015). Power, privilege and rights: How powerful and powerless create a vernacular of rights. *Third World Quarterly*, 36 (6), 1191–1206.

Talbot, A. (2016). Erasing the favela from Vila Autódromo. *RioOnWatch*. Available online at: www.rioonwatch.org/?p=28870

Talbot, A. (2018). Transforming informal communities through discourse intervention: RioOnWatch, favelas, and the 2016 Olympic Games. In: Carter, T. F., Burdsey, D. and Doidge, M. (Eds.) *Transforming Sport: Knowledges, Practices, Structures*. London: Routledge, 167–180.

Talbot, A. (2021). Talking about the 'rotten fruits' of Rio 2016: Framing mega-event legacies. *International Review for the Sociology of Sport*, 56 (1), 20–35.

Talbot, A. (2023). Human rights at the Olympic Games: Policy, protest, progress? *Event Management* 27 (6), 915–930.

Talbot, A. and Carter, T. F. (2018). Human rights abuses at the Rio 2016 Olympics: Activism and the media. *Leisure Studies*, 37 (1), 77–88.

Tarrow, S. (1996). States and opportunities: The political structuring of social movements. In: McAdam, D., McCarthy, J. and Zald, M. (Eds.) *Comparative Perspectives on Social Movements: Political Opportunities, Mobilizing Structures, and Cultural Framings*. Cambridge: Cambridge University Press, 41–61.

Taylor, S. (2018). RioOnWatch launches guide to encourage nuanced news coverage of Rio de Janeiro Olympics. *IJNET*. Available online at: https://ijnet.org/en/story/rioonwatch-launches-guide-encourage-nuanced-news-coverage-rio-de-janeiro-olympics

Teixeira, S. M. (2017). Resistência, pelo direito, história e memória [Resistance, for rights, history and memory]. In: Calabre, L., Cabral, E. D. T. and Siqueira, M. (Eds.) *Memória das Olimpíadas no Brasil: Diálogos e olhares [Memory of the Olympics in Brazil: Dialogues and views]*. Rio de Janeiro: Fundação Casa de Rui Barbosa, 147–164.

Turner, V. (1969). *The Ritual Process: Structure and Anti-structure*. London: AldineTransaction.

Turner, V. (1970). The center out there: Pilgrim's goal. *History of Religions*, 12 (3), 191–230.

Turner, V. (1979). Frame, flow and reflection: Ritual and drama as public liminality. *Japanese Journal of Religious Studies*, 6 (4), 465–499.

Vainer, C. (2011). Cidade de exceção: Reflexões a partir do Rio de Janeiro [City of exception: Reflections from Rio de Janeiro]. Paper presented at XIV Encontro Nacional da ANPUR, 23–27 May, Rio de Janeiro. Available online at: http://memoriadasolimpiadas.rb.gov.br/jspui/handle/123456789/193

Valladares, L. P. (2019). *The Invention of the Favela*. Chapel Hill, NC: University of North Carolina Press.

Venancio, A. R., Barros, J. M. G. and Teixeira, S. M. S. (2018). O museu brasileiro, seus quereres e poderes, para uma improvável definição – o caso do Museu das Remoções [The Brazilian museum, its wants and powers, for an improbable definition – the case of the Museum of Evictions]. In: Soares, B. B., Brown, K. and Nazor, O. (Eds.) *Defining Museums of the 21st Century: Plural Experiences*. Paris: ICOM, 105–111

Vettorazzo, L. (2016). Após derrubar quase toda Vila Autódromo, prefeitura exibe plano [After destroying almost all of Vila Autódromo, City Hall shows plans]. *Folha de São Paulo*. Available online at: www1.folha.uol.com.br/esporte/olimpiada-no-rio/2016/03/1747798-apos-derrubar-quase-toda-vila-autodromo-prefeitura-exibe-plano.shtml

Walford, G. (2007). Classification and framing of interviews in ethnographic interviewing. *Ethnography and Education*, 2 (2), 145–157.

Watts, J. (2015a). Forced evictions in Rio favela for 2016 Olympics trigger violent clashes. *The Guardian*. Available online at: www.theguardian.com/world/2015/jun/03/forced-evictions-vila-autodromo-rio-olympics-protests

Watts, J. (2015b). The Rio property developer hoping for a $1bn Olympic legacy of his own. *The Guardian*. Available online at: www.theguardian.com/sport/2015/aug/04/rio-olympic-games-2016-property-developer-carlos-carvalho-barra

Webb, G. (2013). 'Occupying' our social imagination: The necessity of utopian discourses and an anti-utopian age. *Perspectives in Development and Technology*, 12, 152–161.

Williamson, T. (2016a). Monopoly City vs. Singular City: Competing Urban Visions. In: Carvalho, B., Cavalcanti, M. and Venuturupalli, V. R. (Eds.) *Occupy All Streets: Olympic Urbanism and Contested Futures in Rio de Janeiro*. New York, NY: Terreform, 142–173.

Williamson, T. (2016b). Holding the Olympics in Rio was always a bad idea. *The New York Times*. Available online at: www.nytimes.com/roomfordebate/2016/05/16/should-brazil-postpone-the-olympics/holding-the-olympics-in-rio-was-always-a-bad-idea

Wolfe, S. D. (2024). The juggernaut endures: Protest, Potemkinism, and Olympic reform. *Leisure Studies*, 43 (1), 1–15.

Index

Alencar, Chico 43, 46
anti-Olympic protest 11, 13, 15, 29, 134, 148, 150

Babá 132
Bolsonaro, Jair 119, 145, 146

Cabral, Sérgio 24
Carvalho, Carlos 76, 78, 84, 88, 95, 124, 140, 152
Catalytic Communities 1, 11, 13, 14, 105, 106, 108, 110, *see* RioOnWatch
Cinco, Renato 132
Comitê Popular 6, 11, 13, 14, 32, 35, 42, 46, 48, 59, 65, 69, 74, 85, 86, 91, 102, 103, 133, 152
Conselho Popular 27, 28, 133, 139, 143
Crivella, Marcelo 145, 147, 148

discourse 115, 117, 118
    discourse intervention 115, 116, 117
Duvivier, Gregório 91

ethnography 10–11, 12, 15, 93, 105

favelas
    Barrinha 133, 145
    Estradinha 28, 147
    Favela de Esqueleto 123
    history 20–21, 23, 24, 25, 54, 123, 136
    Horto 133, 145
    Metro-Mangueira 122, 123
    Morro da Providência 20, 21
    Morro do Castelo 136, 137, 138

pacification 25, 81, 145, 147
Rádio Sonda 133, 145
Rocinha 40, 93
Santa Marta 26, 122
translation 8, 24, 108, 115, 117
Vidigal 26
Vila União 129
Foucault, Michel 73–74, 127, 128
Franco, Marielle 146
Freixo, Marcelo 46, 91, 144

gender 6, 73–74

Haddad, Fernando 146
Harvey, David 28, 45, 48, 91
heterotopia 126–128, 131, 139, 144

insurgent citizenship 49, 50, 52, 59, 141
International Olympic Committee 9, 18, 29, 31, 130, 148, 149, 152

Lacerda, Carlos 22, 25, 123, 137, 138
Lefebvre, Henri 16, 45, 65–67, 127, 128
liminality 81, 82–83, 84, 85, 86, 87, 88, 90, 96, 97, 109
    anti-structure 83, 86, 87, 88, 89
    communitas 85, 90
Lula 23, 46, 141, 145, 146, 151, 152

Maia, César 30
Motta, Tarcíscio 132
Museu das Remoções 71, 88, 89, 121–125, 126, 127, 128, 129–130, 131, 132, 133, 134, 135, 136, 138, 153

myth of marginality 9–10, 27, 38, 39, 65, 70, 79, 81, 97, 100, 110, 111, 114, 115, 127, 131, 140, 141, 142, 144, 145, 146, 147, 154

network power 110, 111, 112, 114, 115, 118
Nuzman, Carlos Arthur 24

Ocupa Vila Autódromo 64, 65, 69, 71, 74, 75, 78, 81, 82, 83, 85, 86, 88, 124, 125
 cultural festival 72, 84, 122, 132
 Espaço Ocupa 40, 71, 72, 77, 87, 88, 95, 98, 101, 104, 122
 festa junina 88
 free school of clowns 38, 39, 84, 85
 Plano Popular launch 39–43, 91
 Taça Libertadores da Vila Autódromo 64, 69, 72, 75, 84, 96, 132

Paes, Eduardo 4, 5, 6, 7, 24, 25, 26, 27, 30, 32, 38, 41, 42, 57, 68, 69, 73, 75, 91, 92, 109, 132, 133, 137, 138, 144, 145, 147, 148, 151, 152
Partido dos Trabalhadores 46, 141, 146, 151
Partido Socialismo e Liberdade 43, 46, 91, 132, 146
Pastoral de Favelas 27, 28, 133
Paulo, Pedro 31, 144
Pereira Passos, Francisco 21, 25, 123, 137, 138
Pezão, Luiz Fernando 24, 38
Pitanga, Camila 91
place 81
 and space 87, 88
 placemaking 78, 84, 86, 87–88, 89, 90, 96, 97
 spreading place 90, 91, 92, 95, 96, 97, 100, 104, 105, 108, 109, 110, 111, 118
Plano Popular 32, 38, 39, 42, 43, 44, 45, 46, 49, 57, 58, 64, 86, 88, 89, 91, 92, 129, 130, 131, 141, 144, 147, 153
political opportunity structure 20, 28, 52, 70, 80, 90, 153

positionality 11, 13–14, 93
 language learning 15, 109
protestival 82, 84, 85
public defenders 27, 28, 32, 33, 42, 50, 53, 78, 102, 103, 104, 128, 132, 133, 147

repertoire of removal 10, 26–27, 67, 108, 114, 144
rights 48
 1988 constitution 23, 50, 54, 141
 housing rights 16, 23, 31, 32, 46–47, 49, 50, 51, 58, 59, 75, 86, 97, 110, 114, 124, 125, 126, 127, 128, 129, 130, 132, 138, 139, 140, 150, 151, 153
 human rights advocacy groups 25, 32, 49
 mega-events 8, 19, 148, 149
 paradox of institutionalisation 48, 49, 59
 right to the city 23, 31, 44, 45–46, 58, 59, 86, 88, 125, 126, 127, 145
 sovereign power 51, 52
 unequal distribution 22, 26, 49, 50, 52, 59
Rio 2016 18, 19, 24, 46, 71, 98, 116, 117, 124, 130, 137, 140, 144, 145, 148, 151
RioOnWatch 1, 15, 35, 61, 91, 92, 93, 95, 96, 100, 105–109, 110, 111, 113, 114, 115, 116, 117, 118, 152
Rolnik, Raquel 54, 91
Rousseff, Dilma 22, 24, 38, 46, 145

Santos, Milton 49, 50, 66, 67
social media 38, 74, 90–91, 96, 97, 99, 107, 116, 134
 choreographing 74
 Facebook 41, 63, 64, 74, 91, 105
 Twitter 2, 3, 5, 92, 93, 94, 95, 96, 98, 100, 107, 117
 Urbaniza Já 72, 89, 91, 92, 96, 122
 WhatsApp 1, 2, 121
 YouTube 96
social movements 19, 23, 48, 71, 79, 90, 96, 126

space 65–68
  and place 87
  conceived space 65, 66, 67, 68–69,
    77, 78
  lived space 66, 69, 70, 74, 75,
    87, 97
  perceived space 65, 66, 67, 69, 72,
    74, 89, 92, 132
state of exception 19, 52, 56

técnicas 67, 68, 79, 84
traditional media 110, 111, 114, 118

foreign correspondents 96, 107, 108,
  117, 119
Globo 26, 64, 68, 91, 116, 118
international media 108, 109, 114,
  115, 116, 117, 118
parachutists 107, 110, 114
Turner, Victor 50–51, 82–83, 86

Vargas, Getúlio 21, 22

Witzel, Wilson 146
Wyllys, Jean 91

Milton Keynes UK
Ingram Content Group UK Ltd.
UKHW021257191124
2962UKWH00006B/44

9 781526 156297